THE IMAGE
OF THE FEDERAL SERVICE

The Image
of the Federal Service

FRANKLIN P. KILPATRICK
MILTON C. CUMMINGS, JR.
M. KENT JENNINGS

THE BROOKINGS INSTITUTION
WASHINGTON, D.C.

JK 691
JK 44

To Mary, Nancy, and Holly

THE BROOKINGS INSTITUTION is an independent organization devoted to nonpartisan research, education, and publication in economics, government, foreign policy, and the social sciences generally. Its principal purposes are to aid in the development of sound public policies and to promote public understanding of issues of national importance.

The Institution was founded December 8, 1927, to merge the activities of the Institute for Government Research, founded in 1916, the Institute of Economics, founded in 1922, and the Robert Brookings Graduate School of Economics and Government, founded in 1924.

The general administration of the Institution is the responsibility of a self-perpetuating Board of Trustees. The Trustees are likewise charged with maintaining the independence of the staff and fostering the most favorable conditions for creative research and education. The immediate direction of the policies, program, and staff of the Institution is vested in the President, assisted by the division directors and an advisory council, chosen from the professional staff of the Institution.

In publishing a study, the Institution presents it as a competent treatment of a subject worthy of public consideration. The interpretations and conclusions in such publications are those of the author or authors and do not purport to represent the views of the other staff members, officers, or trustees of the Brookings Institution.

Foreword

THE VOLUME HERE PRESENTED has three broad objectives: (1) to explore the attitudes of various groups in the American public toward the American federal civilian service generally; (2) to analyze what Americans think of the federal government as an employer, in light of the occupational values and attitudes toward work that prevail in their society today; and (3) to set forth for public consideration a series of proposals for changes in federal civilian personal organization, policies, and procedures designed to enhance the appeal of federal employment in the future.

The study was prompted by an interest in exploring the dimensions of the federal government's personnel problems—to identify and to explain the strengths and weaknesses of government as it competes for talented manpower in the 1960's. To do this, personal interviews based on standardized questionnaires were conducted with more than 5,000 people—including a cross-section of the general working public outside the federal government; federal civilian employees themselves; high school and college students and teachers; graduate students; natural scientists, social scientists, and engineers in business, the academic world, and the federal government; and top-level business executives and federal executives.

The present book reports part of a larger study of occupational values and attitudes toward the federal service that was launched by the Brookings Institution in late 1959. Much of the basic data derived from the larger study will be found in the *Source Book of a Study of Occupational Values and the Image of the Federal Service,* published simultaneously with this book. Further interpretive treatments of American attitudes toward work and politics will appear later.

The present book is one of several that the Brookings Institution is undertaking in the general field of leadership, management, and the public service under the direction of George A. Graham, Director of Governmental Studies. The authors and the Institution are grateful to the Advisory Committee, consisting of James A. Bayton, Professor of Psychology, Howard University, Harvey C. Mansfield, Professor of Political Science,

Ohio State University, and James M. Mitchell, Director of the Advanced Study Program, the Brookings Institution, all of whom read the manuscript and made numerous helpful suggestions for its improvement.

The authors, Franklin P. Kilpatrick, a social psychologist, Milton C. Cummings, Jr., a political scientist, and M. Kent Jennings, a political scientist now teaching at the University of Michigan, were all staff members of the Governmental Studies division of the Brookings Institution when the study was made.

The opinions and conclusions presented are those of the authors, and do not purport to represent the views of the Advisory Committee, other individuals whose opinions the authors solicited, or the trustees, officers, and other staff members of the Brookings Institution.

ROBERT D. CALKINS
President

November 1963
The Brookings Institution
1775 Massachusetts Avenue N.W.
Washington 36, D.C.

Authors' Acknowledgments

IN THE PREPARATION OF A BOOK involving the aid and cooperation of as many people as this one, we inevitably incurred more obligations than could possibly be acknowledged individually. Accordingly, we wish to express our thanks to the large group of unnamed individuals whose aid was truly indispensable—the more than 5,000 people who gave an hour or more of their time to be interviewed, and the numerous officials and personnel officers in business firms, schools, and federal installations who facilitated the work of our interviewers. This study is genuinely indebted to them.

Among the many federal officials who assisted us in our research, four were especially helpful: Warren B. Irons, Executive Director, U.S. Civil Service Commission; John W. Macy, Jr., Chairman of the Commission; Dale Rogers, then Executive Vice Chairman of the Interagency Advisory Group, the Civil Service Commission, and now with the Office of Industrial Relations, Department of the Navy; and James E. Smith, then in the personnel Division of the Civil Service Commission, and now with the Philadelphia Region of the Commission. The other members of the Interagency Advisory Group also made a substantial contribution to the study by helping to prepare the way for our interviews with federal employees in their departments and agencies.

Others whom we wish to thank are: Jane M. O'Donnell and Sidney Binder, both of National Analysts, Inc., who contributed in many ways to the interviewing and the coding and tabulating of the questionnaires, and Edwin E. Olson, now at the University of Southern California, who served as a research assistant during much of the project. For help at various stages of the work, our thanks also go to George A. Graham, Director of Governmental Studies, the Brookings Institution, and to Robert D. Calkins, President of the Institution.

At Brookings, we also wish to thank Amy R. Reeves, who did a major share of the secretarial work throughout the project, and Virginia J. Baxter, whose prolonged exposure to the numerous tables and figures contained in this volume failed to dim the enthusiasm and energy with which she checked them for accuracy. To Kathleen Sproul, who edited the manuscript for publication with rare good humor and skill, we are also especially grateful.

The members of our Advisory Committee, already mentioned in the Foreword, gave us the benefit of their careful reading of the manuscript and made numerous helpful suggestions for improving it. During the course of our research and writing, we presented partial summaries of our findings at a number of meetings and conferences; the participants at these meetings invariably made comments which were helpful to us in drafting our report.

We also wish to record a special word of thanks to a small group of individuals who were particularly generous with their time and advice. Their names and their institutional affiliation at the time they met with us are: James A. Campbell, American Federation of Government Employees; Calvin Deal, William T. McDonald, and Phillip W. Schulte, U.S. Civil Service Commission; Charles E. Johnson, Staff Director, House Post Office and Civil Service Committee; William P. Lehman, Bureau of the Budget; James R. Watson, National Civil Service League; Leon L. Wheeless, Department of Defense; and Joseph E. Winslow, White House staff. Busy men all, they spent a full afternoon and evening considering our findings, commenting on a tentative list of recommendations for changes in federal personnel policies and information programs, and suggesting additional recommendations of their own. We gave careful consideration to their advice and found it very helpful. However, like all the others whose aid is acknowledged in these pages, they should not be taxed for any shortcomings of the recommendations or the findings. For those, we alone are responsible.

FRANKLIN P. KILPATRICK
MILTON C. CUMMINGS, JR.
M. KENT JENNINGS

Contents

List of Tables

1

The Problem and the Study

The Problem

THE DISTRIBUTION OF HUMAN EFFORT, skills, and talent among the various enterprises in a society is a significant clue to both the nature and the probable lines of development of that society. It is a matter for grave public concern when any major enterprise essential to social welfare and progress fails to receive its necessary share of these resources. For some time there has been presumptive evidence that the United States government is facing serious difficulties in attracting the numbers of able people it needs to carry out its crucial functions, both at home and abroad.

Many complex considerations are involved in the distribution of people among different occupations. Of basic importance are the kinds, cost, and availability of formal and informal education and job training; the social and geographical mobility of the population; the size of the society; and the stage and rate of scientific and technological development. In most societies with respect to some activities, and in some societies with respect to most activities, coercion, whether of circumstance or law, is a determinant. But in a highly developed, free social order which has high mobility and broadly based opportunity for education and training, individual choice is also an important factor—and becomes increasingly important the higher one goes on the scale of ability and training. Today in the United States the factor of choice is the paramount consideration in the competition for the most able people.

Whenever an individual chooses a specific job and a specific employer, whether for the first time or later, he is the possessor of certain occupationally related abilities; of a complex set of occupational values; of ideas and attitudes concerning perceived characteristics of employ-

1

ing organizations; and of stereotypes or images concerning the kind of people who work for certain categories of employing organizations. Although the process is seldom as orderly as description makes it sound, choice involves a complex blending of the individual's perceptions of the situation—the requirements of the job, his own capacities and skills, the characteristics of the employing organization, the kinds of people with whom he would be identified—with his pattern of occupational values, that is, the kinds of things he hopes both to attain and to avoid in his job.

This study has been designed to assess (1) the patterning of occupational values among a wide variety of key groups in American society and (2) the images these same groups of people have of the United States government as an employer and of federal public servants in their occupational roles. The primary purpose of this book is to examine the competitive position of the federal government as an employer; to provide information that may be useful in modifying federal personnel organization, policy, and procedures; and to suggest means for improved communication concerning these matters.

To measure the appeal of government employment, it is necessary to learn what people want in a job. One can determine what people picture federal employment as providing, but whether or not this appeals to them depends on their basic occupational values. What kinds of things, for example, is a college student looking for as he contemplates taking his first long-term job? How do the features of a job that he may prize compare with the characteristics he sees in federal employment? What is the comparable relationship between the occupational values and perceptions of federal employment of other men and women who will be in the job markets of the 1960's?

Our study has attempted to answer these and many related questions by eliciting from people the image they perceive when federal employment is mentioned—and by exploring the extent to which that image attracts or repels them in relation to the variety of human desires, hopes, intentions, and ambitions which, subtly interwoven, may be said to constitute individual and group patterns of occupational values. To that end, structured personal interviews with employed adults in both federal and nonfederal enterprises and with high school and college students were conducted in all regions of the continental United States.[1]

---

[1] A brief discussion of the design and conduct of the study is presented in the concluding section of this chapter.

The Federal Personnel Problem

To suggest that the federal government should at all times have priority claims on the best of the country's human resources would reflect a distorted view of government's relationship to the other institutions of our pluralistic society. And probably the various operating segments of the society can never reach agreement on what an ideally balanced distribution of skills and talent would or should be. It is clear, however, that the rapid pace of technological and social change has for some time been changing the needs of the government relative to other institutions. A full-scale assessment of the federal government in this regard would have to take into detailed account its present size, personnel composition, and multitudinous functions, as well as possible future trends in each respect. The following brief summary of these matters, however, reveals in broad perspective the major elements in this changing pattern.

The sheer size of the federal establishment, apart from any other consideration, means that a serious malfunction in any part of the government is bound to have an impact throughout the country and the world. In 1963 the administrative expenditures budget was approximately $93 billion, and the civilian federal work force included more than 2.5 million people. Both figures are almost certain to increase. The trend has been upward most of the time since 1910, when the annual expenditure was $694 million and civilian federal employees numbered 389,000; the many scientific, technological, and social developments of recent years would seem to indicate continuing trends in the same direction.

The functions of the central government penetrate all aspects of our domestic economy. Decisions made and procedures followed at the federal level have strong, and often decisive, influence on such matters as the pattern of employment, the amount and kind of scientific research, and the rate and direction of technological development. In its activities overseas, the federal service has assumed responsibilities which involve freedom, and possibly survival, both for ourselves and for a great number of the world's peoples. Thus the United States government can no longer afford to be without the highest capacities for innovation, leadership, judgment, and management in all parts and at all levels of the administrative establishment. The game cannot be played with a second team.

This is not to say that there are not large numbers of highly qualified and devoted public servants in all branches and at all levels of the federal service at the present time. The depression of the 1930's and the exigencies of World War II and, to a lesser extent, of the Korean war drew large numbers of very able people into the federal service, a great many of whom now staff a high proportion of the key positions. These emergencies helped to alleviate the personnel problem, but at the same time tended to obscure the basic, long-run nature of the problem. No longer can we rely on such crises as recruiting measures for able public servants in the numbers that are currently needed. A variety of recent testimony and evidence adds up to a consensus that almost all federal personnel areas which require a high order of training and talent are facing supply problems ranging from difficult to dangerously acute.

Beginning with the Franklin D. Roosevelt administration, every President has experienced increasing staffing difficulties at many levels, in both political and technical fields. During the 1960 hearings of the Senate Subcommittee on National Policy Machinery, which were concerned with personnel aspects of the government's operations in the field of national security policy, a wide variety of experts testified. Their testimony was remarkable for its unanimity on a point which was emphasized by Senator Henry Jackson: "The fact is, we have encountered disturbing difficulties in securing first-rate talent at the very time when the national security calls for the country's 'best brains' to man key posts at home and abroad."[2]

Something of the nature and magnitude of the problem is also suggested by the recent unprecedented upsurge of federal contracting with private or quasi-private organizations for a wide variety of research, development, and other high-level nonproduction activities. Undoubtedly the reasons behind this growth are many and complex, but one prime reason appears to be the inability of the federal government to hire and retain the numbers and kinds of people needed to perform such services within the federal establishment. John Corson, then a management consultant with McKinsey and Company, testified in 1960 before the National Policy Machinery Subcommittee as follows: "I think most nonprofit corporations that have been set up to perform essentially complementary functions for Government were established as a means of attracting tal-

[2] *Organizing for National Security: Mobilizing Talent for Government Service,* Hearings Before the Subcommittee on National Policy Machinery, Senate Committee on Government Operations, 86th Cong., 2d sess. (May 1960), Part III, p. 413.

ent that the Government could not obtain through its normal mechanisms."[3]

To a considerable extent, the urgency of the problem is rooted in the relative composition of the federal and the private work forces, and the rapid change occurring in both. The federal work force, because of the nature of the tasks assigned to it, has historically had a much higher proportion of managerial, professional, technical, and scientific personnel than the nonfederal work force. A 1960 analysis revealed that scientific and engineering tasks were performed by one in every fifty of the nonfederal work force and by one in fourteen of all federal employees. Considering only the people directly employed by the federal government—thus excluding large numbers in the private sphere who are performing scientific and engineering work under contract to the government—one finds that the federal establishment, compared with the general work force, employs twice the percentage of engineers and three and a half times the percentage of professional scientists.[4] Similar considerations apply to managerial and other professional and technical areas.

Technological change is shifting the nature of our manpower needs at a rapid and accelerating rate from production to service, and to ever higher demands for expertise and flexibility. Private industry, the universities and colleges, and the professions are more and more competing for the same kinds of highly trained people that are needed by the government. Since these people are also increasingly in short supply, the government is finding it difficult to meet the competition. Augmenting the federal problem is evidence that government service at all levels is an area of employment which will grow faster than the average rate for the nation, and that the government's rapidly expanding need will be greatest for trained professional and technical employees, and least for semiskilled and unskilled workers.[5]

Agreement on the nature and the urgency of the problem is fairly general, despite a disturbing scarcity of concrete information concerning the types, amounts, and locations of federal personnel shortages. The "pilot" analysis and projection published by the Program Planning Division of the U.S. Civil Service Commission in 1960 for the period 1958 to 1963 covered only physical scientists, psychologists, engineers, and medical

[3] *Ibid.*, p. 526.
[4] U.S. Civil Service Commission, *The Growing Demand for Scientific and Technical Manpower in the Federal Service* (mimeographed; October 1960), pp. 7-9.
[5] U.S. Department of Labor, *Manpower—Challenge of the 1960's* (1960), pp. 9 and 11.

officers (see footnote 4). Some other projections have been made since then, but have not been published in detail. In 1963 the chief of the Program Planning Division commented, "If these [1963] projections are anywhere near the mark, they indicate that not even minimum Federal staffing needs in engineering and the physical sciences will be met."[6] That the situation is comparable for the government's management needs is indicated by a 1960 statement of the chairman of the Civil Service Commission:

> For all agencies, an average of 38 percent of top career executives will be eligible to retire in five years, and 66½ percent in ten years. This does not count the normal losses from death, disability, and resignation. In the face of the urgency of public issues before our administrative agencies, the Civil Service Commission is alarmed and needs help in getting fuller recognition of the threat to effective government that the situation presents.[7]

Something of the magnitude of the need is suggested by the estimate that if the federal government does no more than retain its present size (and, as noted earlier, that seems unlikely in view of the long-time trend toward increasingly broad and complex federal responsibilities at home and abroad), more than 300,000 people must be recruited to the federal public service every year. Progress, and perhaps even survival, demand that there be included in this 300,000 a proper share of the best in human resources that our society has to offer. Yet, according to the Civil Service Commission:

> The reputation of the public service generally . . . is not high enough so that it serves as a positive attraction to people. Any picture of civil service examining procedures as a means of choosing a few of the best from clamoring hordes of officeseekers is as old fashioned as the rolltop desk and the frock-coated dispenser of patronage. Our whole employment system must compete in attractiveness with those of private employers.[8]

Images and Values

The implication of the phrase "compete in attractiveness" is the core of this research. Of what does "occupational attractiveness" consist? It is

---

[6] Harold H. Leich, "Scientific Manpower: Progress and Prospects," *Civil Service Journal*, Vol. 3 (April-June 1963), p. 24.

[7] Roger W. Jones, "The Federal Civil Service Today," *Public Personnel Review*, Vol. 21 (April 1960), p. 118.

[8] *A Report on How People Are Recruited, Examined, and Appointed in the Competitive Civil Service*, Prepared by the U.S. Civil Service Commission for the Subcommittee on Civil Service, House Committee on Post Office and Civil Service, 86th Cong., 1st sess. (April 1959), p. 61.

often thought to connote primarily such matters as rate of pay, opportunity for promotion, retirement benefits, protection from firing and lay-offs, and the like. But this assumes that knowledge about rate of pay, promotion opportunity, and other job characteristics is communicated in an undistorted fashion and in turn will give rise to undistorted perceptions among people in the potential work force. In actuality, communication and perception never achieve such perfection. The difficulty of putting job attributes into precise language, the varying nature, and often lack, of communication channels, and the selecting and modifying aspects of human experience and perception all intervene.

The result is that people usually perceive occupations and employing organizations, not precisely and realistically, but in terms of vaguely generalized cultural pre-judgments, which not only are undiscriminating in application, uncertain as to origin, and resistant to modification, but also tend to be self-perpetuating and self-enhancing by virtue of their selecting and modifying effect on current experience and perception. This is the pattern of stereotypes which, in the vocabulary of this study, add up to the *images* the individual has of kinds of employment and employing organizations. Thus, one of the keys to "attractiveness" is not what *is*, but *how it is perceived*.

Another frequent assumption is that occupational attributes are attractive or unattractive in the same way and in the same degree to most people throughout our society. But the fact is that an occupation's appeal is a function of the individual's perception *in relation to the goals he is striving to attain*. Whether the goals are many or few, immediate or long range, trivial or worthwhile, they are always complex in their patterning of intensity, saliency, and rate of change. Even though the patterns of human striving are rooted in a fairly common biology, their elaboration is a function of learning. They emerge as a compound of the successes and failures and the social prescriptions and expectations to which an individual has been and is exposed as a member of a given family, a given social group, and a given society at a certain time in history.

Thus, the goals or values any individual wants to realize through his occupation are likely to be a patterned blend: some are unique to himself; some are common to members of various cultural groups of which he is, has been, or aspires to be a part; some are common to most members of his society; and some few are common to almost all human beings—and would be in any society at any period. Although particular groups of people in a society tend to share the same values, the amount and kind of variation among individuals and among groups is great.

Therefore, even if it were theoretically possible for everyone in a society to have the same image of federal employment, we would still expect it to vary widely in attractiveness among different elements of the population. And if the variations are not known or understood, efforts to enhance the appeal of an occupation or of an employing organization may miss their target. If we propose, for example, that higher pay will attract certain people to a certain kind of employment, we are *assuming* that these people have a set of occupational values in which such economic considerations are of sufficient concern to influence relative attractiveness and, thereby, choice. Such assumptions could, however, be erroneous.

The Study

Our purpose here is to review briefly the methods employed in the study and the reasons for selecting them. We believe that such a frame of reference will help the reader in assessing the findings and the uses we have made of them.[9]

Within the context of the available resources of theory, method, time, and personnel, the over-all objectives of any research study dictate, or should dictate, the design of the research. Since we wished to explore (1) the patterning of occupational values among key groups of people in American society, and (2) how these same groups perceived both the United States government as an employer and the federal public servant in his occupational role, we established the following six major objectives:

1. *To learn what images people have of the federal government as an employer.* What occupational values are seen as being fulfilled or not fulfilled by the government in its role of an employing enterprise?

2. *To learn what images people have of federal public servants.* Do people have generalized "pictures in their heads" concerning the qualities and traits of federal employees? How do they perceive these civil servants in terms of character, ability, and occupational values?

[9] A more detailed statement of the design and procedures is presented in Chaps. 2 and 3 of this book's companion volume by the same authors: *Source Book of a Study of Occupational Values and the Image of the Federal Service* (Brookings Institution, 1964), hereafter referred to as *Source Book.*

3. *To discover which occupational values are of concern to people and which are of basic importance.* What occupational aims, immediate and long range, are people trying to realize? What are they striving for in their jobs and what are they trying to avoid?

4. *To ascertain the patterns of these images and occupational values among the general public and among federal employees, as well as among a variety of subgroupings of these two populations by occupation, education, age, sex, and other differentiations.* Ideally, we would want to learn these things for all groups which are significant to the productivity and future welfare of our society, but for practical reasons we have concentrated on certain groups which are of special relevance to the personnel problems of the federal government.

5. *To be able to compare the findings for any one group selected for study with those for any other such group, and with the employed public in general.* Only through such comparative analysis can we approach a worthwhile understanding of the factors that go into the occupational decision patterns of given groups.

6. *To provide a base line of data, concerning these images and values, for trend analysis in future research.* A single study, such as this one, is only a snapshot of what *is* at a given point in time. It provides few clues to the direction in which things are moving. But it can be so designed as to offer a reliable comparative base. To provide an adequate base line, a study must be repeatable so that comparable data can be obtained at two or more points in time. This meant not only that the methods we used must be susceptible of fairly exact repetition but also that they and the basic data they yielded must be described with sufficient detail and clarity to enable future researchers to replicate our work on later samples.

General Design

The nature of these objectives in combination suggested that the basic instrument to be used should be a standardized personal interview questionnaire. In such a questionnaire the wording and the order of the questions, the methods of recording responses, and the set of instructions under which the interviewers operate are all prescribed. Without as nearly perfect standardization as possible, neither comparative analysis nor trend analysis would be practicable or reliable, for we would not know whether differences in our results were due to differences in questions and procedure, or to actual differences in images and values.

Once we had decided to rely on standardized personal interviews (rather than on "depth techniques" or mail questionnaires) the objectives of the study told us specific things about the necessary content and form of the questionnaire. Certain broad decisions concerning the composition of the questions were also possible at this point. We knew, for example, that the categorical question—that is, a question which does not permit free response but offers a range of prescribed alternatives—has certain marked advantages in securing information of the kind we needed, and in the considerable range of areas we had to cover. It takes relatively less interviewing time than the free-answer question; is easier to code and tabulate; is more susceptible to precise statistical treatment; and in some forms is an aid in obtaining information which people either cannot, or prefer not to, verbalize.

On the other hand, the categorical question has one great disadvantage; it limits the respondent to choosing his answer from a certain number of preformulated alternatives, and does not permit him to state his answer in his own way. Thus, it eliminates the possibility of learning what the respondent might want to say if he were not obliged to confine himself to a choice of replies. In effect, the categorical question presumes that all the important categories or classes of response are known, and that research need only show how people sort themselves out in their choices of predetermined alternatives.[10] In the area of images and values which we wished to investigate, it would have been foolhardy to presume that we knew enough to be sure of including all of the important areas and categories of questioning and response. But to use only open-end questions would be too time-consuming and would make the entire study liable to a lack of analytic precision.

Our solution was to blend open-end with categorical questions. This promised two advantages. First, if both kinds of questions are asked about the same general topic, it is possible to check the answers against one another. Internal consistency analysis of this kind helps to provide an estimate of the reliability of the responses, and of the degree of cau-

[10] Certain types of highly refined statistical analysis of categorical responses (factor analysis, latent structure analysis, etc.) can yield "new" information, such as common underlying variables, patterns that are differentially characteristic of the individual as opposed to what is being judged, and the like.

tion one must use in interpretation. Second, the dual approach affords the possibility of cross-checking for *concern* and *importance*. Open-end questions tend to yield responses which are *salient* to the individual— that is, the kinds of things that are of current concern to him in his day-to-day transactions with his environment. They can, and often do, miss entirely matters which are of basic *importance* to the indivdual but are not salient.

This distinction can be illustrated by considering the act of breathing. One is rarely "concerned" with breathing, but, if it is interfered with, it immediately assumes great "salience." In response to an open-end question, one would be unlikely to mention "continuing to breathe" as a value, but if one were asked categorically to rate the importance of breathing the rating would probably be very high. Similar considerations apply to occupational values. Security of employment, for example, may be of little concern to most people during an era of continued high demand for the kinds of skills they have to offer, but one should not therefore conclude that security is not important to them. The onset of an economic recession can alter the saliency of employment security very markedly.

Another imperative imposed by the nature of our objectives was that the questions should not be "time-bound." They must be worded in such a way that they could be asked in exactly the same form, and with the same meaning, five years, ten years, or even twenty years from now. Otherwise, the results of the study could not serve as an adequate basis for trend analysis through a repetition of the research, or parts of it, at subsequent points in time, because it would not be known whether observed differences were due to changes in values and images, or simply to alterations in question form or meaning. It is of course difficult to be sure that all topical aspects have been eliminated from a group of questions, but there are certain kinds of questions which are *unlikely* to change very much in meaning over a period of ten or twenty years.

The broad objectives of the study also pointed to some general prescriptions concerning the categories of people (here often termed "populations") to be interviewed, and the manner in which they should be selected. It was clear that we must have a sample of the general employed public, because data from its members concerning occupational values and images of the public service were necessary as a base line for comparison with other groups. This population was also necessary if we were to make generalized statements about the distribution of these values and images in American society. Similar considerations dictated the necessity for obtaining a general sample of civilians presently employed by the United States government.

In addition, since the federal personnel problem is basically a shortage, not of numbers, but of skills and talent, it was important to make separate analyses of certain high-level occupational groups—for instance, natural scientists, social scientists, engineers, and executives. However, no reasonably sized sample of the general employed public would yield enough interviewees in any of these categories to make separate analyses possible; consequently, we needed to draw supplementary subsamples in each of the desired categories.

Of equal importance to our purposes was an understanding of the values and images of young people still in school. Since the above samples would miss this population, it was apparent that we needed to draw special subsamples of such groups as high school students, college students, and graduate school students.

The basic question of the number of interviews to be conducted was resolved according to arbitrary considerations of available time and money in relation to the known approximate cost per interview. We came up with a limit of about 5,000 interviews, which left us with the question of how many groups, which groups, and how to allocate the total number of interviews among them. We decided to make the samples of the general employed public and of general federal employees large enough to support analysis of each of them by such breakdowns as age, sex, geographic region, amount of education, general type of occupation, income, and the like. The minimum number of cases which will permit breaking into such categories and still permit meaningful (though gross) analysis is approximately 1,000. This meant that, out of our total of some 5,000 interviews, we must allocate about 2,000 between our two general samples and distribute the rest among the smaller samples of each of the special subgroups. This imposed restrictions on the study: first, we would have to content ourselves with having too few cases in each of our special subgroups to support any very complex breakdowns by age, school grades, amount of education, and the like; second, we would be unable to obtain samples of all the special groups that ideally should be included, simply because there would not be enough interviews to go around.

It had been apparent from the outset that we must use properly drawn probability samples clearly specified as to the manner of drawing, and drawn in such a way that future investigators would find it possible to repeat our procedures and draw comparable samples. Unless sampling is performed according to proper probability procedures, one cannot safely generalize from the sample to the population from which it was drawn or safely make comparisons among various special populations; furthermore, the results of the study could not constitute a proper basis for subsequent repetition and comparative trend analysis. But if probability sampling procedures are carefully carried out, it is not only possible to generalize and compare but also to estimate statistically the probable degree of error involved.

Development of the Study

In constructing the questionnaire we took into account that our total sample would include three different types of populations: people who are presently employed but not by the federal government; people presently employed by the federal government; and high school and college students who have not yet entered upon full-time employment. Three forms of the questionnaire were therefore prepared, but the differences among the three forms were kept to an absolute minimum. The questionnaire for the nonfederal employed public was developed first as the basic form; then the necessary modifications and additions to this form were made for federal employees and for students.

In developing the basic form, we carried out four successive developmental studies, performing interviewing and extensive analysis each time. Approximately 200 interviews, from one to four hours in length, were conducted during this stage. Finally, the questionnaire was subjected to a pilot study carried out at ten different locations in the United States by the staff of field interviewers who would conduct the final interviews (see following section).

Discussion of the specific content of the basic questionnaire will be confined to those aspects of purpose and procedure which are not immediately apparent from examining the questionnaire itself.[11] The first

[11] The basic form of the questionnaire (for the nonfederal employed public) and the other forms for the federal and student populations, wherein they differ from

matter requiring comment is the use of self-anchoring scaling. Briefly, a self-anchoring scale is one in which each respondent is asked to describe—in terms of his own perceptions, goals, and values—the top and bottom, or anchoring points, of the dimension on which scale measurement is desired. The respondent is then asked to employ this self-defined continuum as a measuring device and as a basis for further questioning concerning his values and goals.[12]

The self-anchoring scaling device, as adapted to probe into occupational values, is so central to this study that a description of how it was used is in order. The first step in the procedure was to ask the following question: "First, I would like you to think of what really matters most to you in your own life. Tell me what kind of a way of earning a living would be ideal for you—that is, the very best way of doing it from your point of view. Maybe no occupation could fit your ideal. But just let yourself dream a bit and tell me the various things *about* an occupation which would make it *absolutely ideal* for you. I am not asking for the name of a specific occupation, but for the *kinds of things about* an occupation which would make it *absolutely ideal* for you."

After the interviewer had encouraged as detailed a response as possible and had recorded as nearly verbatim as possible everything that the respondent said, the next question was: "Now about the worst sort of occupation. What kinds of things *about* an occupation would make it the worst or least satisfying to you." Again, the interviewer encouraged elaboration and recorded the responses.

The respondent was then handed a card showing a ten-step ladder scale. The interviewer said: "Here is a picture of a ladder. Suppose we say at the *top* of the ladder is the *very best,* the absolutely ideal sort of occupation you have just described. At the *bottom* is the *very worst* sort of occupation. Where on this ladder would you put your present occupation, that is, what you are doing now?" In the same manner scale ratings were obtained for where the person felt he (or she) was occupationally

the basic form, are shown in the Appendix. The basic form consists of twenty-two open-end questions; eighty-five items or statements which the respondent sorts onto a ten-step response scale; four self-anchoring scale ratings; six categorical questions; and forty brief classification questions concerning the status and background of the respondent.

[12] The theoretical basis and general areas of usefulness of the method are described in F. P. Kilpatrick and Hadley Cantril, "Self-Anchoring Scaling: A Measure of Individuals' Unique Reality Worlds," *Journal of Individual Psychology,* Vol. 16 (November 1960), pp. 158-173.

five years ago and where he expected to be five years hence. Following this, his reasons for rating his present occupation as he did were explored.

Then came a key question concerning federal employment and the image of the federal service: "Suppose your work or occupation stayed the same but you worked for the federal government, that is, the United States government. How much better or worse would that be? Show me on the ladder, please." The interviewer recorded the step number pointed to by the respondent. In this way we obtained a numerical representation of the degree to which the person felt he would move up or down the scale, *in terms of his own occupational values,* if he were to continue in the same sort of work, but in the employ of the federal government.

To elicit the reasons for this numerical judgment and to explore the individual's image of federal employment, the next two questions were: "What things would be likely to be better?" and "What things would be likely to be worse?" Thus we obtained the individual's feelings about the federal government as an employer, in the context of continuing to perform the same sort of work.

The above questions were phrased for people presently employed in nonfederal enterprises. When federal employees were interviewed, occupational values and ratings of their own occupations were secured in the same fashion. Then they were asked how much better or worse would it be on the ladder rating if they continued to do the same sort of work but did it *outside* the government, and what things would be likely to be better or worse.

Another procedural matter also requires some comment: the fact that the purpose of an open-end question is not always apparent from simply reading the question. For example, all respondents were asked: "If you were to describe your general idea of a United States civil service employee, what sort of a person would that be?" Since of course there are all kinds of people working for the government, the only really logical answer is simply to say so, and perhaps express a little anger that such a stupid question has been asked. But the fact remains that, in varying degrees, most respondents did have evaluative pictures or stereotypes in their minds, and they expressed them in response to the question.

The purpose of the question was to learn the degree and content of stereotyping in various segments of the population, and to learn whether the stereotyped images are predominantly favorable, unfavorable, or neutral. Therefore, the individual who responded, "That is a stupid question, for there are all kinds and types of people in the civil service," supplied us with valuable information directly relevant to the objectives of the study. Similar considerations apply to almost all the open-end questions concerned with the nature, type of work, and motivations attributed to civil service employees.

A third matter requiring discussion is the scale sort we employed in Item 17 of the basic questionnaire. The fifty-five statements used in the scale sort are identical for all three questionnaires (see Appendix). This scale sort does not involve scaling in the technical sense of the term, but is simply a way of getting reliable numerical responses on a ten-interval agree-disagree scale to fifty-five separate statements in a very short amount of interviewing time. The statements are concerned with such matters as the importance of certain occupational values, with the evaluation of certain aspects of federal employees and federal employment, and with attitudes toward government and politics.

Each item was printed on a separate small card. In the actual interview situation, the interviewer shuffled the small cards in order to insure random presentation, thus eliminating possible order bias due to presenting the items in the same order time after time. The interviewer then said: "Please take the small cards and place each one in turn on the large card (the scale) according to how much you agree or disagree with the statement on it." When the interview was over, the interviewer recorded the number of the scale space (1 through 10) into which a given item had been sorted.

Another slightly modified version of the scaling procedure was used at a later point in the questionnaires, with thirty items on individual small cards. The large printed scale on which the cards were sorted was labeled "Extremely High" at the top and "Extremely Low" at the bottom. Each item, instead of involving just one dimension, involved two dimensions of judgment. The respondent was asked, first, to consider a specific category of people and, second, to rate them on a prescribed personal quality. For example: "Consider: People in the top-level jobs in the federal civil service. On the average, how would you rate them on *honesty?*" And, "Consider: People in the top-level jobs in private business. On the average, how would you rate them on *ability?*"

In this fashion respondents rated general civil servants, people in the top-level jobs in the federal civil service, and people in the top-level jobs in private business on ability, honesty, how well respected they are, their interest in serving the public, and their drive to get ahead.

The Conduct of the Study

Interviewing

The standardized questionnaires were administered to 5,078 respondents in the continental United States. The personal interviews ranged in length from slightly less than one hour to as much as two and a half hours, averaging, as expected from pilot study results, about one hour and twenty minutes. They were conducted by the interviewing staff of a commercial research organization that specializes in "custom design" survey research, rather than in simple, routine, repetitive polling.[13]

The first phase of interviewing—for the nonfederal populations—began in April 1960 and was almost entirely completed in May, with a few remaining interviews done in June. The total of completed interviews obtained in this phase was 3,576, conducted by a force of approximately 100 of the most experienced and skilled personnel on the research firm's roster.[14]

The second phase involved 1,502 interviews with federal employees, conducted from the middle of November 1960, through January 1961, with a very small number carrying over into February. Again, about 100 interviewers were employed, about 60 of whom had worked with the first phase.[15]

[13] National Analysts, Inc., Philadelphia, Pa. The staff of about 500 trained interviewers is distributed throughout the United States, for the most part located near 100 sampling points in the organization's master sample. The interviewers are part-time employees—preponderantly housewives with some college education—personally selected and trained either by local field supervisors or by central office staff. The firm's volume of research is such that most members of this corps are kept busy for a large share of their available time. On the average, they have had about five years of interviewing experience; they have also had extensive interview training, conducted both as a routine matter and as a means of acquainting them with novel assignments involving new or modified procedures.

[14] In accordance with standard practice, each interviewer had been provided with an instruction booklet pretested for clarity, accuracy, and completeness in the pilot study phase of the research. It described the general purpose of the study, told exactly how respondent selection procedures were to be carried out, and gave question-by-question instructions on how the questions were to be asked and the answers recorded. In addition, before the interviewing began the interviewers were assembled in small groups at various conveniently located points around the country and given two days of intensive training by central staff members. These sessions involved general instructions, practice interviewing, review of the practice interviews, and individual corrective instruction.

[15] Instruction booklets revised to accommodate the special problems of interviewing federal employees were provided, and once again, personal training sessions were held.

Sampling

A carefully devised, up-to-date, national (continental United States), general purpose sample provided the basic framework for all the samples of the populations studied. Technically, this master sample may be described as a two-stage, stratified random sample in which each primary sampling unit (a county or a group of counties) has a known probability of selection. Within this general framework, probability samples of different categories of people were interviewed in the numbers shown in Table 1-1.[16]

An element in sampling which must not be overlooked in this discussion is the specification for each sample of the larger group or "universe" from which the sample is drawn. The essential parts of the numerous universe definitions used in this study must be repeated here in order to make clear what we are talking about when we refer, for example, to the "general employed public," to "natural scientists in business," and so on.

The universe from which the sample of the general employed public was drawn was defined as regularly employed persons, male and female, 18 to 60 years of age inclusive, either self-employed or working for someone else (35 hours per week or more), exclusive of the federal government.

---

[16] The master sample was National Analysts, Inc., National General Purpose Sample, 1960. Details of the procedures for drawing each sample are given in the Source Book, Chap. 3, and are not repeated here. However, it should be mentioned that our sample of general federal employees was drawn in accordance with our master framework from a larger sample of federal employees made available to the Brookings Institution by the United States Civil Service Commission. This consisted of the names and installation addresses of 5,000 civilian federal employees in the continental United States drawn by a random sampling procedure from the St. Louis Central Registry. (CIA and FBI employees were excluded from the list.) Also, at all stages in the federal employee phase of our work, we had the active and inventive support of the Interagency Advisory Group, the Civil Service Commission, installation personnel officers, and the chief personnel officers of almost all the major departments and agencies in the federal government.

In addition, with rare exceptions, the schools, the colleges, the business organizations, and the federal installations permitted interviewing to be conducted on site and during school or working hours. This was a main factor in achieving a high proportion of satisfactorily completed interviews with the people selected by the sampling procedures. In none of the nineteen groups did the completion rate, as conventionally calculated, fall below 85 percent; for all but two of them the rates were over 90 percent, and in a number of instances 95 percent or higher.

TABLE 1-1. *Population Samples and Numbers of Interviews in Each*

Populations	Sample Size
Nonfederal and Federal Populations (total)	5,078
Nonfederal Populations (total)	3,576
General employed public	1,142
Students	
High school juniors and seniors	359
College seniors	404
College graduate students	383
Groups in education	
High school teachers	203
High school vocational counselors	80
College teachers[a] (total)	470
Natural scientists	121
Social scientists	106
Engineers	87
Humanities	56
Other	100
Groups in business	
Executives	287
Natural scientists	85
Social scientists	73
Engineers	90
Federal Populations (total)	1,502
General federal employees[b]	948
Special federal populations	
Executives	273
Natural scientists	92
Social Scientists	90
Engineers	99

[a] The sample of 470 college teachers was purposely drawn in an unbalanced fashion, to obtain approximately 100 each of natural scientists, social scientists, and engineers. Before tabulation of the total college teacher interviews, the sample was statistically adjusted to the known distribution of college teachers in the five categories shown in the table. Details are given in the *Source Book*, Chap. 3.

[b] The sampling of general federal employees resulted in an under-representation of Postal Field Service employees. Before tabulating, this under-representation was statistically adjusted. Details are given in the *Source Book*, Chap. 3.

The universe for the samples of high school juniors and seniors, high school teachers and vocational counselors was defined as all such people in high schools—public, private, and parochial—in the continental United States. Schools teaching grades 10, 11, and 12 were included, whether they taught one or more other grades or no other grades.

The samples of college seniors, graduate students, general college teaching faculty, and college natural scientists, social scientists, and engineers were taken at 100 institutions of higher education drawn by probability procedures from a listing of all four-year degree-granting colleges and universities in the continental United States.[17] Conventional definitions of seniors, graduate students, and teaching faculty were used. College teachers of natural science, social science, and engineering were defined in terms of specific lists of subjects in each of the three areas.

The business respondents were drawn from a sample of business organizations selected by random procedures from a list of such organizations.[18] A business executive was defined as one whose duties are primarily administrative (supervising, planning, organizing, coordinating, reporting, delegating, etc.). In organizations of over twenty employees, only those personnel above the supervisor or foreman level were included in the executive population; in organizations with twenty employees or less, only those at the level of manager or vice president and above were included. A natural scientist in business was defined as a person in a business organization who has had more than four years of college with a major or graduate degree in one of the listed natural science disciplines, and no higher degree in any subject not on the list. Social scientists were defined in the same way, in terms of the listed social sciences. In the case of engineers, however, the definition required only a four-year degree in one of the listed engineering disciplines and no higher degree in another subject.

The universe for the sample of general federal employees was defined as all regularly employed federal civilian personnel (except CIA and FBI) in the continental United States working 35 hours or more per week. Federal executives were defined as GS 12 or above (or equivalent based on salary) whose duties are primarily administrative. Definitions of federal natural scientists, social scientists, and engineers were the same as the above definitions for their counterparts in business.

Preparation of the Code

Whenever more than a small number of questionnaires are used in a research project, it is impossible to analyze the results simply by examining the questionnaires. The information must be classified, tabulated,

---

[17] U.S. Office of Education, *Education Directory, 1958-1959: Part 3, Higher Education,* Theresa Birch Wilkins, editor (1960).

[18] *McKittrick Directory of Advertisers Classified, 1960* (1959).

and manipulated, in order to extract its meaning. Therefore, once enough interviews to provide a good sample had been returned from the field and had been checked and edited for quality and completeness, work began at the Brookings Institution on the next phase in the research— the preparation of a code whereby relevant, discrete items of information in the completed interviews are identified and assigned numbers. Our task was to turn the questionnaire data into a number code so it could be punched on standard 80-column IBM cards for machine reading and manipulation.

The categorical questions in the questionnaire presented relatively few problems, since a large percentage of them had been precoded by numbers appearing on the questionnaire beside the categories. Those which were not precoded involved only the relatively simple problem of managing the coding procedure with care so that the rate of error was kept within an acceptable limit.

The free-response questions, however, presented a very specific problem. One of the main purposes of open-end questioning is to permit the emergence of new information; consequently, the codes for such questions must emerge from the responses themselves. Yet the responses alone do not dictate the categories. Any given code must strike a balance between the hypotheses to be tested and the answers contained in the interviews. In some cases, the proper code may be dictated almost entirely by the nature of the hypotheses; in other cases, the content of the answer plays a dominant role. In all cases, however, the underlying nature of the code is a function of the hypotheses to be tested. This is true simply because there are innumerable ways of coding any given answer, and the only basis for choosing among them is to make the decision in relation to the hypotheses which the resulting data must test.

For example, the responses to the questions on occupational values could have been coded for the *number* of values mentioned without regard to their content; for the *kinds of names used to describe* the values; for the *quality or nature* of the values; and in many other ways. How were we to decide among these possibilities? If one of the hypotheses in our research had been that "fullness of response to questions on occupational values is associated with level of education, age, and other factors," then we might have constructed a code based on the length of response, or on the number of different occupational values mentioned, without regard to the qualitative nature of the responses. But since that hypothesis was not a part of our study, such a code would have been irrelevant.

We did hypothesize, however, that the *kinds* of occupational values mentioned in response to open-end questions would be differentially patterned according to occupation, age, education, and other factors. This meant that we had to construct a code based on the different *kinds* of values described by the respondents, the dimension for categorization thus being the distinction in their qualitative nature. But we did not know completely in advance the nature of the values that would be mentioned by people as matters of concern. Therefore, we had to let the code emerge from an analysis of actual responses to the questions.

As illustration, here is a brief recounting of the procedure used in deriving the code of occupational values. First, we drew a sample of about 300 interviews for analysis, turning our attention to all the questions which were designed to elicit occupational values. For coding purposes, the responses to each question were broken down into individual statements which described a single occupational value. Each value mentioned was then entered on an index card in the respondent's own words as recorded by the interviewer. One respondent, for instance, answered the question about what would make an occupation absolutely ideal this way:

> Well, pleasant work; that is, not all kinds of noise and dirt. I want it to pay fairly well. There would have to be variation in work; not monotonous. I would want pleasant companions around me. A good place to eat at work would be important, as well as good working hours, and interesting work.

For this response seven different cards were filled out, as follows: (1) Pleasant work; that is, not all kinds of noise and dirt; (2) I want it to pay fairly well; (3) Variation in work, not monotonous; (4) I would want pleasant companions around me; (5) A good place to eat at work would be important; (6) Good working hours; (7) Interesting work.

From the eight occupational value questions on the 300 sample questionnaires, over 7,200 of these individual cards were prepared, each containing a statement about a discrete occupational value, using the same phrasing as in the recorded responses. The next step was to use the 7,200 cards to prepare a set of value categories and a set of coding instructions with concrete examples. Two people, both of whom were thoroughly acquainted with the aims of the study, independently sorted, combined, and recombined the cards to obtain a set of categories. Then they compared and reviewed their results and resolved their differences in consultation with the third member of the study team. The final result was a fifty-category code, with which it was possible to classify virtually all of the responses to the free-answer questions concerning occupational values according to the same set of categories and according to identical criteria. The nature and variety of the values are illustrated by the following summary headings of the thirty-six that were mentioned most frequently.

1. Financial reward
2. Financial reward (qualified by an explicit statement that it is not of primary importance)
3. Social motives: interpersonal relations with supervisors
4. Social motives: passive relations (having co-workers and other people around one who are congenial)
5. Social motives: active relations (having a chance to work or deal with people in an active, positive sense as part of one's occupation)
6. Doing work that is worthwhile or useful (not specifying the way in which it is worthwhile or useful)
7. Doing work that is worthwhile or useful (in the sense of serving others—without specifying the exact nature of the contribution to others that is to be made)
8. Doing work that is worthwhile or useful to others (in the sense of making others happy or giving them pleasure)
9. Doing work that is worthwhile or useful to others (in the sense of contributing to their training, or to their mental, social, or physical development)
10. Doing work that provides a sense of achievement or accomplishment
11. Obtaining recognition from others for one's work
12. Doing work of a religious, spiritual, or ethical nature
13. Doing work that is interesting or enjoyable (not specifying a particular type of work)
14. Doing work of a specific type that is interesting or enjoyable
15. Having adequate time off for leisure or recreation
16. Doing work that affords security, stability, or fringe benefits
17. Doing work that contributes to one's self-development (through which one can develop one's own capacities, talents, or knowledge)
18. Doing work that calls for self-expression and creativity
19. Having freedom from restrictions affecting one's work (having control over the work or over the way one does it)
20. Avoiding work where there is excessive pressure or tension
21. Avoiding an excessive work load
22. Doing work that is challenging (overcoming obstacles, keeping goals ahead)

23. Having work with responsibility and authority (the power to make decisions)
24. Avoiding work with responsibility and authority (avoiding the necessity to make decisions)
25. Doing work that has prestige
26. Doing work that provides opportunities for self-advancement and progress
27. Doing work that fits one's capacities or training
28. Having the equipment, facilities, or the wherewithal to do the job
29. Avoiding work that is too hard
30. Having good general working conditions (including a satisfactory physical environment in which to work)
31. Working in a desirable location
32. Doing work that is routine and ordered
33. Doing work that is varied and not routine
34. Doing work that provides opportunities to travel
35. Doing mental work
36. Avoiding physical or manual work

The next step after the categories of occupational values had been decided upon was to create the coding instructions.[19] This involved setting down in words the nature and content of each category, along with concrete examples drawn from the actual questionnaires, so that a trained coder would be able to classify any response in the intended way. It was recognized, of course, that a certain amount of slippage from one category to another is inevitable, but great effort went into making the instructions so clear and unambiguous as to reduce such slippage to a small percentage of the total.

This same procedure was followed in creating the codes for all the open-end questions where the nature of the code was not completely dictated by the nature of the hypotheses. In the entire operation, over 14,000 cards were prepared, sorted, and classified as a means of preparing the code and coding instructions. The result was a coding instruction booklet of more than 200 pages, the major portion of it devoted to the open-end question codes.

The actual coding operation—the reading of the responses and the assignment of code numbers to the responses—was carried out jointly by National Analysts, Inc., and the Brookings Institution. The important question arises, "How accurate was the coding?" The question cannot be

[19] Both the creation of the codes and the preparation of the coding instructions were done by the Brookings Institution; however, much invaluable help and advice were given by Mrs. Genevieve Timm, of National Analysts, Inc.

answered with a single set of statistics, because two quite different considerations are involved. In the case of the categorical questions, which require no judgment in assigning a code number, the accuracy of the operation can be checked against an objective standard quite easily. Errors of this kind were kept well below 1 percent. For the open-end responses, the problem is entirely different. Both interpretation and judgment are involved, and there is no objective standard with which to compare the results in order to get an absolute measure of error. The appropriate measure for evaluating such coding, therefore, is the degree of agreement between two sets of coders who have each performed the entire coding and checking operation independently. Independent tests of intercoder agreement were performed on two samples of questionnaires for all of the open-end coding. Both samples showed an average of 93 percent agreement for all of the codes combined, with agreement on individual questions being 82 percent or higher in all cases and in some instances reaching 100 percent.

Punching and Tabulating[20]

Once the coding operation was completed, the coded responses to all of the questions in all of the questionnaires were punched onto standard 80-column IBM cards; a complete verification of all keypunching was performed. As a beginning step, question-by-question tabulations of responses were performed on all the questions for each sample population separately. They showed, as was expected, that many of the free-response code categories were mentioned too infrequently to permit analysis by smaller subgroups (e.g., age, income, etc.), even if the analysis were confined to the two large general samples (nonfederal employed public and federal employees). Consequently, some of the codes were combined into more inclusive categories, and others which could not logically be combined to form larger categories were eliminated.

Following this, numerous further tabulations were performed. These were designed to permit analysis and comparison of the patterns of responses in a considerable number of subdivisions of the sample populations (for instance, by age, patterns of occupational values, attitudes toward federal civil servants, educational levels, geographic regions, occu-

[20] The punching and machine tabulating were performed under contract by National Analysts, Inc.

pations, and income levels). Since the number of subgroup tabulations that are *possible* in a study of this kind is almost astronomical, judgment and considerable restraint had to be exercised to avoid being drowned in a deluge of data, some of it of little or no value.

In general, we confined our cross-tabulations to those which offered a chance of providing enough cases in the various subcategories to make analysis statistically feasible, and which at the same time had a clear bearing on significant hypotheses. Consequently, we made only about twenty sets of subgroup tabulations for each of the two large samples, and two or three additional sets of breakdowns for each of the smaller samples. Even so, the result was approximately 5,000 complex tables containing over 1,000,000 items of information, all of which had to be examined for analytic value, abstracted, summarized, and finally reduced to the basic number we believed were needed to reveal the significant results with force and clarity.[21]

THE MATTERS with which this book is concerned—the images that people have of the federal public service and how these images are distributed in various segments of American society; occupational values and how they are distributed in American society; and the relationships between these two sets of factors as they shed light on the appeal of federal employment—have been the subject of much prior discussion, published and unpublished, and of a certain amount of previous research. This material was highly instructive to us when we were exploring the dimensions of the problem to be investigated, formulating the plan for the research, and interpreting our findings. How the federal service and the American public's attitudes toward it have varied with social change through the years of the Republic's existence is the subject of Chapter 2. The other main stream of previous material that was helpful to us in formulating the present study—informal commentary on and more formal research into both the public service and occupational values—is briefly noted at the end of that chapter.

[21] The basic tables are presented in the *Source Book*.

2

Public Service and American Society

THE PROBLEM of obtaining able men and women to hold positions of public responsibility is as old as government itself. Pericles alluded to it in his Funeral Oration: "We are the only community who regard a man who holds himself aloof from politics not as one who minds his own business, but as a useless citizen."[1] To Pericles, the willingness and the capacity of his fellow citizens to assume public duties was one of the crowning achievements of Athenian democracy. But to present-day analysts of social institutions, these traits also indicate that the Athenian intellectual aristocracy considered employment by the state both desirable and appropriate to their status.

There is probably no country—of whatever size—where public attitudes toward civil employment have not had a bearing on the difficulty or ease of staffing the government. The matter is further complicated by the fact that the attitudes change with changes in the society. In the pages that follow, we shall examine briefly how such social change in the United States has affected the occupational standing of the federal service since the founding of the Republic.

The Founding of the American Federal Service

The task of attracting outstanding individuals into the government has been a persistent concern of government leaders since 1789. To George Washington, shortly before he began his first term as President, the problem seemed especially acute, for he believed that the fate of the federal experiment hinged in part on the quality of the new federal

[1] *Speeches in Thucydides and Funeral Orations,* translated by Arthur S. Way (London: Macmillan, 1934), p. 47.

service.[2] It is difficult today to realize just how venturesome this attempt to create a general government for the new United States seemed in 1789. Never in the history of the world had a government based on republican principles attempted to organize and administer so vast a territory. And never before had the administration of so large an area been so directly dependent upon elected representatives of the people.

Nor were all the talents of American society at President Washington's disposal as he began his formidable task. Then, as now, some individuals were reluctant to leave private life to take a post in the federal service, and many of those who did have a positive interest in government employment found the longer-established public service of the states more appealing than the new and untried government of the Union. Moreover, as Congressman Fisher Ames noted:

> In other countries, where their Governments had been of long standing, persons were trained up with a view to public employments; but in this country this had not been the case, and, therefore, the President found the circle from which to select proper characters for office was very confined.[3]

The purge and flight of the Tories, some of whom had had governmental experience, further curtailed the list of citizens who were suitable for public office.

In spite of these obstacles, Washington and his immediate successors hoped to establish and maintain a federal public service of the highest caliber. Their objective, in Washington's words, was to draw "the first characters of the Union" into the national government.[4] In large part they were successful.

> The call to public service in these formative years was sufficiently compelling to bring to office some of the ablest men of the generation—not

[2] Shortly before leaving Mount Vernon to take up his duties as Chief Executive, Washington wrote: "It is the nature of Republicans, who are nearly in a state of equality, to be extremely jealous as to the disposal of all honorary or lucrative appointments. Perfectly convinced I am, that, if injudicious or unpopular measures should be taken by the Executive under the New Government with regards to appointments, the Government itself would be in the utmost danger of being utterly subverted by these measures." See Washington to Samuel Vaughan, March 21, 1789, *The Writings of George Washington,* John C. Fitzpatrick, ed. (Government Printing Office, 1931-1944), Vol. 10, p. 240.

[3] Quoted in Leonard D. White, *The Federalists* (Macmillan, 1948), p. 318. For a summary of the development of the federal service, see Herbert Kaufman, "The Growth of the Federal Personnel System," in Wallace S. Sayre, ed., *The Federal Government Service: Its Character, Prestige, and Problems* (The American Assembly, Columbia University, 1954).

[4] Washington to James Madison, September 25(?), 1789, *The Writings of George Washington,* Vol. 10, p. 414.

merely Washington, Hamilton, and Jefferson, but John Adams and his son, Wolcott, Steele, Pickering, King, Benjamin Hawkins, Tench Coxe, Higginson and Stoddert, John Marshall and C. C. Pinckney. Seldom has the country been served by more gifted men in posts official and diplomatic. The first precedents of officeholding in high place were honorable ones.[5]

The occupants of lesser offices in the new federal service were, of course, less distinguished. Nonetheless, the competition for such posts was keen—on several occasions Washington first learned of the death of an officeholder upon receiving an application from a would-be successor—and the record of performance of those who held them was generally good.[6] Yet as a product of the eighteenth century, the administrative system of the Federalist era differed profoundly from the public service of a later day. "Its temper and outlook," according to White, "were influenced by the class distinctions of the mother country; its work habits were those of a relatively leisurely era; its tools were of the simplest kind."[7]

It was also a remarkably small public service. In 1792, 780 employees and a small number of deputy postmasters sufficed to run the federal establishment. In 1800 the office of the Secretary of the Navy comprised, in addition to the Secretary himself, a chief clerk, four or five subordinate clerks, a single messenger, and a total pay roll of $9,152. And though the service as a whole grew steadily during its first decade, the entire civil government of the Union in 1801 could be manned by 2,120 regular employees and 880 deputy postmasters.[8]

Nor was the state of the administrative art far advanced in the eighteenth century.

> Most civil servants were engaged in finance, record keeping, and the ordinary type of clerical operations, chiefly plain copying. The professional side of the service was modest indeed, comprising the judges, the district attorneys and an occasional legal counsel elsewhere, and a small number of physicians and surgeons in the army, navy, and marine hospitals. Add a few surveyors in the western wilderness, a few engineers in the army and a naval constructor, and the roll of professionally trained officials is complete. Science—other than the professions—was absent. Statisticians were unknown and professional economists could not be found on the North American continent, much less in the departments of state. It was not an age of experts.[9]

[5] White, *op. cit.*, p. 320.
[6] *Ibid.*, pp. 320-322, 512-516.
[7] *Ibid.*, p. 303.
[8] *Ibid.*, pp. 159, 255.
[9] *Ibid.*, p. 303.

Even so, this new public service of the American Union compared favorably with any the world had yet known. It enabled the national government to organize and administer a territory greater than Caesar's Rome or the dominions of France at the height of Napoleon's power; it weathered the initial challenges to federal authority and thus made the prospects for the preservation of the Union more secure; and it set standards of excellence for the service that could be revived at a later day. Yet the administrative system which the Federalists created with such skill had one weakness that limited its capacity to survive: it was based on an aristocratic tradition that in the context of America's rapidly changing society had but one more generation to endure.

Federalist defeats in the elections of 1800 and the elevation of Thomas Jefferson to the Presidency in 1801 were accompanied by pressures for change in the federal service. Efforts were made to secure a "due participation of office" for deserving Republicans, and a certain number of Federalist incumbents were removed for partisan purposes.[10] Yet under Jefferson and the two other "Virginia dynasty" Presidents who succeeded him the upper-class nature of the service was not fundamentally changed. Thus, from 1789 to 1829, standards of appointment conformed to a single pattern.[11] Like Washington, the Presidents from Jefferson to John Quincy Adams found it hard to conceive of a public service based on principles other than relative tenure, unbending honesty, and reasonable competence.[12]

The Jacksonian Revolution

The years from 1789 to 1829 were a time of far-reaching changes in American society. Within these four decades, the population increased from less than 4,000,000 to nearly 13,000,000. Through the acquisition of Florida and the Louisiana Purchase, the national domain more than doubled. By 1829 men were at work clearing the way for the first steam railroads, white manhood suffrage had been established in most of the

[10] The phrase "due participation of office" is Jefferson's. See "Jefferson to Elias Shipman and others, a Committee of the Merchants of New Haven," in Saul K. Padover, ed., *The Complete Jefferson* (Tudor, 1943), p. 518.

[11] Leonard D. White, *The Jeffersonians* (Macmillan, 1951), p. 368.

[12] Paul P. Van Riper, *History of the United States Civil Service* (Row, Peterson, 1958), p. 25.

states, and thousands of Americans were crossing the mountains each year to establish settlements on the western frontier. Eleven new states—nine of them west of the Appalachians—had been added to the original thirteen. In the election of 1828, all nine of the new western states supported Andrew Jackson, himself a westerner, in his successful bid for the Presidency.

The expansion of the federal service during this period more than matched the phenomenal national growth. The number of employees reached 4,000 by 1810, then climbed to 7,000 by 1820 and to nearly 11,500 by 1830.[13] President Jackson favored limited government and as small a public service as possible, but he also considered it essential that the holders of federal offices should be sympathetic to the ends of his administration and party. In his inaugural address, he made his views explicit:

> The recent demonstration of public sentiment inscribed on the list of Executive duties, in characters too legible to be overlooked, the task of *reform*, which will require particularly the correction of those abuses that have brought the patronage of the Federal government into conflict with the freedom of elections, and the counteraction of those causes which have disturbed the rightful course of appointment and have placed or continued power in unfaithful or incompetent hands.[14]

To Jackson's followers it must have been clear that this declaration had two major implications for the nation's civil employees. The federal service should be made more democratic to mirror the society it was called upon to serve, and it should provide a reservoir of patronage positions that the party in power could distribute among its followers. If there were any doubts about these implications, they were soon dispelled. In his first message to Congress the President enunciated a philosophy of public administration that was to be dominant in America for more than half a century:

> The duties of all public officers are, or at least admit of being made, so plain and simple that men of intelligence may readily qualify themselves for their performance; and I can not but believe that more is lost by the long continuance of men in office than is generally to be gained by their experience.[15]

[13] U.S. Bureau of the Census, *Historical Statistics of the United States, Colonial Times to 1957* (1960), p. 710.

[14] James D. Richardson, ed., *Messages and Papers of the Presidents* (Bureau of National Literature and Art, 1905), Vol. 2, p. 438. The italics are Jackson's.

[15] *Ibid.*, p. 448.

In practice, the proportion of federal officeholders removed by Jackson was not greatly larger than the proportion Jefferson had removed twenty-eight years before. Nevertheless, a profound change took place in the character of the federal service, at both its upper and lower levels. Alexis de Tocqueville, upon his arrival in the United States in 1831, noted that he was "surprised to find so much distinguished talent among the citizens and so little among the heads of the government." He added:

> It is a constant fact that at the present day the ablest men in the United States are rarely placed at the head of affairs; and it must be acknowledged that such has been the result in proportion as democracy has exceeded all its former limits. The race of American statesmen has evidently dwindled most remarkably in the course of the last fifty years.[16]

This change in the quality of the federal service was reflected in the government's lower ranks as well. In Tocqueville's judgment, the general run of American public officials were "frequently unskillful and sometimes contemptible."[17]

Both moral standards and office efficiency declined during the Jacksonian years. Yet these negative consequences were not the only legacy of Jacksonian democracy to American public administration. Stopping short of destroying the administrative system which had been established by the Federalists and, for the most part, maintained by the Jeffersonians, the Jacksonians took the machinery of government their predecessors had left them and added to it a new element of democracy. The result was a public service well adapted to the needs and character of the society which produced it, and one that fostered and reflected the vitality and independent spirit of its people.[18]

Alexis de Tocqueville, coming as he did from a society where aristocratic and autocratic conceptions had shaped the character of the public service, saw this plainly:

> Public officers in the United States are not separate from the mass of citizens; they have neither palaces nor guards nor ceremonial costumes. This simple exterior of persons in authority is connected not only with the peculiarities of the American character, but with the fundamental principles of society. . . . A public officer in the United States is uniformly simple in his manners, accessible to all the world, attentive to all requests, and obliging in his replies. I was pleased by these characteristics of a demo-

---

[16] Alexis de Tocqueville, *Democracy in America* (Vintage Books, 1958), Vol. 1, p. 207.

[17] *Ibid.*, p. 250.

[18] Leonard D. White, *The Jacksonians* (Macmillan, 1956), pp. 554, 566-567.

cratic government; I admired the manly independence that respects the office more than the officer and thinks less of the emblems of authority than of the man who bears them.[19]

NOT UNTIL 1861 was this new type of federal service, based on democratic standards of admission and the partisan rotation of offices, put to a severe test. But then it underwent the greatest ordeal of all—civil war. Faced with the fact that many federal employees were disloyal to the Union and with the need to preserve the unity of the Republican party in order to prosecute the war, President Lincoln made greater use of the spoils system than any of his predecessors had.

Of 1,639 presidential officers, 1,457 were replaced; and removals of subordinate employees in the rest of the civil establishment were almost equally widespread.[20] Appointments to the military forces were also used freely for partisan purposes, and the dismal performance in the field of some of the North's political generals cost the Union more than one battle. All of this took place at a time when enormous new demands were being placed on the public service, and when for the first time, civilian employees of the Union government may have numbered 100,000, with perhaps another 70,000 in the civilian service of the Confederacy.[21] Yet in the end the Union was preserved. The cruel dilemma the President faced between 1861 and 1865 has been summed up by Carl R. Fish: "If Lincoln had made appointments for merit only, the war might have been shortened; on the other hand, he might not have preserved a united North to carry on the war."[22]

Reform Movements and Technological Change

During the era of reconstruction that followed the Civil War the federal service probably reached its lowest point—in prestige, moral stand-

[19] Tocqueville, op. cit., pp. 214-215.
[20] Carl R. Fish, The Civil Service and the Patronage (Longmans, Green, 1905), p. 170.
[21] The estimate of the size of the Union government during the Civil War is taken from Lionel Murphy, "The First Federal Civil Service Commission: 1871-75 (Part I)," Public Personnel Review, Vol. 3 (January 1942), p. 31. For this, as for most estimates of the size of the federal service in the nineteenth century, the margin of error is probably as large as 20 percent. The figure given for the size of the Confederate government appears in Van Riper, op. cit., p. 58.
[22] Fish, op. cit., p. 172.

ards, and level of efficiency. The majority of federal employees were honest and efficient, yet the dominant tone of the Grant administration, during a period when the ethical level of other segments of American society was none too high, was undistinguished. The patronage system, according to White, had "rendered the public services unstable, ignorant, clumsy, expensive, partisan, and at times corrupt."[23]

> During the 1870's there was both incompetence and dishonesty in the large custom houses; discipline and integrity among the navy-yard labor forces were at a low ebb; the Indian service had been roundly condemned by Garfield; land agents connived at irregularities, and surveyors made fraudulent claims for work not performed.[24]

These very excesses, however, led to a countermovement of opinion. The scandals that took place during the Grant administration were accompanied by the first sustained attack on the spoils system in half a century. Led by men like Carl Schurz, E. L. Godkin, and George William Curtis, the New England Yankee who became political editor of *Harper's Weekly* and founder of the National Civil Service Reform League, a determined group of articulate individuals began to press for a new reform of the public service—this time by substituting merit for political partisanship as the basis for appointment of federal officeholders. Under Grant's successors in the White House, Rutherford B. Hayes and James A. Garfield, the tone of the public service slowly began to improve. Finally a number of circumstances—the dramatic assassination of Garfield by a disappointed office seeker, the continuing agitation of the reformers, the obvious need for competence in the management of the public's business, and the growth of Republican fears that the GOP would lose the President's appointive power at the next election—combined to bring about passage of the Pendleton Civil Service Act of 1883.

Designed to make merit the basis for appointment to certain governmental positions, the Pendleton Act was a landmark in the development of the American public service. Its immediate impact was modest—initially the merit system covered only about 14,000 positions. But it created a bipartisan Civil Service Commission to insure that jobs covered by the act would be filled by open, competitive examinations, and it empowered the President to extend the coverage of the merit system by

---

[23] Leonard D. White, *The Republican Era, 1869-1901* (Macmillan, 1958), p. 18.
[24] *Ibid.*, p. 367.

executive order. Successive Presidents, most frequently toward the end of their term in office, gradually extended the plan's coverage.[25] (By 1940 more than 90 percent of the positions in the federal service had been placed under the merit system.)

Thus the foundations for a nonpartisan public service were laid. Yet the original role of the Civil Service Commission, as created by the Pendleton Act, was essentially negative. The Commission was supposed to insure that the agencies of government did *not* do certain things, rather than to assist them in the application of creative techniques to personnel management. Nevertheless, since in 1883 the idea that government positions should be filled on the basis of merit was still considered a radical departure, its implementation in any degree was bound to be salutary.

For the federal service the closing years of the nineteenth century were a period of transition, during which the character of government employment was gradually altered by a number of fundamental developments in the society. New concepts of efficiency in the administration of large-scale organizations were beginning to be applied, a trend symbolized by the occasional appointment of an outstanding businessman as the head of a government department. With the gradual extension of the merit system, the public service was becoming less the pawn of partisan politics. The post-Civil War prejudice against employing southerners as public servants was also on the wane. Once again the federal establishment was becoming a national, rather than a sectional, service.[26]

During the 1880's and 1890's another development began to assume importance—the unionization of certain types of government employees. The growth of federal employee unions paralleled and was influenced by the gains being registered at this time by the labor movement outside the government. For the most part it occurred among skilled and unskilled workers in industrial activities and among postal employees. Thus, the National Association of Letter Carriers, a group that was to take a particularly active role in the fight for better working conditions in the federal service, was formed in 1889.

In its size, too, the national government was changing, as the expansion that had proceeded at an almost uninterrupted rate since 1789 con-

---

[25] Leonard D. White, *Introduction to the Study of Public Administration* (4th edition, Macmillan, 1955), pp. 311-312. For a detailed account of the civil service reform movement, see Ari Hoogenboom, *Outlawing the Spoils: A History of the Civil Service Reform Movement, 1865-1883* (University of Illinois Press, 1961).

[26] White, *The Republican Era*, pp. 387-389.

tinued. By the turn of the century the number of federal employees had reached nearly 240,000.

Yet perhaps the most important change of all during these years stemmed from what White has called the "dawn of the age of the technician." That centuries-old institution, the copy clerk, began to give way to the employee trained in the use of the typewriter and other office machines. In the government's new and rapidly growing scientific agencies, an even greater transformation was taking place: the geologist's hammer, the chemist's reagents, and the plant pathologist's microscope were becoming the marks of a new kind of public service.[27]

The Federal Service in the Twentieth Century

When Theodore Roosevelt, who had been a notably effective member of the Civil Service Commission from 1889 to 1895, succeeded to the Presidency on William McKinley's death in 1901, 42 percent of the positions in the federal service had been placed under the merit system. When he left office in March 1909, the figure stood at 60 percent, and he had been instrumental in raising the public service to a level of importance and excellence that had not been known since its earliest days.[28] But T. R. contributed more than this to the nation's public life: his capacious conception of the power and scope of the Presidency inevitably enhanced the prestige of the entire federal service.

For those involved in the work of the government, it was a time of new departures—in the regulation of business, in the building of national strength, in the administration of colonial dependencies, in the conservation of the nation's resources. The new challenges and excitement, coupled with the dynamic leadership of the President himself, attracted to government service some of the ablest young people of the day. This was when men such as Gifford Pinchot, Felix Frankfurter, and Henry L. Stimson first came to Washington, and their *élan* was infectious. The spirit of the public service at this time made a strong impression on Britain's Lord Bryce: "Never in any country," he said, had he "seen a more

[27] *Ibid.*, pp. 390-391.
[28] Van Riper, *op. cit.*, pp. 202-203; and Commission on Organization of the Executive Branch of the Government [hereafter termed the Second Hoover Commission], Task Force on Personnel and Civil Service, "Highlights in the Growth of the Merit System," *Report on Personnel and Civil Service*, Appendix B (1955), p. 151.

eager, highminded, and efficient set of public servants, men more useful and creditable to their country, than the men doing the work of the American Government in Washington and in the field."[29]

The return of the Democrats to power for the first time in sixteen years, with Woodrow Wilson in the White House, brought an increased demand for patronage appointments to the federal service. For a time, in fact, the administration made skillful use of the appointment process to get its program through Congress, but this soon gave way to the problems engendered by the war in Europe. Finally, with the active participation of the United States in a war of global dimensions, the expansion of the government's activities and responsibilities was staggering. The task of mobilizing the country for war forced the federal service to hire—and to hire quickly—on a scale unequaled before. Of necessity, much of this expansion took place under rules which had been modified for the period of the emergency, outside the regular competitive system.[30] Between 1916 and 1918, the size of the civil establishment nearly doubled, rising to 917,000 by November 1918. Delays occurred and errors were made—but the country's latent strength was organized, an army of more than 2,000,000 men was put in Europe, and the war was won.

This great outpouring of energy was followed by a relatively placid period for the federal service in the 1920's. Both the size and the range of government activities contracted from their wartime peak. By 1922 the number of positions in the Executive branch had shrunk to 560,000, of which 77 percent were under the merit system. Throughout the rest of the decade, these figures remained fairly constant.[31]

In 1920 the basis for a federal retirement system had been established, a move that was one in a series of steps to enhance the security of public employment.[32] Over the years, other fringe benefits were gradually added to the service. For employees who attained career status, various elements of job protection were also provided. In 1912, the La Follette Act had specified that civil servants should have a written statement of the charges against them before they were fired. In 1944 the Veterans Preference Act went considerably farther, requiring that any veteran faced

[29] Quoted in William D. Lewis, *The Life of Theodore Roosevelt* (United Publishers, 1919), p. 258.

[30] Second Hoover Commission, Task Force on Personnel and Civil Service, *op. cit.*, p. 174.

[31] *Ibid.*, p. 175.

[32] Van Riper, *op. cit.*, p. 276.

with removal had the right to appeal to the Civil Service Commission and that the decision of the appeal hearing would be binding on his agency.[33]

The combination of the Great Depression and Franklin D. Roosevelt's New Deal brought a virtual revolution in the role of government in American life. The expansion of public activities was enormous, as the administration grappled with vast and complex problems, ranging from the provision of relief for the unemployed to attempts to rekindle the spark of economic recovery, and from the enforcement of new measures for the regulation of business to the creation of a comprehensive system of social security. With these new functions came a dramatic increase in the size of the federal service, and also new pressures for patronage appointments. Between 1932 and 1936 the number of civilian employees in the federal government grew from 605,000 to 867,000. Yet in 1932, 80 percent of the positions were under the merit system; four years later only 60.5 percent were.[34]

For the government recruiter, the early days of the New Deal were the golden age. The challenge and importance of what the government was trying to do, the urge of many citizens to perform public service, and the absence of jobs elsewhere combined to give the recruiter an unprecedented opportunity to pick and choose among talented applicants. To Rexford Tugwell, one of those who left academic life in response to a call from FDR to come to Washington, this was the "renaissance spring" of American government—and one that left an indelible imprint on the federal public service. The impact of the period is suggested in this vignette by a leading historian of the New Deal:

> The memories would not soon fade—the interminable meetings, the litter of cigarette stubs, the hasty sandwich at the desk or (if there was time) the lazy lunch along sun-drenched wharves by the Potomac, the ominous rumour passed on with relish, the call from the White House, the postponed dinner, the neglected wife, the office lights burning into the night, the lilacs hanging in fragrance above Georgetown gardens while men rebuilt the nation over long drinks, the selflessness, the vanity, the mistakes, the achievement. At his worst, the New Dealer became an arrant sentimentalist or a cynical operator. At his best, he was the ablest, most intelligent, and most disinterested public servant the United States ever had.[35]

[33] Second Hoover Commission, Task Force on Personnel and Civil Service, *op. cit.*, p. 194.
[34] *Ibid.*, p. 176.
[35] Arthur M. Schlesinger, Jr., *The Coming of the New Deal* (Houghton Mifflin, 1958), pp. 19-20.

In the last years of Roosevelt's second term a strong movement developed to extend the coverage of the civil service system to most of the new and exempted positions created by the New Deal. In 1940, the Ramspeck Act authorized the President to issue a series of executive orders which brought more than 90 percent of the permanent positions in the federal government under the merit system. During the years of crisis in the 1940's and 1950's the majority of the positions that were created were included within the regular competitive civil service.

Like Woodrow Wilson, Franklin Roosevelt was forced during the later years of his Presidency to turn increasingly to problems of foreign relations and of preparing the United States to survive in a world at war. The major changes in the federal service from 1939 to 1945 were a reflection of this basic fact. Again the expansion of the government's responsibilities was enormous—ranging from the administration of a comprehensive price-control system to deploying the nation's resources for a two-front war and the successful development of the atomic bomb. At the height of this wartime effort, 3,800,000 people—one in every 15 members of the nation's labor force—were employed in the civilian federal service. At the same time another 12,000,000 men and women were in uniform.

The postwar demobilization of civilians reduced the size of the federal service by nearly half. Yet 1,960,000 people were still working for the government in 1950—nearly a million more than the figure in 1940. With the advent of the Korean war the number rose to 2,400,000; in 1962 it had become 2,514,000. The federal government's responsibilities had, of course, declined somewhat following 1945, but new responsibilities seemed continually to appear. With the Marshall Plan, new programs to provide technical assistance for underdeveloped areas, and the continued maintenance of most of the domestic welfare activities stemming from the New Deal, the range and scope of government activities were larger than in any previous peacetime period in history.

Long-Term Changes

By the early 1960's, a number of basic changes that had reshaped the character of the federal service since 1789 could be identified. They may be summarized as follows:

Growth of the federal work force. In 1801, one American in every 2,000 worked for the federal government. By 1957 one American in every 80 was a federal employee, and of every 30 members of the civilian labor force, one was employed by the federal government. Yet even these figures give an inadequate picture of the present impact of federally supported employment on the nation's economy. Today many services supported by the federal establishment are done on contract by private individuals and groups. According to one estimate, there are nearly 6 million people who are not formally employed by the federal service but who work on activities paid for by the national government through contracts, grants, and other similar arrangements.[36] Nearly 3 million more men and women are in the armed forces. Thus a total of 11 million people—or one among every 6 gainfully employed Americans—occupy jobs that depend directly upon the scope and nature of the activities of the federal service.

Changing social composition. Although a meticulous investigation would be necessary to document the point, it is also likely that the social composition of the federal work force has undergone a marked change since 1789. In its early days the federal service had distinctly aristocratic overtones, particularly in its upper echelons.[37] Today, the government recruiter draws from the total spectrum of American society, and the appointment of members of various minority groups to some of the highest posts the government can offer is one of the principal characteristics of the nation's democratic political system.

Changes in the appeal of federal employment. The appeal of the federal service compared with the appeal of other occupations in the society is another aspect of the history of the American public service that would benefit from detailed further study. Although the documentation is neither definite nor complete, undoubtedly the appeal of public employment has varied considerably—both during different phases in the nation's history and among different groups in the population. In the Federalist era, as we have seen, even the subordinate positions in the federal service were keenly sought, and the call to serve the public

[36] Victor K. Heyman, "Government by Contract," *Public Administration Review,* Vol. 21 (Spring 1961), p. 59.

[37] For a description of the upper-class social and economic position of federal office holders in New York State during the early days of the American Republic, see Arthur Jay Alexander, "Federal Patronage in New York State: 1789-1805" (Ph.D. dissertation, University of Pennsylvania, 1945). See also Anson E. Morse, *The Federalist Party in Massachusetts to the Year 1800* (Princeton: The University Library, 1909), and Charles S. Sydnor, *Gentlemen Freeholders: Political Practices in Washington's Virginia* (University of North Carolina Press, 1952).

in the top-level posts of government attracted some of the ablest statesmen that this country, or any other country, has ever produced. In the period following the Civil War, when the nation's energies were harnessed to the twin objectives of westward expansion and industrial development, the appeal of the public service for the most talented groups in American society declined sharply. New York City, not Washington, was the center where the great decisions affecting American life were made. The scramble for patronage positions at nearly all levels of government was unseemly, and the over-all quality of the federal service dropped markedly. During the New Deal era, by contrast, there was a resurgence of interest in public service, and the federal recruiter did very well in the competition for talent with other segments of American society. Yet, even then, the variations in the attitudes of different groups in the population toward public employment were no doubt extensive.

Increased need for skilled personnel. The relative simplicity of public administration in the eighteenth century has already been noted. In contrast, by the late 1950's the federal government was recruiting cryptographers and electrical engineers, bacteriologists and cartographers, and one of every seven federal white-collar positions required professional training. This trend toward specialization and complexity is, of course, reflected throughout American society, but it has special importance for the government, because the proportion of highly trained people in the federal service is larger than in the work force as a whole.[38]

Relative size of the civilian and the military services. In recent years the historic relationship between the size of the civilian service and the size of the military establishment has also changed. Throughout the second half of the nineteenth century the American aversion to standing armies was reflected in a peacetime military force that was always much smaller than the civilian public service, and, although during the first half of the twentieth century the peacetime military force grew larger than it had been earlier, it was still substantially smaller than the civilian service. The change came with the end of the Korean War in 1953. Since then the number of men and women in uniform has exceeded the number of civilian federal employees.

---

[38] See the two U.S. Civil Service Commission pamphlets *Occupations of Federal White-Collar Workers* (1958), p. 4, and *The Growing Demand for Scientific and Technical Manpower in the Federal Service* (October 1960), pp. 7-9. According to the latter's analysis, approximately 2 percent of the national work force held positions in science or engineering in 1960. The comparable figure for the federal work force was 7 percent.

A formal civil service system. In the early days of the Republic, the departments were sufficiently small that appointments could be made at the discretion of the department head—and in many cases by the President himself. The federal personnel system was both small and flexible. Even when the service as a whole began to grow in size, for many years of the nineteenth century the determination of who should be hired still rested with the heads of the operating agencies. This flexibility was used both for good and for ill by administrators during the heyday of the patronage system. When the Civil Service Commission was created by the Pendleton Act of 1883, qualified applicants began to be certified for positions covered by the act. Gradually the number of positions under the Commission's jurisdiction was expanded, and a relatively centralized system of personnel administration took shape.

Increased fringe benefits. With the creation of a federal retirement scheme in 1920, the basis for an extensive system of fringe benefits for government employees also emerged. Benefits presently include generous vacation and sick leave policies (which existed before the Retirement Act was passed) and the programs for group life insurance (legislation of 1954) and health benefits (1959) which are financed in part by the government. The health program, which provides coverage for most federal employees and their dependents—in all, nearly 5 million people—is the largest employer-sponsored health insurance plan in the world.[39]

Veterans preference. The first statutory provision for preferential treatment of war veterans was made in 1865. It applied to disabled men only, stipulating that they "shall be preferred for appointments to civil offices, provided they are found to possess the business capacity necessary for the proper discharge of such office."[40] At the end of World War I, the scope of this preference was greatly expanded: legislation of 1919 granted preferential treatment to nondisabled veterans, to wives of veterans too disabled to work, and to veterans' widows.[41] In 1944, Congress anticipated the end of World War II by passing an act which codified and extended all previous regulations designed to benefit veterans seeking employment after demobilization. But, whereas previous statutes had

[39] Elizabeth F. Messer, "Health Benefits—Where They Count the Most," *Civil Service Journal,* Vol. 3 (January–March 1963), p. 5.

[40] Quoted in U.S. Civil Service Commission, *Growth of Veterans Preference in the Federal Service* (mimeographed; 1957), p. 1.

[41] *Ibid.,* p. 2.

left the Executive branch wide discretion in administering the program, the 1944 Act strictly specified many details of the program. Veterans, and in certain cases their dependents, were given not only wide preference in obtaining employment, but also special protection against layoffs and extra privileges in cases of disciplinary action.[42]

Growth of federal employee unions. The union movement began to assume importance among postal employees and government industrial workers in the late nineteenth century, but the unionization of other federal employees lagged until World War I and, in some cases, until the depression years. During the 1930's there was friction among several unions which competed for a service-wide membership. In 1963 the largest unions of this type were the American Federation of Government Employees (affiliated with the AFL-CIO) and the National Federation of Federal Employees (not affiliated). In the federal service as a whole, about a third of the employees were union members. Outside the postal service, the proportion was 16 percent.[43] Though the situation has never been carefully studied, the political power of certain of the federal employee unions is undoubtedly considerable. From 1910 to 1960, for example, there were thirty-one successful discharge petitions designed to pry legislation loose from the Committee on Rules in the House of Representatives; six of these—all between 1949 and 1960—had the active backing of the National Association of Letter Carriers. Five of the six led to pay raises for government employees.[44]

Decreasing spread between the top and bottom pay levels. The American federal service has never been the place to amass a fortune. ("A democratic state," Alexis de Tocqueville wrote in 1835, "is most parsimonious toward its principal agents."[45]) And in recent years there has been evidence that most federal salaries lagged behind the compensation outside the government—particularly for people in the upper-level positions in the federal service. This situation has been accentuated by the tendency to raise the pay scales for lower-level government employees proportionately more than the scales at the top. From 1939 to 1960,

[42] In 1962, Congress granted nonveterans already in the federal service rights identical to those of veterans to appeal adverse personnel actions to the Civil Service Commission.

[43] O. Glenn Stahl, *Public Personnel Administration* (fifth edition, Harper & Row, 1962), pp. 224-228.

[44] William C. Doherty, *Mailman U.S.A.* (David McKay, 1960), pp. 217-225.

[45] Tocqueville, *op. cit.*, p. 225.

TABLE 2-1. *Ratio of the Top Salary to the Bottom Salary in the Federal Civil Service, 1924-1964*[a]

Year	Top Salary	Bottom Salary[b]	Ratio of Top Salary to Bottom Salary
1924	$ 7,500	$ 900	8.3
1928	9,000	1,020	8.8
1942	9,000	1,200	7.5
1945	9,800	1,440	6.8
1946	10,000	1,690	5.9
1948	10,330	2,020	5.1
1949	14,000	2,120	6.6
1951	14,800	2,420	6.1
1955	14,800	2,600	5.7
1956	16,000	2,690	6.0
1958	17,500	2,960	5.9
1960	18,500	3,185	5.8
1962	20,000	3,245	6.2
1964[c]	20,000	3,305	6.1

[a] Sources: For 1924–1956, U.S. Civil Service Commission, Federal Employment Statistics Office, *Pay Structure of the Federal Civil Service* (June 30, 1960); for 1958–1964, relevant reports of the House Committee on Post Office and Civil Service.
[b] The minimum rate for CPC-2 is used as the bottom salary through 1951. This schedule was abolished in 1955; for 1955 and after the bottom salary figures denote the minimum rate for GS 1.
[c] The 1964 figures are those authorized to go into effect on January 1, 1964, by the 1962 Pay Reform Act; they are subject to alteration by new legislation in 1963 or 1964.

for example, the pay of a clerk carrier in the Postal Field Service increased by 155 percent, that of a GS 1 by 152 percent, and that of a GS 5 by 117 percent. During this same period a GS 11's pay went up by 98 percent and a GS 15's by only 71 percent.[46]

This situation, however, is nothing new. Tocqueville noted long ago that "in America the secondary officers are much better paid and the higher functionaries much worse than elsewhere."[47] Nevertheless, the top salary in the federal service of the 1960's was substantially less in relation to the minimum federal salary than it was forty years earlier (see Table 2-1). More and more the pay structure of the federal service has tended to resemble a mud pie, not a pyramid.

In 1962, Congress passed a new Federal Pay Reform Act which in time could lead to an important change in the structure of federal salaries. In this legislation Congress accepted the principle that an attempt

[46] U.S. Civil Service Commission, *Questions and Answers Regarding the New Federal Pay Reform Act* (mimeographed; October 1962), p. 3.
[47] Tocqueville, *op. cit.*, p. 225.

should be made to bring all General Schedule salaries through the GS 15 level into line with the compensation for similar jobs in private enterprise. The measure also called for an annual survey of salaries inside and outside the government, to serve as a guide line for future salary legislation. But enunciating the salary comparability principle is not the same thing as implementing it. The actual pay raises contained in the 1962 Act again fell short of achieving comparability with the private enterprise rates for mid- and upper-level government employees. And, as of late summer 1963, pay legislation that would actually bring upper-level government salaries into line with those outside had yet to be enacted.

Altered role of the Civil Service Commission. The new demands placed on the public service during World War II stimulated the Civil Service Commission to decentralize many of its activities to the operating agencies—a trend that has continued during the postwar years. At the same time the Commission began to concern itself increasingly with the broader aspects of personnel management. Its traditional function of resisting encroachments on the merit system remains important, but, as one close student of public administration has put it, "The decade and a half since World War II has seen greater and greater efforts to modify the role of the central governmental personnel agency from that of a policeman to that of a major staff assistant to line management."[48]

Increased scope and complexity of administrative functions. Underlying all of these trends has been an enormous growth since 1789 in the scope and complexity of the functions the federal service has been called upon to perform. Although the development of any of the older agencies could be traced to illustrate this growth, the U.S. Weather Bureau will serve here as our example.

The first federally financed meteorological effort in the United States was spurred by an interest in the weather's potential effect on the fortunes of war: during the War of 1812, the Surgeon General of the Army directed all hospital surgeons to make regular weather observations and to keep climatological records.[49] Later efforts to organize a weather reporting service through the nation's telegraph companies were disrupted

[48] Van Riper, "Public Personnel Literature: The Last Decade," *Public Personnel Review,* Vol. 22 (October 1961), p. 227.

[49] Donald R. Whitnah, *A History of the United States Weather Bureau* (University of Illinois Press, 1961), p. 9. We have drawn on this book for the facts that follow in this and the next three paragraphs.

by the Civil War. In 1870, however, Congress authorized a national weather system under the Army Signal Service, and since that time the federal government has been the public's chief source of information about the weather. Renamed the Weather Bureau, the system later became a civilian agency, first in the Department of Agriculture, then in the Department of Commerce.

Like the operations of many other government agencies, the activities of the Bureau have undergone a technological revolution. Initially a federal weather expert made most of his observations with the naked eye, and had only a few—and relatively crude—instruments to supplement this visual information. In 1900, the Bureau conducted experiments with the wireless telegraph and from then on the pace of technological innovation accelerated. The development of the airplane soon made it possible to collect data far above the earth's surface. Beginning in the late 1930's, airplane observations were largely replaced by data obtained by radiosonde, a radio meteorograph which could be sent to altitudes of more than 50,000 feet. And on April 1, 1960, the successful launching of Tiros I, the world's first meteorological satellite, opened a new era in man's quest for knowledge about the weather.

Through the years, each technological development was reflected in a marked change in both the number and the kind of personnel employed by the Weather Bureau. In 1871 there were 233 full-time employees; in 1960 there were 4,754. Over the same time span, the Bureau's annual appropriation grew from $15,000 to $51,355,000. Recruitment standards have also changed greatly. Although even in the earliest years operations were built around a corps of trained scientists, many observers with a relatively low level of specialized training were also employed. Today the average senior scientist on the staff is the product of a vastly complex training, often in a field that was unknown ninety years ago— and the typical observer or junior forecaster coming new to the staff is a college graduate, with a major in meteorology or, at the very least, a strong background in basic physics and mathematics.

The present activities of the Weather Bureau are of such range and scope that few Americans are unaffected, either directly or indirectly, by them. The farmer, the vacationer, the fruit grower, the traveler about to board a plane, the hundreds of thousands of citizens who for a host of reasons dial "Weather" each day all make use of the services provided by this agency of the United States government.

In the years ahead, the functions performed by the agencies and departments of the federal service will, in all probability, continue to grow in magnitude, importance, and complexity. The social needs and demands—for worldwide economic development programs, urgent domestic social services, and maintenance of the United States' position of leadership in the world—which in the past two decades have brought about the tremendous expansion of government functions are not likely to diminish in the foreseeable future. The men and women in the federal service of the 1960's confront awesome responsibilities.

PREVIOUS INVESTIGATIONS of the twofold theme with which this study is concerned—the relationship of people's basic occupational values to their attitudes about government employment—parallel the historical evolution of the American public service. As the federal service has grown from the initial very simple administrative machine, manned by a few hundred employees, to what is probably the largest and most complex administrative establishment in the world, so too have appraisals and investigations of both the government service and general occupational values changed.

Appraisals of the American federal service began in the late eighteenth and early nineteenth centuries with comments in the journals, letters, or books of contemporary observers—Europeans and Americans alike. Through the years since then we have had documents, steeped in controversy, prepared both by men (in and out of government) who sought to change the nation's administrative system and by men defending the status quo; internal reviews of the government's operations, conducted by the Executive branch and its various agencies and by Congress; the testimony of experts as to the efficiency and drawing power of the public service in relation to other occupations; scholarly studies of specific aspects of the public service; statistical profiles of the composition of the federal bureaucracy; a few recent projections of the government's future manpower needs; the contributions of modern industrial psychology and sociology to an understanding of the workings of large-scale organizations, whether in private industry or government; and surveys, by university researchers and by public opinion polling organizations, designed to probe the attitudes of the American public toward the politician, public vs. private employment, and the role of the public servant in our society.

The oldest sources of information concerning American occupational values also stem from observations made by foreign visitors and by Americans themselves. And even today the first-hand impressions of perceptive observers of the American scene are of primary importance. After World War I, however, new kinds of analyses began to appear. The result was a series of new approaches and insights into man's attitudes toward his work: studies of the prestige enjoyed by different occupations; investigations of employee morale and related problems by those concerned with human relations in industry; examination of particular motives, such as a desire for high pay, that were believed to be of prime importance on the job; investigation of the entire process by which the individual chooses an occupation; studies by business corporations designed to indicate the steps that should be taken to attract high quality personnel; studies of the full range of occupational values common to particular social classes or groups and of the distribution of these values among different groups in the society; general interpretive works such as C. Wright Mills' *White Collar* or William H. Whyte's *The Organization Man;* works that attempt to synthesize the now extensive literature on occupational values; and the cross-cultural comparisons that have been made in recent years of occupational values in a number of different societies.

The foregoing summary indicates something of the variety of the subject matter and methodology that these two main streams of previous appraisal and research contain.[50] But perhaps it also signifies something more—the thread of development in the way Americans have studied their public service and occupational values. Over the years, appraisals of the nation's administrative system and attitudes toward work have increasingly been supplemented by more systematic investigations of these topics.

Yet given the advances of recent years in the methods of social analysis, the gap between what could be studied with profit and what has been studied remains large. Shortly after we began our research, two distinguished students of public administration, Wallace S. Sayre and Frederick C. Mosher, called for a study of "public attitudes and the public service" as an important element of research in public personnel administration. They pointed out:

> The prestige of the public service is a much discussed phenomenon. Although there exists relatively little comprehensive or systematic informa-

[50] For a detailed discussion of these materials, see the *Source Book*, Appendix A.

tion about the matter, there is a widely held assumption that public service prestige does not rank favorably with nongovernmental employment prestige. The information available is mainly concerned with the attitudes of aggregate, undifferentiated publics toward an aggregate, undifferentiated public service. The most promising assignments for future research would seem to be those which are directed at discovering the attitudes of carefully defined and precisely identified publics toward specifically defined segments of the public service, perhaps supplemented by inquiries intended to elicit the attitudes of the special publics toward the public service as a whole. Such research needs also to aim at a deep penetration into the nature and intensity of the attitudes being measured. Out of a series of such studies a more realistic measure of the prestige and status of the public service might emerge.[51]

Prestige, of course, is but one aspect of the public's attitudes toward the government service. Yet the above statement summarizes both the need and the opportunities for research on public attitudes toward the public service that existed when we began the present study. The standing and appeal of the federal service had not been examined in detail on the basis of a national survey of the American population and several of its component parts. Nor had there been a comprehensive analysis that presented an over-all view of the strengths and weaknesses of the federal government as it competes for talented manpower in the job markets of the 1960's. In the pages that follow, we have tried to provide new findings and data of this kind.

[51] Wallace S. Sayre and Frederick C. Mosher, *An Agenda for Research in Public Personnel Administration* (National Planning Association, 1959), p. 61.

3

Job Satisfaction, Sense of Progress, and Expectations

WHEN THE RESPONDENTS in the nonfederal populations were describing their occupational values, assessing the appeal and the positive and negative features of federal employment, and judging the characteristics of federal employees, how were they themselves feeling about their own occupations? Were they disillusioned, dissatisfied, or pessimistic, or was the general context one of satisfaction and optimism? And what about the federal employee populations? How did their assessments of their job situations compare with those of their counterparts outside government?

Answers to these questions provide a useful frame of reference for understanding and evaluating the subsequent material this study presents on the patterning of occupational values and on the ways in which people, both within and outside the federal government, perceive federal employment and federal employees. Consequently, we begin the discussion of our research findings with a brief chapter on the respondents' assessments of three aspects of "how they are doing" occupationally—their present satisfaction, sense of progress, and expectation for the future.[1]

General measures of these aspects were derived from the judgments made by respondents on a ten-point self-anchoring occupational value scale. Each respondent was handed a card showing the ten-step ladder, and the interviewer said, "Here is a picture of a ladder. Suppose we say

[1] The basic tables in which these findings and all others referred to in this volume are shown may be found in the *Source Book*. In the chapters that follow, occasional specific reference is made to the *Source Book;* where such reference is not made, and where tabular material is not furnished in this present volume, the reader can assume that the data involved are shown in the companion volume.

at the *top* of the ladder is the *very best*, the absolutely ideal sort of occupation you have just described. At the *bottom* is the *very worst* sort of occupation. Where on this ladder would you put your present occupation, that is, what you are doing now?" Next, the interviewer said, "Now think of what you were doing five years ago. Where on this ladder would you put what you were doing as an occupation five years ago?" And finally, "Thinking now of your occupational future. Where on the ladder do you expect to be five years from now?" Table 3-1 shows the mean scale ratings given by the various nonfederal and federal employed groups.[2]

A glance at the "present occupation" column suggests that occupational satisfaction is substantially high on the average in all the employed populations studied.[3] Without exception, the scores fall in the upper third of the ten-point scale. It is equally clear that all the groups indicate a marked sense of being better off now than they were five years ago; in each one of the employment categories ratings are significantly higher for "present occupation" than for "five years ago." Occupational optimism would also appear to be the keynote; again without exception, the "five years from now" scores exceed the "present occupation" scores by significant amounts.

These results have several important implications for the research as a whole. It is clear, for example, that most of the interviewees were responding to the questionnaire in an attitudinal context that was quite the reverse of occupational unhappiness, disillusionment, and negative expectation. It appears also that when people think of making changes in employment, most of them are far more apt to think of the positive appeal of a new job rather than of escape from an old one. In addition, since the general findings indicate that basic occupational values are being satisfied to a considerable degree, the range of occupational values with which people can concern themselves is greatly broadened. And it would seem that both the average nonfederal employee, when asked to

[2] All figures in this study are, of course, subject to sampling error. Tables helpful in assessing their statistical significance are provided in the *Source Book*, Chap. 3, section on "Sampling Error." In most cases, differences between means (scale scores) of roughly 0.5 to 0.7 scale points, and differences between percentages of roughly 5 to 10 percent begin to be large enough to merit interpretive consideration. However, this is merely a "rule of thumb." In our evaluations of the figures, we have taken account not only of sampling error but also of such matters as the nature of the question, interviewing accuracy, coding consistency, the patterning of related results, and so forth.

[3] We recognize that making this absolute judgment on the basis of absolute scale scores is risky. However, free responses also showed a balance heavily on the side of over-all occupational satisfaction, indicating that the conclusion is warranted.

TABLE 3-1. *Respondents' Ratings of Where They Are Now Occupationally, Were Five Years Ago, and Expect To Be Five Years Hence.*[a]

Employed Groups	Average Number Answering	Five Years Ago	Present Occupation	Five Years from Now
Nonfederal Populations				
General employed public	(1,063)	6.4	7.1	8.1
By sex				
Men	(837)	6.3	7.1	8.0
Women	(226)	6.8	7.4	8.3
By educational level[b]				
High school not completed	(308)	6.4	7.0	7.4
High school completed	(478)	6.2	6.9	8.1
Some college	(120)	6.5	7.4	8.5
College graduate	(129)	6.9	8.0	8.9
Groups in education				
High school teachers[c]	(259)	7.4	8.4	9.0
College teachers (total)	(448)	7.7	8.7	9.2
Natural scientists	(115)	7.7	8.8	9.3
Social scientists	(101)	7.2	8.3	8.9
Engineers	(81)	7.5	8.4	9.1
Groups in business				
Executives	(270)	6.8	8.1	8.9
Natural scientists	(82)	7.0	8.0	8.9
Social scientists	(72)	6.2	8.0	9.1
Engineers	(86)	6.9	8.1	9.0
Federal Populations				
General federal employees	(896)	6.1	7.0	8.1
By sex				
Men	(633)	6.0	6.9	8.0
Women	(263)	6.4	7.1	8.3
By educational level[b]				
High school not completed	(181)	6.1	6.9	8.0
High school completed	(339)	5.9	6.8	7.9
Some college	(172)	6.1	6.8	8.1
College graduate	(152)	6.7	7.4	8.4
Executives	(262)	7.0	8.0	8.9
Natural scientists	(85)	6.5	7.9	8.7
Social scientists	(85)	6.5	7.7	8.8
Engineers	(89)	6.4	7.6	8.4

[a] Mean ratings on the ten-step, self-anchoring "ideal occupation" scale; the higher the score, the nearer to "ideal." Student populations are not included here; the questions put to them differed from those for the presently employed groups.

[b] The number of respondents by educational level is less than the number for the population as a whole, because a small percentage of respondents could not be safely fitted into any of the four levels. This is true also of subsequent tables that carry this breakdown.

[c] For purposes of analysis, high school vocational counselors have been included in the high school teacher population, and not tabled separately, in this and subsequent tables in this volume.

appraise federal employment, and the average federal employee, when asked to appraise nonfederal employment, are apt to base their judgments not only on their perceptions of *present* occupational standing but also on a marked sense of occupational progress in the past and a strong positive expectation for the future.

With respect to expectation for the future, the findings for high school students, college seniors, and graduate students merit presentation. These groups are not shown in Table 3-1 because, with rare exceptions, the individual students had no present or previous full-time employment to rate. They were asked instead to rate where on the ten-step ladder scale they expected to start out occupationally, and where they expected to be five years later. As the following figures indicate, the expectations are positively related to present educational level, and the respondents in each group are relatively modest about where they expect to start out—but far from modest about where they expect to be five years later.

	Number Answering	Expect To Be At Start	Expect To Be Five Years Later
High School Students	(358)	5.5	8.0
College Seniors	(404)	6.3	8.2
Graduate Students	(381)	6.8	8.4

They show a far higher degree of optimism concerning their occupational progress over a five-year period than do any of the employed groups. In addition, the scores show a positive relationship with academic grades; the higher the grade, the higher a student expects to be at the start and also five years later.[4] One may well wonder how their ideas of what federal employment has to offer fit such a pattern of expectation.

The results shown in Table 3-1 for the groups employed in education also merit special brief mention. The high school and college teachers give the highest ratings of any group, nonfederal or federal, for occupation at present, five years ago, and five years hence. At the very least, this raises interesting questions concerning the place of financial reward in the scales of occupational values of the various populations. Certainly the teachers must have had something other than financial reward in mind, since their scores, especially on present satisfaction, substantially

[4] See the *Source Book,* Chap. 19, Table 19-2.

exceed those of even the four business groups, who on the average are much more highly paid than the teachers.

For the federal employee populations, we may note with particular interest the pattern of scores for the general federal work force. Over all, their scores and those of the general employed public are very similar— "five years ago" ratings are 6.1 and 6.4 respectively, "present occupation" almost the same at 7.0 and 7.1, and "five years from now" identical at 8.1. Breakdowns by sex are similarly parallel, with women showing slightly higher scores in both instances. However, the similarity disappears when we compare the patterns by educational levels, especially on the ratings for "present occupation" and "five years from now."

When we examine the "present occupation" figures according to educational level we see that people in the general employed public who have had some college experience, and especially those who are college graduates, rate their present occupations substantially higher than people at the two lower levels: moving up the four levels, the scores are 7.0, 6.9, 7.4 and 8.0. For the general federal employees the comparable figures are 6.9, 6.8, 6.8 and 7.4. Thus, the federal employees at the two lower educational levels rate their present occupations nearly as high as do their nonfederal counterparts. But those who have had some college experience or are college graduates rate their present occupation more than 0.5 scale points lower than do their nonfederal counterparts.

The comparative results are even more extreme in the case of the ratings for "five years from now." In the nonfederal general work force there is a sharply graduated score rise—from 7.4 at the lowest educational level through 8.1, 8.5, and 8.9 at the other three levels. Comparable figures for general federal employees at the four levels are 8.0, 7.9, 8.1 and 8.4. Thus federal employees with less than a high school education rate their expectations 0.6 *higher* than their nonfederal counterparts, whereas the expectation rating for college graduates in government work is 0.5 *lower* than that given by college graduates in the general employed public.

In sum, federal employees at the two lower educational levels yield scores equal to or above those given by people of comparable educational level in the general employed public on occupational past, present, and future. However, federal employees with some college experience show ratings that are not appreciably higher than those of the less-educated government employees, and both the some college and college graduate groups show markedly lower ratings of occupational past, present, and future than those of their nonfederal counterparts. Even among the "elite" federal groups—the executives, natural and social scientists, and engineers—these negative comparative results do not entirely disappear. It is true that the executives and both groups of scientists show occupational past, present, and future scores equal to or only slightly lower than those of their business world counterparts, but the scores of federal engineers are significantly lower than those of engineers in business. And the federal natural and social scientists and, especially, the engineers show scores that are markedly lower on all three measures than those of the comparable groups in the colleges.

These findings are disconcerting in view of the nature of the federal government's present and projected "high-level" personnel problem, but cannot be said to be unexpected. They confirm, at least in tentative fashion, that the problem has its correlate in the occupational outlook of the present upper-level federal employee, but of course do not tell us why this is so. Thus, they place a major explanatory burden on our subsequent analysis. What can we say about occupational values and the perceived nature of federal employment which would help to account for such a pattern of results?

4

Occupational Values

In describing the patterning of occupational values among the nonfederal and federal populations studied, we will confine our attention mainly to those findings that are most significant in relation to perceptions of federal employment and of the federal civil servant. Two sources of data are drawn upon. The first is the result of the analysis of answers to two free-response questions which were designed to elicit descriptions of "the kinds of things about an occupation that would make it absolutely ideal" and "the kinds of things about an occupation which would make it the worst or least satisfying."[1] These questions tend to bring out positive and negative occupational values which are of *concern* to people; the results therefore should not be interpreted as reflecting the *importance* attached to the values.[2]

The other data drawn upon are the rating scores obtained when respondents sorted thirty "occupational value" statements on the ten-point agree-disagree scale. The statements, either as single items or clusters of several items, concerned such matters as financial reward, occupational involvement, status and recognition, personal relations on the job, occupational competitiveness, self-development, opportunity vs. security, sense of duty, and so on.[3]

The results from these two types of inquiry—free-response questions and item scaling—supplement each other in assessing the pattern of occupational values. They also complement each other's reliability; on all points where comparisons of results can be made, the findings from the two approaches are highly consistent.

[1] The two questions also served to anchor the top and the bottom of the self-anchoring ten-step occupational value scale.
[2] The distinction between the concepts "concern" and "importance" was discussed in Chapter 1.
[3] For the thirty statements (part of the fifty-five statements noted in Chapter 1) see Item 17 of the basic questionnaire in the Appendix.

Some General Considerations

In considering the free-answer responses as a whole, one is impressed with the wide variety of occupational values with which people are concerned. The listing of the thirty-six most commonly mentioned values presented in Chapter 1 does not by any means encompass the variety of occupational aspirations and fears mentioned by significant numbers of people in the various populations. No list can accurately characterize the complexity of occupational values and their great variations from person to person and group to group, for any listing of the types of responses in order of frequency which may be valid for one group has little validity for any other group that differs in education or occupational level. Nevertheless, there are certain occupational values which rank near the top in frequency of mention by almost all groups, even though the precise rank order usually differs from one group to another: financial reward, the general physical aspects of the working environment, personal relationships with other people at work, and the amount of self-determination and freedom in the job. Beyond these, there is little consensus. The amount of challenge, for example, offered by the work is very important among highly educated groups, but is mentioned hardly at all by those with little education. Similar variability from group to group is seen in estimations of such values as the worthwhileness of the work, the variety afforded, and the degree of opportunity offered for self-development and self-expression.

Of considerable interest is the fact that the patterns of negative values and positive values are not simply mirror images. To be sure, there is a rough parallel between the two patterns, but the significant differences are many. Personal relationships with people at work is a case in point. As a positive value, all groups give considerable emphasis to the active aspect of personal relations—that is, being associated with stimulating, interesting people; on the negative side, however, this concern with the active aspect appears hardly at all. Instead, the focus of concern is not on the *lack* of interesting and stimulating personal relationships, but on the difficulties of working with unpleasant, disagreeable people.

Concern with the nature of supervision differs in like manner. In all groups more concern is expressed about the negative aspects of bad supervision than about the positive aspects of good supervision. Another example is the reference to routine as a negative value; frequency of mention is high in all groups, ranging from about 20 to over 60 per cent. Yet variety and lack of routine and monotony in one's work is rarely cited as a positive value.

An almost uniformly high proportion of respondents in all groups—from about two thirds to over three fourths—mention as a positive occupational value the interest, enjoyment, or satisfaction of doing work one is interested in, wants to do, or likes to do; yet in one sense this common response is not an occupational value at all. Rather, it is a global summary of many of the values with which the respondent is concerned, and tells us nothing about the content of what is regarded as interesting, satisfying, or enjoyable. In a large share of the interviews, the response is clearly an opening gambit, an attitudinal summary which lays the groundwork for further, more precise specification. Because of such limitations, this global category has not ordinarily been treated in the subsequent analyses.

Considered by itself, however, the commonness of such a response is of great interest. It shows that a majority of people in all walks of life in the United States feel that, ideally, their occupations should satisfy their personal, individual occupational aims. Such overwhelming free mention of personal, self-oriented motivation suggests a broad cultural acceptance of the legitimacy of having personal occupational aims apart from those of any organization or of the society as a whole.

The General Employed Public

Major Occupational Concerns

The occupational values mentioned by 10 per cent or more of the respondents in the general work force when they were asked to describe the kinds of things about an occupation which would make it "ideal" are presented in rank order in Table 4-1. Topping the list with almost equal percentages are money and having a physical working environment that is pleasant, clean, and safe. Good personal relations with people at work is the third most frequently cited consideration. The desire to be one's own master, to be free from heavy supervision, to have freedom of thought and action in one's work also is a pervasive concern as indicated by the 29 percent figure for "self-determination."

Following the four highest ranking values, there is a sharp drop to security of job and income, mentioned by 15 percent. Since the *importance* of job and income protection to a major share of the work force can scarcely be doubted, we must conclude that the feeling of job secur-

TABLE 4-1. *Attributes of the "Ideal" Occupation Mentioned by 10 Percent or More of the General Employed Public*

Attributes of the "Ideal" Occupation		Percent of 1,136 Respondents Mentioning[a]
High or good financial reward		43%
Good physical environment and working conditions		41
Good personal relations with people (not supervisors) at work		30[b]
Passive (e.g., being around pleasant, agreeable people)	12%	
Active (e.g., meeting stimulating people; making good contacts)	19	
Miscellaneous	1	
Self-determination		29
Security, stability, fringe benefits		15
Doing work that is worthwhile, useful, constructive		14
Doing work that fits one's capacities and/or training		14
Good superior, supervisor, boss		11
Variety in the work, absence of monotony and routine		10
Leisure, recreation, time off, vacations		10
Self-development, self-expression, and creativity		10

[a] Percentages add to more than 100 owing to multiple replies.
[b] Subcategory percentages add to more than the category total owing to multiple replies.

ity is sufficiently pervasive among these respondents to enable them to consider other positive occupational concerns.

Tied for sixth place in the hierarchy of positive occupational values (and not significantly lower than job security) is the desire to do work that is worthwhile, useful, constructive. Subsumed under this heading were responses dealing with work which makes a contribution both to specific kinds of people and to society in general. Many of the replies were highly specific in emphasizing goals of increasing the happiness, the training, or the mental, social, or physical development of others. This value is of special interest because of the relevance of the service motive to the nature of public employment.

The attributes of the "worst sort" of occupation mentioned by 10 percent or more of the general employed public are presented in rank order in Table 4-2. Notable by its absence from the list is the category of "absence of, or insufficient job security, stability, protection, fringe benefits (retirement, illness, income protection)." Only 9 percent of the respondents in the general employed public give replies falling in this category. Perhaps the wording of the question suggested that, no matter

TABLE 4-2. *Attributes of the "Worst" Occupation Mentioned by 10 Percent or More of the General Employed Public*

Attributes of the "Worst" Occupation		Percent of 1,135 Respondents Mentioning[a]
Bad physical environment and working conditions		48%
Poor or inadequate financial reward		27
Too much routine in the work; monotony; not enough change, variety		21
Bad or inadequate relations with people (not supervisors) at work		19[b]
Passive (e.g., being around unpleasant, disagreeable people)	11%	
Active (e.g., not meeting stimulating, worthwhile people)	3	
Miscellaneous	7	
Bad superior, supervisor, boss		18
Lack of self-determination		15
Excessive work load; hard work		12
Physical work; work that is menial or manual		10

[a] Percentages add to more than 100 owing to multiple replies.
[b] Subcategory percentages add to more than the category total owing to multiple replies.

how bad the "worst" occupation was, one would at least have a job, and thus it inhibited replies concerned with job and other security. In any case, the 9 percent figure indicates that at the time of the interviews (the early 1960's) there was no widespread apprehension about job and income security among employed adults.

Looking now at the replies that *were* made by at least 10 percent of the respondents, the composite picture of the "worst" occupation involves working conditions which are unpleasant, dirty, unsafe or otherwise physically undesirable; low pay; monotonous, routine work; disagreeable associates; bad supervision; little freedom; excessive work; and work that is physical or menial. These negative elements have a rock-bottom quality. They are the kinds of things which can violate a human being physically, mentally, and socially and invade the sense of individuality. We might characterize them as attributes of occupational equilibrium—that is, they are anchored in basic human motives which must not be excessively violated if the individual is to be free to pursue "higher-order" occupational goals.

Variations by Education, Income, and Occupation

Occupational values vary in the general work force according to education, income, and occupation. Many of the variations are large, and they form a coherent pattern that is basically similar for all three measures.

Considering first the descriptions of the "ideal" occupation as they relate to educational level (Table 4-3), we find that the higher the level, the less frequent are the references to good physical environment and working conditions and a good and understanding supervisor or boss. At the same time, the higher the educational level, the more likely is the respondent to cite associations with stimulating, worthwhile peo-

TABLE 4-3. *Education in the General Employed Public, Related to Mention of Attributes of the "Ideal" Occupation*

Attributes of the "Ideal" Occupation	High School Not Completed	High School Completed	Some College	College Graduate
Positive Relationship to Education				
Good *active* relationships with people (not supervisors) at work	12%	18%	26%	34%
Doing work that is worthwhile, useful, constructive	9	10	22	32
Sense of achievement or accomplishment	7	7	9	15
Self-development, self-expression, and creativity	6	7	16	22
Sense of challenge, overcoming obstacles, keeping goals ahead	1	5	16	18
Negative or No Relationship to Education				
High or good financial reward	40	44	39	44
Good physical environment and working conditions	39	48	35	25
Good superior, supervisor, boss	12	13	10	4
Security of job, income, retirement	12	17	15	12
NUMBER ANSWERING	(330)	(508)	(129)	(139)

ple; opportunity for self-advancement; opportunity for self-development, self-expression, and creativity; an occupation that offers challenge; and being able to do worthwhile, constructive work.

Similar variations by educational level occur in descriptions of the factors that would characterize the worst sort of occupation (Table 4-4). The higher the level, the less likely is the mention of such negative occupational values as doing a specific kind of work one especially dislikes,

TABLE 4-4. *Education in the General Employed Public, Related to Mention of Attributes of the "Worst" Occupation*

Attributes of the "Worst" Occupation	High School Not Completed	High School Completed	Some College	College Graduate
Positive Relationship to Education				
Lack of self-determination	13%	13%	23%	23%
Monotony, routine, lack of variety	7	22	30	45
Lack of self-development, self-expression, and creativity	1	2	3	13
Little or no sense of achievement or accomplishment	0	3	4	11
Negative Relationship to Education				
Bad physical environment and working conditions	54	51	46	24
Poor or inadequate financial reward	30	29	20	20
Excessive work load; hard work	20	10	5	4
Absence of, or insufficient, security of job, income, retirement	11	9	7	5
NUMBER ANSWERING	(327)	(512)	(129)	(137)

poor physical environment on the job, excessive workloads, and insufficient security of job or income. On the other hand, the higher the level, the more likely is the respondent to note such negative concerns as being unable to do the particular kind of work one likes; being unable to engage in worthwhile, constructive work; lacking opportunity for self-determination and freedom, and for self-development, self-expression, and self-advancement; and doing routine and monotonous work.

Examination of the scores by educational level on the occupational value scale items confirms the general nature of the results obtained on the open-end questions. This is illustrated by the first five items in Table 4-5, which show a strong positive relationship between educational level and desire for self-development, authority, challenge, and (as opposed to security) opportunity, and a negative relationship with the identification of money as a necessary ingredient in success. The scores on the last two items in Table 4-5, however, add an additional element to the pattern. Agreement with the statement "To me, work is nothing more than a way of making a living" declines dramatically from 5.6 among those who have not completed high school to 2.6 among college

TABLE 4-5. *Education in the General Employed Public, Related to Ratings of "Occupational Value" Statements*[a]

Occupational Value Statements	High School Not Completed	High School Completed	Some College	College Graduate
"To me, it's important to have the kind of work that gives me a chance to develop my own special abilities"	7.6	8.1	8.5	8.9
"It is satisfying to direct the work of others"	6.0	6.5	7.1	7.6
"Work is most satisfying when there are hard problems to solve"	5.6	6.4	7.6	7.8
"It is more important for a job to offer *opportunity* than *security*"	5.3	5.7	6.6	7.2
"To be really successful in life, you have to care about making money"	6.6	5.7	5.5	4.6
"To me, work is nothing more than a way of making a living"	5.6	4.0	3.2	2.6
"I like the kind of work you can forget about after the work day is over"	7.5	6.7	6.0	5.3
AVERAGE NUMBER ANSWERING	(304)	(495)	(123)	(135)

[a] Mean ratings on the ten-step "agree-disagree" scale; the higher the score, the more agreement.

graduates. Similarly, on the item "I like the kind of work you can forget about after the work day is over" the range of scores fall from 7.5 to 5.3. Occupational involvement, both as an attitude toward present occupation and as a desire, increases sharply with increasing education.

Considered as a whole, the results show clearly that the lower the educational level, the greater is the emphasis on the more tangible, material aspects of the job such as physical environment, money, and security. Conversely, the higher the level, the greater is the degree of occupational involvement and the emphasis on the more intrinsic, nonmaterial, and ego-rewarding attributes such as achievement, challenge, self-development, and the chance to make a positive contribution to society.

This same general pattern, with but minor variations, prevails according to income level and by occupational levels classified as unskilled and semiskilled, skilled and clerical, and professional and managerial (Tables 4-6 and 4-7). There are significant score differences between

TABLE 4-6. *Family Income in the General Employed Public, Related to Ratings of "Occupational Value" Statements*[a]

Occupational Value Statements	Family Income			
	Under $4,000	$4,000– 5,499	$5,500– 8,499	$8,500 and Over
"To me, it's important in an occupation to have the chance to get to the top"	7.3	7.6	8.0	8.3
"It is more important for a job to offer *opportunity* than *security*"	5.5	5.6	5.8	7.0
"It is satisfying to direct the work of others"	6.0	6.3	6.8	7.1
"To me, it's important to have the kind of work that gives me a chance to develop my own special abilities"	7.6	7.9	8.3	8.8
"Work is most satisfying when there are hard problems to solve"	5.6	6.1	6.7	7.7
"To me, work is nothing more than a way of making a living"	5.5	4.4	3.9	3.2
"I like the kind of work you can forget about after the work day is over"	7.5	6.9	6.7	5.6
"To be really successful in life, you have to care about making money"	6.4	6.0	5.4	5.4
AVERAGE NUMBER ANSWERING	(210)	(312)	(323)	(204)

[a] Mean ratings on the ten-step "agree-disagree" scale; the higher the score, the more agreement.

skilled and clerical workers on many items. But there is no consistent progression from one to the other, and both occupational groups consistently show scores falling between the unskilled and semiskilled on the one hand and professional and managerial on the other.

Variations by Sex

The evidence is clear that men and women differ significantly in the positive and negative occupational values they describe as being of con-

TABLE 4-7. *Occupation in the General Employed Public, Related to Ratings of "Occupational Value" Statements*[a]

Occupational Value Statements	Occupation[b]			
	Unskilled and Semiskilled	Skilled	Clerical	Professional and Managerial
"It is more important for a job to offer *opportunity* than *security*"	5.5	5.6	5.6	6.8
"It is satisfying to direct the work of others"	5.9	6.8	6.5	7.2
"To me, it's important in an occupation for a person to be able to carry out his own ideas without interference"	6.2	6.6	6.6	7.2
"Work is most satisfying when there are hard problems to solve"	5.7	6.7	6.7	7.4
"To me, work is nothing more than a way of making a living"	5.2	4.4	3.8	3.1
"I like the kind of work you can forget about after the work day is over"	7.4	6.6	6.7	5.9
AVERAGE NUMBER ANSWERING	(369)	(176)	(177)	(290)

[a] Mean ratings on the ten-step "agree-disagree" scale; the higher the score, the more agreement.

[b] Farmers do not fit neatly into the occupational hierarchy, and are not included here. Results for them can be found in various occupational tables in the *Source Book*.

cern to them. Of the positive values, men more than women tend to emphasize job and income security, opportunity for self-advancement, self-determination, and freedom on the job, and, to a somewhat less extent, financial reward. Women, more than men, emphasize personal relationships with people at work, good and understanding supervision, and doing work that is worthwhile and constructive. In discussing negative aspects of employment, men refer more often to lack of employment security and give somewhat more emphasis to poor or inadequate financial reward. Women emphasize far more the factors of poor personal relationships on the job (especially being associated with unpleasant, disagreeable people) and of bad or unfair supervision.

Analysis of the ratings given by men and women on the scale statements not only confirms a number of important elements in this matter, but adds some important dimensions on which the sexes differ. With respect to occupational involvement, women show less desire to integrate work with other activities of their lives. They also subscribe less to the idea that it is important to have a chance to get to the top, place less emphasis on doing a better job than the next person, are less apt to see the challenge of hard problems as a satisfying aspect of work, and are perhaps slightly less inclined toward the belief that it is important to be able to carry out their own ideas without interference. On the other hand, they are more inclined than men to emphasize social relationships on the job, even, perhaps, at the expense of getting ahead or of having power over others. And, to a greater degree than men, they tend to see work as a means of forgetting about personal problems.

Summing up, then, the over-all pattern suggests that the occupational values of men are more associated with a career outlook as well as a sense of responsibility and involvement—perhaps all related to their traditional social role of "breadwinner." Thus they tend to emphasize opportunity, drive to get ahead, competitiveness, challenge, and autonomy as well as the practical considerations of financial reward and job and income security. Women are somewhat more inclined to view work as an escape partially divorced from life's other activities, and the values they stress are primarily social—personal relationships, supervision, and service to others.

It may be questioned whether these variations by sex are due to actual differences in outlook or to the fact that the majority of women are concentrated in certain types and levels of occupation, and are thus merely reflecting in their replies the characteristic values of people, male or female, in such occupations. However, the sex differences described persist (although varying in degree) regardless of occupation, income, or education.

Variations by Age

Does age make a difference in the stress placed upon work values and perspectives in our sample of the nonfederal work force? For the most part, it does not. There are, however, a few elements which are moderately related to advancing age, especially in the area of values that involve the ethics of work. Older people agree more that work should be the most important part of one's life, that there must be constant striving for success, that work helps one forget personal problems and is also a way of being of service to God. Older people also place slightly more emphasis on doing work that is worthwhile and that helps other people. Increasing age, then, seems to be associated with greater stress on the inherent goodness and primacy of work, plus some stress on altruistic motivations.

Groups in Education and Business

The patterning of values previously described as being associated with a high level of education is in general shown by all of the groups in education and business. Any other finding would be not only surprising but disconcerting, since all but the business executive group have at least four years of college as a condition of qualification for inclusion in the study, and the business executives have, on the average, an education approaching the college graduate level. Beyond this common framework of values, however, there are a number of significant variations associated with both occupation and type of organization.

High School Teachers

In comparison with the other special high-level groups and with college graduates in the general employed public, high school teachers place special stress on good personal relationships with the people involved in their occupation, and emphasize active, stimulating relationships rather than passive, agreeable relationships. This is not surprising, in view of their teaching function and the importance of their relationships with students, but it is worth noting that they place even more stress on such matters than college teachers do.

The high school teachers are also more concerned about experiencing a sense of achievement or accomplishment through seeing the results of their work, and show an especially strong leaning toward being able not only to help others, but also to do something that is worthwhile to society in general. Combined with these major elements are less pronounced, but still significant, differential tendencies to see hard work as a duty and to place less stress on financial reward and various aspects of status. On the average, then, the responses indicate that these teachers approach their work with a strong sense of duty, a positive interest in people, an altruistic outlook, and relatively low concern with materialistic and status aspects.

College Teachers

An especially high degree of occupational involvement and a liking for the interweaving of work with life's other activities is shown by the college teachers as a group. Coupled with this is a very strong positive concern with self-determination and freedom and the opportunity for self-development, self-expression, and creativity. On the negative side, concern is strong about loss of self-determination, lack of challenge, and lack of opportunity to do worthwhile, constructive work.

Almost no reference is made to occupational security either as a positive or negative concern, and little attention is given to either good or bad supervision. In the case of security, it is reasonable to suppose that college tenure practices plus the continuing high demand for teachers are the conditioning factors. In the case of supervision, it seems likely that most faculty members simply don't see themselves as being "supervised"; if they did, it is hardly possible that their free-agent, ego-oriented outlook would permit them to feel neutral about this value.

The faculty groups are also quite extreme—in comparison to all other groups in or out of government—in their *disagreement* with the idea that to be really successful in life one must care about making money, and in their *agreement* with the idea that after one is making enough money to get along, making more is not very important. Paralleling this is their low expression of regard for the material aspects of status.

College Natural and Social Scientists and Engineers

Natural scientists, social scientists, and engineers in colleges yield a pattern essentially the same as that of the general college teacher population (in which they are included in their proper proportions). However, all three of these special groups show on both the scale scores and the free responses one highly significant difference from the general college teacher population—a markedly higher degree of concern with the occupational value of self-determination and freedom. As an aspect of the "ideal" occupation, self-determination is mentioned by 48 percent of both the natural scientists and the social scientists, and by 56 percent of the engineers, whereas the figure for the general college teacher population is 38 percent. Related to this is the fact that the natural scientists, in describing the "worst" occupation, are more inclined than their colleagues to mention loss of opportunity for self-development, self-expression, and creativity.

Groups in Business

Compared with their counterparts in colleges and the federal government, the business groups rate the importance of financial reward considerably higher. There is also a suggestion that they rate status a little higher as an occupational value. This is definitely true when they are compared with college teachers, but the case is more doubtful when the comparison is with the special federal groups or the college graduate group in the general employed public. In addition, the business groups appear to be somewhat less concerned about social goals as occupational values.

Further generalizations about groups in business are impossible, because there is a major cleavage within the groups. The executives and engineers show one rather consistent pattern, while the natural and social scientists show another. The executives and engineers, for example, compared with the scientists, show a lower degree of occupational involvement, and place greater emphasis on money as a necessary ingredient of success. The cleavage is apparent, too, with respect to status: the executives and engineers give significantly higher scores to the aspects of respect and material possessions. They also place higher value on the opportunity to make friends at work, on finding satisfaction in directing the work of others, on competitiveness, and on seeing hard work as an avenue to success.

The Student Population

Variations by Present Educational Level

Among the student groups occupational values vary in accordance with present educational level in much the same way that they vary by educational level in the general work force. As one might expect, the differences are relatively small between college seniors and graduate school students, whereas they are fairly large between these two groups on the one hand, and high school juniors and seniors on the other. When the "ideal" occupation is discussed, the college groups, far more often than the high school students, speak of such attributes as self-development, self-determination, sense of achievement, and sense of worthwhileness and usefulness in the work. Also worth noting is that 14 percent of them, compared to 6 percent of the high schoolers, qualify their mention of financial reward by saying explicitly that money is not of primary importance in a job and that one needs only to be paid enough to meet an adequate standard of living.

A similar association with educational level is seen in the responses about the "worst" occupation. High school students more frequently mention inadequate financial reward and bad physical environment and general working conditions, but cite lack of opportunity for self-expression, self-determination, challenge, and achievement significantly less often than the college seniors and graduate students. All three groups note monotony and routine very often, but the marked difference by level still holds: frequency of mention for the high schoolers is 34 percent, for college seniors and graduate students, 57 and 59 percent.

On the rating of scale items, too, results by educational level parallel those in the general employed public. Thus, we find that college seniors and graduate students, compared to high school students, desire more involvement in and more recognition for their work; place less emphasis on respect and keeping up with the Joneses as aspects of status; wish more strongly to direct the work of others; more often emphasize opportunity as opposed to security; are more inclined to see satisfaction in the challenge of hard problems; are significantly more interested in autonomy and the opportunity to carry out their own ideas; and agree much *less* that money is a necessary ingredient of success and much *more* that, once you are making enough money to live adequately, other occupational values are more important.

Despite this similarity between the student groups and the general employed public in the *pattern* of their scores by education, the striking fact is that the two sets of scores are very different in absolute magnitude. It is particularly revealing to compare students presently in high school with the members of the general work force who completed high school but went no further in their education. The comparison shows clearly that current high school students have a configuration of occupational values which resembles the pattern of the college-educated in the general employed public more than it does the pattern of those who curtailed their education on receiving a high school diploma. How much of this is due to age differences, intergenerational culture change, or the fact that our high school sample contains a high proportion of potential college-level youngsters is not revealed by our data.

Another of our sets of comparative results for the students and the general work force is extremely interesting, but difficult to interpret definitively. The data strongly suggest that present-day college students, compared both with high school students and with people at the college level in the general employed public, approach work more often with an idea of deriving fun and personal satisfaction out of it; perhaps with equal or greater desire for opportunity; and with a hint of less willingness to strive and to be dedicated to work at the expense of other things. In the absence of trend data, it is impossible to say whether this difference in value patterns between present college students and college-level people now at work is a product of social change or merely a reflection of the different situation in which the college students find themselves as compared to people who are facing the facts of being presently employed.[4]

Variations by Academic Grades

We approached analysis according to academic grades with considerable trepidation, since this measure is subject to many sources of unreliability. Not only are unreliabilities associated with the grading process itself but also, in our case, these are compounded (1) by variability in standards from one high school to another and one college to another, and (2) by the fact that we had no choice but to rely on the reporting by students of their own grades. In spite of these limitations, we did find a strong pattern of association between occupational values and academic grades.

Considering first the free responses, we find that in general the "A" students, compared with the "B" students, and the "B" students, in turn compared with those with lower grades, express more concern with doing work that fits one's capacities, that allows self-determination, that provides opportunities for self-development, self-expression, and creativity, that enables one to enjoy *active* relations with people at work, and that is worthwhile and constructive—but are less concerned about physical environment and working conditions, having good *passive* rela-

[4] In the usual order for discussing variations within groups, sex differences would follow here. However, among all three student populations the variations in occupational values by sex so closely parallel those found in the general work force that presentation of the results would be unnecessarily repetitious.

tions at work, and high financial rewards. Not all the differences referred to are linear. There tends, for example, to be more distance between "A" and "B" students in both high schools and colleges than between "B" and "C" students; the differences are greater in the high school population; and among graduate students almost all the differences are so small that they would be insignificant were it not for the fact that they parallel those in the other two student groups.

TABLE 4-8. *Students' Academic Grades, Related to Ratings of "Occupational Value" Statements*

Occupational Value Statements	High School Juniors and Seniors			College Seniors			Graduate Students	
	A	B	C and Below	A	B	C and Below	A	B and Below
"To me, work is nothing more than a way of making a living"	1.8	3.1	2.8	1.8	2.1	2.4	1.9	2.2
"I like the kind of work you can forget about after the work day is over"	3.6	5.0	5.3	3.4	3.9	4.1	3.3	3.8
"To be really successful in life, you have to care about making money"	3.9	4.1	4.7	3.4	3.5	4.7	3.2	3.9
"After you are making enough money to get along, then making more money in an occupation isn't very important"	5.3	5.4	4.6	6.5	6.1	4.9	6.7	6.3
"Work is most satisfying when there are hard problems to solve"	8.0	7.1	6.5	8.3	7.9	7.6	8.3	8.1
"It is more important for a job to offer *opportunity* than *security*	6.5	5.6	5.1	7.4	6.9	7.4	8.0	7.4
"To me, almost the only thing that matters about a job is the chance to do work that is worthwhile to society"	7.2	6.5	6.2	6.9	7.1	6.3	6.6	6.8
"The main satisfaction a person can get out of work is helping other people"	8.7	8.2	7.8	7.6	7.9	7.3	7.3	7.4
AVERAGE NUMBER ANSWERING	(51)	(142)	(161)	(89)	(203)	(105)	(153)	(205)

When we examine the scale statements (Table 4-8), we find that, as the grade averages of each student population climb, there is less agreement that work is nothing more than a way of making a living, that the kind of work you can forget about at the end of the day is preferable, and that to be really successful you have to care about making money. On the other hand, the higher the grade average, the greater the agreement that after a given minimum of income is achieved making more is not important, that work is most satisfying when there are hard problems to solve, that opportunity is more important than security, that doing work which is worthwhile to society is important, and that the main satisfaction a person can get out of work is helping other people.

It is apparent here, as in the free-response results, that with each rise in the educational hierarchy the divergencies by grade averages narrow. There is more difference in relation to varying grade averages among high school students than among college seniors, and more among the college seniors than among graduate school students. No doubt this is partly a result of successive selection, and partly a reflection of increasing homogeneity of exposure and experience at successively higher levels of education.

Summing up, the pattern by academic grade average parallels quite closely the pattern by educational level noted in the general work force and among students. The higher the grade average, the more likely is the student to look with favor upon closer and more complete involvement with work, and also to be concerned about the ego-rewarding, nontangible values of an occupation rather than the more tangible, physical, and passive features.

General Federal Employees

The responses of all of the federal populations to the open-end questions concerning the "ideal" and the "worst" occupations were greater in number than those of the nonfederal groups and covered a wider range of attributes. This would not be disturbing if we could safely assume that it reflects a tendency for government workers to have a greater variety and complexity of occupational concerns. However, we are inclined to believe that the result is, for the most part, a methodological artifact. Most of the federal respondents, in contrast to the nonfederal, were interviewed at work, during working hours, and after arrangements had been made with their superiors. Most important of all, they knew that our research mainly concerned federal employment and federal employee. We believe, therefore, that the greater volubility of the federal groups is accounted for, to a large degree, by one or more of these factors. Consequently, we have exercised restraint in making comparisons between the nonfederal and federal responses to these two questions, and offer as comparative results only those that are confirmed by supplementary analytic procedures.[5] Fortunately, the scale items on occupational values are not subject to this methodological difficulty, and thus permit differences between federal and nonfederal groups to be explored with greater precision.

Major Occupational Concerns

Despite the above limitations, we can point with some surety to the significance of certain differences in emphasis in the responses of the two general employee populations. Federal employees, on the average, show more concern about the "ideal" attributes of having various aspects of job security; good equipment and facilities; good supervision; good personal relationships on the job—especially passive relationships; doing work that fits one's capacities and training; opportunity for self-development; and the chance to do worthwhile and constructive work. On the other hand, they evince somewhat less concern with financial reward and self-determination. A similar pattern of differences is shown in the responses regarding the "worst" possible occupation. Federal personnel, far more than nonfederal employees, put emphasis on bad supervision and bad personal relations on the job; they also give more stress to lack of self-advancement, lack of personal recognition, and having to do routine and monotonous work.

The differential concern with the nature of supervision is outstanding. Approximately 20 percent of the federal employees, vs. 11 percent of the nonfederal, mention good supervision as an "ideal" value; the relationship is about the same for the mention of bad supervision as an occupational drawback—31 percent vs. 18 percent. Even more striking are the attitudes toward personal relationships on the job; as a positive attribute, this ranks first among federal employees with a figure of 47 per-

---

[5] Major supplementary procedures were the use of relative rank orders of the responses in the federal and nonfederal groups, and percentages calculated by using total *responses* (as opposed to number of respondents answering) as a base.

cent, in contrast to the third-place ranking with a figure of 30 percent in the general employed public. Mention of bad personal relationships as a negative attribute shows a similar pattern; in the federal population, 33 percent mention it, compared to 19 percent of the nonfederal population.

Also worth comment because of its particular relevance to the federal personnel problem is the category of financial reward. Despite the tendency for nearly all categories to be mentioned with higher frequency by federal employees, in this case it is the nonfederal population that shows the higher frequency, on both the positive (43 vs. 40 percent) and negative (27 vs. 24 percent) sides. The result is that for the general employed public financial reward is given first ranking as a positive value, and second ranking as a negative value, while among general federal employees, it ranks third and fifth. The evidence is therefore clear that concern with financial reward is significantly less among federal employees. The over-all result, however, conceals within it a differential pattern by educational level, a matter which will be discussed later.

When we turn to consider a comparison of the scale ratings given to various occupational value statements by general federal employees and the general employed public, the major impression is that the scores of the general federal work force differ from those of the general employed public by significant amounts on a large share of the items. A number of items illustrating the nature and magnitude of the differences are shown in Table 4.9. The following analysis, however, is not confined to the tabled results but includes other items, as well as patterns by sex and education where appropriate.

Particularly striking, in comparison to the general public's ratings, are the higher degree of occupational involvement, more Spartan approach to work, and stronger subscription to duty shown by the general federal group over all, by both men and women, and by all four educational levels. This is seen in the federal group's much stronger disagreement with the idea that work is nothing more than a way of making a living; that the kind of work one can forget about after the work day is over is an advantage; that anyone has a *right* to expect his work to be fun; and that it is a person's own business if he does not want to work hard (Table 4-9).

Federal employees are far less likely to see money as a necessary ingredient of success, and this is true for both men and women and at all four educational levels. With respect to status as an occupational value, the federal and nonfederal groups differ only slightly on the factors of respect and material possessions, but the federal group places somewhat more emphasis on getting recognition for one's work.

Especially noteworthy are the scores on the statement, "Work is most satisfying when there are hard problems to solve." When the scores of

TABLE 4-9. *Ratings Given by General Federal Employees and the General Employed Public to "Occupational Value" Statements*[a]

Occupational Value Statements	General Federal Employees	General Employed Public
"To me, work is nothing more than a way of making a living"	3.3	*4.2*
"I like the kind of work you can forget about after the work day is over"	6.2	*6.7*
"If a person doesn't want to work hard, it's his own business"	4.3	*5.4*
"To be really successful in life, you have to care about making money"	5.0	*5.8*
"It is more important for a job to offer *opportunity* than *security*"	5.7	*5.9*
"Getting recognition for my work is important to me"	*8.2*	7.6
"It is satisfying to direct the work of others"	*7.1*	6.6
"It would be hard to live with the feeling that others are passing you up in your occupation"	*6.4*	6.1
"To me, almost the only thing that matters about a job is the chance to do work that is worthwhile to society"	*6.2*	5.6
"A person should constantly try to succeed at work, even if it interferes with other things in life"	*6.6*	6.0
"Even if you dislike your work, you should do your best"	*8.8*	8.3
AVERAGE NUMBER ANSWERING	(930)	(1,087)

[a] Mean ratings on the ten-step "agree-disagree" scale; the higher the score, the more agreement. (The higher score of each pair of ratings is italicized.)

federal employees—over all, by sex, and by educational level—are compared with those of the general employed public, we find that the federal group shows consistently higher agreement. It appears from this that the general worker in government is more likely than his counterpart outside to respond positively to the challenge of difficult problems. Another significant comparison between the two groups is on their subscription to social goals as an occupational aim. Here we find that agreement is about equal that "the main satisfaction a person can get out of work is helping other people." However, federal employees show significantly stronger agreement with the broader, less personalized statement, "To me, almost the only thing that matters about a job is the chance to do work that is worthwhile to society." Differences on this item are especially great for men and for the three lower educational levels in each population.

In view of some of our other findings which show that many people tend to stereotype federal employees as lacking in competitiveness, it is interesting to note that federal employees score as high as the general employed public on the three value statements designed to get at competitiveness, and slightly higher on two of them. Paralleling this finding are the comparative scores for the statement which pits opportunity against security as an occupational value. Although it was noted earlier that, in their free responses, federal employees evince a greater concern with security of job and income, on the statement, "It is more important for a job to offer *opportunity* than *security*," we find that the scores for federal employees and for the general employed public are almost alike (5.7 and 5.9), and that there appears to be no significant differences by sex or by educational level between the two populations. Such results certainly do not accord with the stereotype of the federal employee who is primarily interested in security *as opposed to* opportunity.

Summarizing the findings on the scale items, we may say that the general federal employees, compared with members of the general employed public, show a higher degree of concern with the values of occupational involvement and of subscription to duty; place less emphasis on money; indicate a somewhat stronger desire for personal recognition in their work; and place more emphasis on challenge and worthwhile social goals.

Variations by Sex

In describing the attributes of the "ideal" and "worst" occupations, men in the general federal work force place much more emphasis than women do on financial reward, job security, and self-determination; women differentially emphasize such socially related factors as personal relationships on the job—especially passive relationships—worthwhile and constructive work, and intelligent and sympathetic supervision.

On the scale statements, too, we find that the differential patterning of occupational values by sex closely parallels the results in the general employed public. Compared with their male colleagues, federally employed women show markedly less agreement that they have a right to expect their work to be fun; express stronger liking for the kind of work that can be forgotten about after office hours; score significantly lower on all three status items; express less agreement about the satisfactions of directing the work of others; accord less importance to having an opportunity to get to the top; agree less that "it's important to do a better job than the next person"; and assign less importance to self-determination and autonomy.

On financial reward, there is a difference between men and women in the federal population that is not found in the general public. In the federal population the scores in response to the statement, "To be really successful in life you have to care about making money" are 5.2 for men and 4.3 for women, whereas in the general public they are 5.8 and 5.8. Another male-female difference found in the federal population and not in the general public is found in the responses to the statement, "To me, almost the only thing that matters about a job is the chance to do work that is worthwhile to society." Women in federal work show less agreement with this than men—5.6 vs. 6.4—whereas in the general employed public both men and women score 5.6. It should be noted that the federally employed women and women outside government score the same; the difference is entirely due to the scores of the federally employed men, which are markedly higher than those of their nonfederal counterparts.

Variations by Education, Income, and Occupation

In most respects the responses of the general federal work force to the open-end occupational value questions display the same patterns according to education, income, and occupation previously described for the general employed public. Here, as in the nonfederal work force, values dealing with the physical, tangible, extrinsic elements of work show a negative relationship or no relationship with these three variables, but values associated with personal emergence and ego-satisfaction tend to show moderate to strong positive relationships.

Consider, for example, the category of wanting to have responsibility for making decisions on the job as it is related to federal grade level. The frequency of its mention ranges from lows of 5 percent for the postal service and the unskilled and semiskilled wage board employees and 7 percent for GS 2 to 4 respondents, to a high of 21 percent for

GS 12's and above. An even more extreme polarity occurs for the category of challenge of the job; while only 7 percent of the unskilled and semiskilled wage board workers mention it as a positive attribute, 41 percent of the GS 12's and above do. Further illustration of the hierarchical, or graduated, patterning of values is furnished by Table 4-10,

TABLE 4-10. *Attributes of the "Ideal" and "Worst" Occupations Mentioned More Frequently by General Federal Employees as Educational Level Rises*[a]

Attributes	High School Not Completed	High School Completed	Some College	College Graduate
Attributes of "Ideal" Occupation				
Self-determination	19%	23%	21%	31%
Doing work that is worthwhile, useful, constructive	11	15	22	30
Self-development, self-expression, and creativity	11	16	25	33
Sense of achievement or accomplishment	9	14	21	20
Self-advancement	6	14	18	20
Sense of challenge, overcoming obstacles, keeping goals ahead	4	11	23	23
Attributes of "Worst" Occupation				
Routine, monotony	14	25	45	49
Lack of self-determination	8	12	19	25
Lack of self-advancement	5	14	15	15
Lack of self-development, self-expression, and creativity	2	6	8	15
Lack of challenge	1	3	7	10
NUMBER ANSWERING	(190)	(356)	(180)	(162)

[a] Percentages for both positive and negative values may add to more than 100 owing to multiple replies.

which presents a number of the positive and negative occupational values for which frequencies of mention in the federal work force rise with increasing education.

However, there are two major federal-nonfederal differences when results are compared by educational levels—the emphasis on financial reward and on personal relationships on the job. The better-educated federal employees show a more pervasive concern with financial reward, both as a positive occupational feature and as an occupational drawback, than the less-educated employees do. This variation by education is not found in the general work force.

Even more striking are the figures on personal relationships on the job. Among federal employees, both positive and negative references to this characteristic are very high and show little difference by educational level. Approximately one half of all federal employees at all educational levels mention personal relationships as a positive value, and one fourth to one third of them mention it as a negative occupational value. In the general employed public, references to personal relationships show a sharp positive relation to education; as a positive occupational value it rises from 22 percent among those with less than a high school degree to 42 percent among college graduates.

Also worth noting is the relatively greater emphasis that federal personnel, compared to nonfederal, give to passive rather than active personal relationships, especially at the upper educational levels. For example, in the general work force, the active/passive ratio rises from 1 to 1 at the bottom of the educational ladder to almost 4 to 1 among college graduates, whereas in the federal work force the ratio is approximately 1 to 1 at all four educational levels.

Thus, in the general employed public, increase in educational background is accompanied by rising concern with personal relationships on the job, as well as a marked shift in emphasis away from simply being around pleasant, agreeable people to a desire to associate with stimulating, interesting, worthwhile people. Among federal employees, on the other hand, concern with personal relationships is not only more pervasive but also equally high at all educational levels. In addition, the better-educated federal employees evidence no greater interest than their less-educated colleagues in having stimulating, positive relationships. In about equal degree, they express the more passive outlook of wanting to avoid unpleasantness and to have an agreeable, if not stimulating, social situation on the job.

Discussion of the relationship between scale scores on occupational value items and educational, income, and occupational levels among federal employees can be brief because, for the most part, we need only refer to the earlier discussion of the relationship between occupational values scores and these three factors in the general employed public. While the absolute values of the scores often are different for the federal and nonfederal populations, the internal relationships between the scores parallel one another, with only minor exceptions, in the two populations. Thus, among federal employees, the higher the level of education, income, or occupation, the greater is the degree of occupational involvement and the greater is the emphasis on the nonmaterial and ego-rewarding attributes of work.

Variations by Age

As in the general work force, age differences among general federal employees appear for only a modest number of occupational values. Mainly they show that age is positively associated with emphasis on striving and duty, and on the importance and inherent value of work.

Federal Executives, Natural Scientists, Social Scientists, and Engineers

When the four special groups of federal employees are considered as a whole in comparison to their counterparts in business and higher education, gross differences emerge which closely parallel those found when federal employees in general were compared with the general work force. The special groups likewise place significantly more stress on the nature of supervision and on personal relationships on the job, giving far greater emphasis to passive, rather than active, relationships. Also, although they do not mention employment security frequently, they cite it more often than do the nonfederal groups.

In addition, the four groups display in even more marked degree the pattern of responses on money matters we noted earlier as characterizing upper-level, compared to lower-level, general federal employees. That is, they express more *concern* with financial reward, but at the same time are less likely to see it as a necessary element in success and are more likely to feel that, once you are making enough money to get along, making more money in an occupation is not very important. In this they differ from the patterns of both the business and academic groups. The business groups exhibit lower *concern* with money, but are much stronger in their identification of it as an element in success and subscribe the least to the notion of being satisfied with an "adequate" income. The college groups also show lower concern with money, but are strongest of all in their rejection of the "money-success" equation and in their agreement that, once income is adequate, other occupational values count more.

In our earlier examination of the scale item scores of the four business groups, we found that on many statements the scores of executives and engineers tend to be alike, differing substantially from the scores of the natural and social scientists, whose scores also tend to be alike. Among federal executives, natural and social scientists, and engineers we find the same phenomena with respect to exactly the same items that differentiated the business pairings.

If it is kept in mind that the four special federal groups share the value patterns of highly educated groups generally, as well as those which especially characterize federal employees, the following generalizations about the groups individually have validity.

1. The mean score of federal executives on the statement, "To me it's important in an occupation for a person to be able to carry out his own ideas without interference," is lower than that of any group, federal or nonfederal, at a comparable educational or occupational level. In some instances the differences are not great, but they are all in the same direction. It is quite possible that to a considerable extent, this represents the executives' adjustment to the realities of governmental administration.

2. There are considerably more similarities in the values of the three groups of natural scientists (federal, business, college) than there are differences. To the extent that there are significant differences, they tend to be between the federal and business groups, and not between the federal and college groups. For example, federal natural scientists, in their lesser emphasis on money, striving, and competitiveness and in their greater emphasis on altruistic motives, display values which more closely approximate those of college natural scientists than those of natural scientists in business.

3. The preceding generalization applies to social scientists as well, but with slightly less exactitude.

4. To the extent that the value responses of federal engineers are significantly different from those of either the business or academic engineers, they bear more resemblance to the responses of the engineers in business. Thus, in comparison with college engineers, both the federal and business engineers score lower on occupational involvement and the importance of doing socially worthwhile work, and place more stress on money, status, and the more competitive aspects of striving.

Summary

1. The number of occupational values and their variability from group to group is impressive. There is a modest general consensus of concern with financial reward, physical environment and working conditions, personal relationships on the job, and self-determination, but otherwise the keynote is diversity.

2. Occupational values display a consistent hierarchical patterning by level of attainment, as measured by education, income, and occupation in the employee samples, and by academic grades among students. The lower the attainment level, the more simple is the structure of occupational concerns and the greater is the emphasis on the physical, material, immediate, and extrinsic values. The higher the attainment level, the higher is the personal involvement with work, the more complex is the value structure, and the greater is the emphasis on abstract, long-term, ego-rewarding, and intrinsic values.

3. Men and women in both the nonfederal and federal populations differ significantly in the occupational values they emphasize, with men differentially stressing "breadwinner" and career-related values and women stressing socially related values.

4. All the special high-level groups (teachers, executives, natural scientists, social scientists, and engineers) share the pattern of values common to those at the upper levels of attainment. Within this common framework, however, two basic types of variation are clear—those associated with *type* of employment or profession (e.g., executive, natural scientist, engineer), and those associated with *situs* of employment (e.g., college, business, the federal government). Both types of variation suggest that occupational values tend to be channeled in common directions both within occupations and within institutions. Probably the channeling process involves numerous stages of self-selection and of being selected, as well as social reinforcement within the groups.

5. Federal and nonfederal employees display similar hierarchical patternings of values by attainment level, but there are many highly significant differences within and beyond this common structure. Federal employees in general display greater occupational involvement and subscription to duty; display far more concern with supervision and with personal relationships, especially passive relationships, on the job; place

somewhat more emphasis on challenge, self-development, and worth-while social goals; and evince somewhat less concern with financial re-ward and self-determination. In addition, while they display slightly more concern with security of job and income considered by itself, they do not do so when security is put in the context of being opposed to op-portunity.

In the above pattern, the greater emphasis put on supervision and personal relationships, especially of the passive sort, is especially out-standing. It may be that high concern with these matters is simply char-acteristic of personnel in large organizations. If true, this might account for the federal-nonfederal differences, as our nonfederal employee sam-ples contain personnel from organizations of all sizes in their proper pro-portions. But this does not banish the fact of the marked concern of the federal employee with supervision and with passive personal relation-ships.

One other item requires comment. Federal employees show less over-all concern with financial reward, but this concern is differentially con-centrated among upper-level employees. This is not the case in the non-federal populations. However, paradoxical as it may sound, the greater *concern* with financial reward of the upper-level federal employee is ac-companied by a basically less materialistic outlook. This suggests that these individuals are experiencing a feeling of relative financial depriva-tion, even though material considerations do not rank as high in their hierarchy of values.

6. Security of job, income, and the like, despite its undeniable occupa-tional *importance*, is a matter of only modest concern among all of the groups and at all levels. Apparently twenty years of generally pervasive prosperity has had its effect in permitting the great majority to take job security for granted. In addition, the differential structuring by attain-ment level of security and certain other values strongly suggests that se-curity tends to be thought of by employees at the lower levels in terms of external guarantees, and by employees at the upper levels in terms of maintaining and further developing one's qualifications and capacities. Stating the case in extreme form, the physicist, in contrast to the assem-bly-line worker, can feel great assurance that, if he maintains a high level of qualification for his work, his services will be in high demand regardless of the fate of any particular organization, project, or technol-ogy with which he might be presently associated.

7. There is some indication of a cultural change in certain clusters of

occupational values. One piece of evidence is the fact that the work-related values of today's high school juniors and seniors are much like those of the college-educated members of the present work force. Another indication lies in the finding that subscription to certain values, especially those involving the inherent goodness, primacy, and social value of work, show a moderate positive relationship with age. A third line of evidence results from the comparison of present college seniors with members of the general work force who are college graduates. The college seniors on the average seem to regard work with the idea of deriving fun and personal satisfaction from it, and appear to be somewhat less willing to strive and to dedicate themselves to work at the expense of other things. It is quite possible, of course, that the differences observed in all three instances are due, not to any cultural shift, but simply to the difference between the situation of being a student and young and the situation of being an employed breadwinner and older. In the absence of trend data we can only say that there is suggestive, but not conclusive, evidence of cultural change in occupational values.

5

The Appeal of Federal Employment

ESTABLISHING THE DEGREE OF ATTRACTIVENESS of federal employment is a cornerstone of this study. In the first place, this will indicate
how the appeal of federal work may differ among a variety of groups—
a significant objective in itself. Given the government's increasing need
and demand for highly educated personnel, for example, it is important
to know to what extent federal employment may appear attractive to
people of this kind. Second, ascertaining the appeal factor sets the stage
for examining the underlying rationale of the attitudes that are expressed about federal employment, as we search out the relationship between a person's basic occupational values and the image he holds of
the federal service.

Because the appeal factor was so important to our research, we believed that relying on a single approach to it would be unwise; therefore we used a variety of measures. These several measures provided us
with a cross-check on the consistency of the results, and also allowed us
to take into account the different vantage points from which federal employment appeal would be judged by nonfederal employees, students,
and federal employees themselves. Using this cross-check, we have
found that the patterns of results from measure to measure within and
between groups tend to be highly consistent. Consequently, it is possible to state with confidence the considerable number of general conclusions that follow about the comparative appeal of federal employment,
in one group compared to another, and within groups according to such
factors as sex and socioeconomic and attitudinal variables.

The General Employed Public

Present Employment vs. Federal Employment

Let us first consider the responses given by the general work force when they were asked, "Suppose your work or occupation stayed the same but you worked for the federal government—that is, the United States government—how much better or worse would that be? Show me on the ladder, please."[1] The results are especially revealing when compared with the ratings given to "present occupation" on the same scale. Table 5-1 shows both sets of mean scores, as well as the differences between them, for the general public as a whole and also according to a number of demographic characteristics.

The 6.5 rating given by the over-all general work force to federal employment seems to be somewhat on the favorable side, but this judgment must be tempered by the fact that it is 0.6 below the 7.1 rating accorded present occupation.[2] These global figures for the general work force are useful as a comparative base to keep in mind, but are otherwise not especially enlightening. It is when we examine the score patternings within the work force according to several variables that vital findings emerge.

The breakdown by sex shows that women rate federal employment higher than men do by more than a full scale point.[3] Women appear to feel that a change to federal employment would leave them on a par with their present employment, whereas men see a significant decline. Compared to men in corresponding categories, the women who would feel least disadvantaged by going to work for the government are younger in age, with lower education, and doing clerical work; these kinds of women employees tend, in fact, to feel that government employment would improve their situation.[4]

[1] The "ladder" is the ten-step "ideal occupation" scale; the higher the placement, the nearer to "ideal."

[2] There is a further complicating factor in judging whether federal employment appeal is positive or negative, high or low, in any absolute sense. In almost all the measures, including this one, a change of employers is suggested directly or by implication; therefore a slight negative reaction to the idea of change per se probably intrudes upon the measurements.

[3] Further analysis shows that this holds true with little variation at all levels of education, income, occupation, age, etc.

[4] More details on the male-female comparisons, as well as further discussion of other socioeconomic variables mentioned here, are presented in the *Source Book*, Chap. 14.

TABLE 5-1. *Socioeconomic Characteristics of the General Employed Public, Related to Ratings of Present Occupation vs. Doing the Same Work, but for the Federal Government*[a]

Characteristics	Average Number Answering[b]	Present Occupation	Same Occupation, but for the Federal Government	Difference: "Federal" Minus "Present"
General Employed Public	(1,120)	7.1	6.5	−0.6
Sex				
Men	(862)	7.1	6.3	−0.8
Women	(258)	7.4	7.4	0.0
Educational Level				
High school not completed	(324)	7.0	7.1	+0.1
High school completed	(503)	6.9	6.5	−0.4
Some college	(128)	7.4	5.7	−1.7
College graduate	(137)	8.0	6.3	−1.7
Occupation				
Unskilled and semiskilled	(386)	6.6	7.0	+0.4
Skilled	(181)	7.1	6.8	−0.3
Clerical	(178)	7.3	7.0	−0.3
Professional and managerial	(297)	7.7	6.0	−1.7
Family Income				
Under $4,000	(230)	6.8	7.2	+0.4
$4,000–5,499	(318)	6.9	6.7	−0.2
$5,500–8,499	(324)	7.2	6.5	−0.7
$8,500 and over	(206)	7.7	5.7	−2.0
Age				
Under 33	(308)	6.9	6.7	−0.2
33–39	(207)	6.9	6.5	−0.4
40–48	(295)	7.2	6.4	−0.8
49 and older	(302)	7.5	6.6	−0.9
Race				
White	(978)	7.2	6.3	−0.9
Negro	(116)	6.4	7.8	+1.4

[a] Mean ratings on the ten-step, self-anchoring "ideal occupation" scale; the higher the score, the nearer to "ideal."
[b] Entries represent the average number of respondents for the two questions involved. A similar rule for computing the average number of respondents applies to other tables in this chapter in which an average number answering is given.

Of great significance is the patterning of the difference scores (last column, Table 5-1) by education, income, and occupational levels. The story is the same in each case: the higher the level, the greater the net difference to the disadvantage of federal employment.[5] For example, respondents with family incomes under $4,000 indicate that changing from their present employment to doing the same thing for the federal government would result in an upward movement of 0.4; respondents at the other extreme of $8,500 and over calculate a downward movement of 2.0. Similarly, unskilled and semiskilled workers see a modest upward movement while the professional and managerial group see a downward plunge.

The pattern by age presents a somewhat different picture. True, the "'federal' minus 'present'" scores become increasingly negative with increasing age. But this decline in the comparative appeal of federal employment is accounted for, not by declining ratings of federal employment, but by rising scores for "present occupation." This, as well as some further evidence to be discussed later, strongly suggests that age, per se, has little relation to absolute judgments concerning federal employment appeal; however, since increasing age is positively associated with occupational satisfaction, the attractiveness of working for the government suffers increasingly by comparison.

The sharp differences on both absolute and comparative scores between the white and Negro populations are noteworthy. White workers see a downward movement of −0.9, while Negroes see an upward movement of +1.4. This is accounted for in part by the moderately higher ratings whites give to their present occupations, but in greater part by the much higher rating Negroes give to federal employment. It is true that, among the interviewees, the Negroes included a larger component of those with low education and income. As we have seen before, people on the lower levels are more favorable to government employment than higher-status individuals. In an effort to take this weighting at least partially into account, we compared whites and Negroes with annual incomes under $4,500 and those with over $4,500. The differences still remained, mitigated somewhat, but present nevertheless.[6]

[5] Perhaps an exception, in this case farmers (not shown in Table 5-1), proves the rule. It is hard to know where to place farmers in an occupational hierarchy, but probably it would not be at the top. In any case, their rating for doing the same work, but for the federal government, is a whopping 3.0 below their present work situation.

[6] Since the number of Negroes in the $4,500 and over category is small (N = 23), this statement applies primarily to the comparison made between whites and Negroes at the level below $4,500.

WHEN THE PATTERNING OF APPEAL SCORES elicited by the "change of employer" question is related to certain other attitudes of the general employed public, further interesting results emerge. Table 5-2 shows, for example, such an association between the scores and (1) opportunity vs. security orientation and (2) evaluation of general civil servants. To arrive at indexes for the attitudes, we divided the population into three roughly equal groups, in the first instance according to their low,

TABLE 5-2. *Two Attitude Classifications of the General Employed Public, Related to Ratings of Present Occupation vs. Doing the Same Work, but for the Federal Government*[a]

Attitude Classifications	Average Number Answering	Present Occupation	Same Occupation, but for the Federal Government	Difference: "Federal" Minus "Present"
Opportunity vs. Security				
Low on opportunity	(335)	7.0	7.1	+0.1
Medium on opportunity	(361)	7.1	6.4	−0.7
High on opportunity	(379)	7.3	6.1	−1.2
Evaluation of General Civil Servants				
Low	(343)	7.0	6.0	−1.0
Medium	(398)	7.2	6.6	−0.6
High	(313)	7.2	7.1	−0.1

[a] Mean ratings on the ten-point, self-anchoring "ideal occupation" scale; the higher the score the nearer to "ideal."

medium, and high agreement (on the ten-point scale) with the statement, "It is more important for a job to offer *opportunity* than *security*," and in the second instance according to the low, medium, and high ratings given to civil servants on three qualities—honesty, ability, and interest in serving the public.[7]

Looking at the results on the opportunity vs. security classification, we note that there is little difference among the low, medium, and high groups in their "present occupation" ratings, but the scores on doing the same work for the government move sharply and progressively downward with increasing opportunity orientation. In short, the more a re-

[7] The attitudinal indexes are described fully in the *Source Book*, at the beginning of Chap. 14.

spondent is oriented to opportunity, as opposed to security, the worse off he feels he would be, both absolutely and relatively, were he to go to work for the government. As will be demonstrated in later chapters, a hallmark of the federal service image is an emphasis on security. That the respondents who are more interested in the opportunity a job offers than its security show decidedly less attraction toward federal work is no coincidence: they feel that their greater opportunity orientation would not flower in the federal environment.

The second index, "evaluation of civil servants," also shows a significant relationship with appeal scores: the higher the estimate respondents have of federal civil servants, the higher they rate the appeal of working for the federal government, both absolutely and in relation to their present employment. This suggests that the relative appeal of federal work is likely to be based, in part at least, on evaluations of some aspects of the federal environment—in this case federal employees. However, even those who are the most favorable in their judgments of civil servants still give a slight deficit to shifting to federal employment.

Another variation in attitude is also related to the enthusiasm with which people contemplate a shift to government employment. Dividing members of the general employed public into three groups according to how they rated their own jobs on the self-anchoring occupational value scale—low, medium, or high—reveals a significant relationship between occupational satisfaction and the appeal of federal employment. People in the lowest third of occupational satisfaction feel that their lots would be improved significantly by a shift to federal employment ($+0.9$); those in the highest third feel they would suffer a serious loss (-2.2). The conclusion is inescapable—on the average, the more occupationally satisfied a person is, the greater the loss he sees in shifting to federal employment, and vice versa. Only the least satisfied feel that becoming a federal employee would improve their satisfaction levels.

It is worth noting that the profiles on these indexes are also highly related to socioeconomic characteristics. In general, the lower the opportunity orientation and the higher the evaluation of federal employees, the lower is the socioeconomic level. People rating the appeal of government highest according to these attitudinal variables *tend* to represent the qualitative ranks needed least by the government.

A further perspective on the attractiveness of government work was gained when respondents were asked whether their families would consider a switch to government employment (doing the same work) as a move up the occupational ladder or down. Replies were recorded as "up the ladder," "down the ladder," and "no difference." (Developmental research showed that this is primarily a projective question, since a respondent usually had little basis for assessing family reaction beyond assuming that it would be about the same as his own. Therefore, the results should be interpreted more as a representation of the respondent's feeling rather than his family's.)

Perhaps the most significant finding is that, by every classification used in the analysis, a substantial proportion of respondents—ranging from one fourth to one half—replied "no difference." Implicit here is the suggestion that many people, even at the upper levels of education, income, and occupation, find it of little relevance whether their employment is with the government or with some other organization.

But the percentage distribution of "up the ladder" and "down the ladder" replies is important too. Almost without exception it parallels the pattern reported above for the comparative scale scores on the original questions. Again we find women giving the more favorable responses; here, too, additional analysis revealed that the favorable differences for women, although prevailing at all levels, tend to be concentrated more heavily among women in the less-educated, younger, clerical, and lower-income brackets.

Further illustrating the consistency of the results with those previously described is the distribution of replies according to education, income, and occupation. In each case, the higher the level, the higher the percentages for "down the ladder," and the lower the level, the higher the percentages for "up the ladder." The disparities are most graphic by education and especially by family income. In the latter instance, 53 percent of workers with incomes under $4,000 report moving up, and only 11 percent down; in sharp contrast, 23 percent of those in the highest bracket reply moving up, while 43 percent record moving down.

One other highly significant result must, however, be pointed out. Despite the consistent negative relation between the assessment of the appeal of federal employment and levels of education, occupation, and the like, in no instance does the figure for "up the ladder" fall below 17 percent, the figure for college graduates. Even in the highest brackets, by every classification used, there are significant percentages who indicate a positive reaction to the idea of federal employment. While these *percentages* are often not large in comparison to the percentages for "down the ladder" or "no difference," it is clear that large *numbers* of people in even the highest brackets look with favor on working for the federal government.

With respect to the indexes of opportunity vs. security and of evaluation of civil servants, again the findings coincide with the results reported in Table 5-2. The lower the orientation for opportunity as opposed to security and the higher the evaluation of civil servants, the more the pattern of replies favors federal employment.

ANOTHER APPROACH TO APPEAL ASSESSMENT involved the agree-disagree ratings on the parallel statements, "All things considered, working for the federal government appeals to me," and "All things considered, working for a large private business firm appeals to me."[8]

The results on the first statement are consistent with our findings from other measures of appeal, but in the scores for the appeal of large private business and in the difference scores we find new information of value (Table 5-3). Of particular interest is the fact that, in contrast to the federal appeal scores, the business appeal scores vary little according to the demographic and attitudinal index classifications. And even the few statistically significant variations are small compared to the variations in federal appeal scores—and in some instances move in the opposite direction: for example, business appeal scores rise slightly with increasing opportunity vs. security orientation, while federal appeal scores decline sharply.

The net result of all this is that most of the difference scores by all the classifications favor large private business, usually by very large amounts. Differences favoring federal employment are very small and for the most part are found in those at low levels of education, occupation, income, opportunity orientation, and occupational satisfaction. One exception is the positive valence shown by Negroes, even with income levels held constant.

It is a plausible hypothesis that the more a person perceives an employment sector as offering opportunities for success, the more that sec-

---

[8] These were among the fifty-five statements to be sorted by a respondent on the ten-step scale. To eliminate "order effect" the cards were shuffled between interviews. Consequently, only occasionally and by chance were these two items adjacent in the deck.

TABLE 5-3. *Occupational Appeal of the Federal Government vs. Large Private Business, Related to Various Classifications of the General Employed Public*[a]

| Classifications | Average Number Answering | Appeal of Working for | | Difference: "Federal" Minus "Business" |
		Large Private Business Firm	Federal Government	
General Employed Public	(1,081)	5.7	5.3	−0.4
Sex				
Men	(832)	5.8	5.2	−0.6
Women	(248)	5.6	6.0	+0.4
Educational Level				
High school not completed	(301)	5.8	6.1	+0.3
High school completed	(495)	5.6	5.4	−0.2
Some college	(122)	5.9	4.6	−1.3
College graduate	(134)	5.8	4.2	−1.6
Family Income				
Under $4,000	(210)	5.6	5.9	+0.3
$4,000–5,499	(310)	5.8	5.6	−0.2
$5,500–8,499	(320)	5.9	5.3	−0.6
$8,500 and over	(204)	5.5	4.2	−1.3
Race				
White	(947)	5.7	5.2	−0.5
Negro	(102)	6.1	6.8	+0.7
Opportunity vs. Security				
Low on opportunity	(332)	5.8	5.7	−0.1
Medium on opportunity	(364)	5.4	5.5	+0.1
High on opportunity	(374)	6.0	4.8	−1.2

[a] Based on mean ratings assigned to the statements, "All things considered, working for the federal government appeals to me," and "All things considered, working for a large private business firm appeals to me," on the ten-step "agree-disagree" scale; the higher the score, the more agreement.

tor is likely to appeal to him. The data shown in Table 5-4 indicate that this is, indeed, the case. There is a very strong positive relationship between the ratings given the government on the chances it offers for success and its appeal as an employer. Similarly, those who feel optimistic about chances for success in private employment evince more attraction toward working for a large private firm.

It also is true that those who are more sanguine about success in government are slightly more attracted toward business than those who are less sanguine; similarly, seeing opportunity for success in the business sphere is associated with moderately higher ratings on the appeal of federal employment. But it is notable that these relationships do not approach the magnitude of those which are complementary to each other—that is, they are not nearly so strong as the relationships between perceptions of success opportunity in one sector (say government) and the appeal of that sector. This is further and vividly demonstrated in the difference scores shown in Table 5-4. As the belief in the chances of achieving success in private employment *increases,* the comparative appeal of federal work *decreases* to the point of a substantial negative score. Conversely, as the belief in gaining success in the government *increases,* the comparative appeal of federal employment also *increases* strongly and progressively, to a point of moderately strong positive valence. Quite clearly, a person's attraction toward federal employment is related to the strength of his feeling that the pinnacles of success can be attained therein. It should be pointed out, however, that the respondents who are the most positive about the chances for success in government come disproportionately from the lower socioeconomic levels.

TABLE 5-4. *Occupational Appeal of the Federal Government vs. Large Private Business, Related to the General Employed Public's Perceptions of Avenues to Success*[a]

| Avenues to Success | Average Number Answering | Appeal of Working for | | Difference: "Federal" Minus "Business" |
		Large Private Business Firm	Federal Government	
Large Corporation Employment				
Low agreement	(303)	4.7	4.9	+0.2
Moderate agreement	(380)	5.5	5.4	−0.1
High agreement	(390)	6.8	5.7	−1.1
Federal Employment				
Low agreement	(337)	5.5	3.8	−1.7
Moderate agreement	(392)	5.6	5.2	−0.4
High agreement	(334)	6.2	7.0	+0.8

[a] "Appeal" statements are quoted in the footnote to table 5-3. The two sets of "success" categories are derived from ratings on the ten-point "agree-disagree" scale for the following statements: "For a young man of ability, his best chance for being *really successful* lies in working for (a large private business corporation) (the federal government)"; the higher the score, the more agreement.

The principal message of the foregoing findings in regard to the general employed public is incisive. While substantial *numbers* of people in all the subgroups analyzed look with favor on federal employment (or at least without disfavor), the *ordering* of appeal tends to flow opposite to the present and expected critical personnel needs of the federal establishment. There is direct evidence for this in terms of education, occupation, and income levels and indirect evidence from various attitudinal indexes.

An addendum to this conclusion is needed. We observed that women compared to men and Negro employees compared to white employees are more positive in their appraisals of federal work. This does not necessarily accord with our contention that the ordering of appeal flows opposite the ordering of critical needs. However, it must be reiterated that it is largely the women at the lower educational and occupational levels who demonstrate more favorable attitudes toward federal employment than do comparable men. Furthermore, even if women at higher levels were inordinately attracted toward federal work, the pure lack of numbers in needed areas, coupled with the channeling effects presently operating to remove many of them from the job market, mean that women could not fill the government's needs. Similarly, the Negro population is only a fraction of the total population from which federal employees are recruited, and, unfortunately, the number of highly trained and well-educated personnel in the Negro population is still meager. As a general proposition, then, our statement about the inversion of appeal and need still stands.

Groups in Education and Business

To a great extent the findings concerning the attractiveness of federal employment for persons in the education and business group samples parallel those found for upper-stratum employees in the general public. There are, however, some important variations within and among these groups. The importance of the attitudes of teachers and the business groups toward federal employment cannot be overemphasized: these people not only constitute a critical pool of manpower supply, but are also conditioners of thought and opinion for the students, clients, and colleagues with whom they associate.

High School Teachers

Of all the special groups in education and business, the high school teachers most nearly resemble the general employed public in the way they view the appeal of federal employment. The difference score between their present occupational rating and the rating for the same job if it were with the federal government is quite close to that of the general public (−0.9 for teachers compared with −0.6 for the general employed public). Similarly, their rating on the absolute appeal of working for the federal government ("All things considered, working for the federal government appeals to me") is virtually identical to that of the larger general public (5.2 compared with 5.3).

A likely reason for this close approximation is that, in socioeconomic and status terms, high school teachers are more like the working public than are other groups in education and business. Their frame of reference in evaluating employment sectors is thus more likely to be similar. In any case, the result is that high school teachers, most of whom have college degrees, exhibit considerably more favorable attitudes toward government employment than do comparably educated employees in the general employed public and in other educational and business groups. Since a high proportion of high school teachers are already public employees working in public institutions, it is probable that they see the switch to federal employment as less of a change than do comparably educated people in other pursuits.

This is apparently why so many of them (59 percent) said there would be "no difference" in their families' feeling if the teachers became federal employees. It also helps explain why this group gives a nod to the appeal of government vs. large private business employment. As noted earlier, the absolute attractiveness of federal work is as high for the teachers as for the general employed public. But since the teachers assign substantially lower scores to large private employment, their difference score shows a moderate advantage for federal work (+0.8), compared to the slight disadvantage on the part of the general public (−0.4) and the large disadvantage among the college graduates in the general public (−1.6).

A closer look at high school teachers reveals no large variations among them as far as federal appeal is concerned. One interesting note is that, in contrast to all the other populations, there is virtually no difference between men and women on federal appeal, and on one of the appeal measures men show a slightly higher score than women.

College Teachers, Natural and Social Scientists, and Engineers

College teachers are significantly less favorably disposed toward federal employment than are high school teachers. In many respects they resemble the college-educated employees of the general public, although there is one important difference which we shall describe presently. Their views about federal work are indicated by the following figures derived from ratings on the ten-step occupational satisfaction scale:

College Teachers	N	Present Occupation	Same Occupation, but for the Federal Government	Difference: "Federal" Minus "Present"
Total Teachers	(453)	8.7	7.1	−1.6
Natural Scientists	(115)	8.8	7.0	−1.8
Social Scientists	(101)	8.3	6.6	−1.7
Engineers	(86)	8.4	6.9	−1.5

Similarly, when asked whether their families would think they were moving up or down the occupational ladder if they became federal employees, a range of 27 to 33 percent say "down," compared to a range of 10 to 15 percent saying "up." As with all populations, however, a high proportion (50 percent or more) say their families would perceive no difference.

On the two statements about the appeal of working for a large private business or for the federal government we encounter an instance where the college teachers depart from highly educated people in the general work force and, as we shall see later, deviate radically from the business groups. Like the high school group, the college teachers give a net advantage to the appeal of federal employment. Their absolute scores for federal appeal are not high (from 4.3 to 5.1 on the ten-point agree-disagree scale), but are a bit higher than the absolute scores for private employment. While their value structures do not lead college professors to a high positive orientation toward federal employment, their preferences are even less in the direction of employment with a large private business firm.

Actually, a caveat is in order here. The above statement is true of college teachers in general and of the natural scientists and social scientists, but it does not apply to college engineers, who place the appeal of government employment somewhat lower than that of private business. Yet even in this instance the net disadvantage for government (−0.8) is not nearly so large as that shown by college graduates in the general work force (−1.6).

By most standards, however, college teachers do not appear to be highly drawn toward federal employment. Only in comparison to the appeal of large private business does the federal sector come off relatively well. All in all, this climate of opinion does not augur well for the federal government from a personnel standpoint. Certainly the general mood of the academic community is not especially conducive to leaving academia and entering federal service. More important, however, is the influence, both of a direct and a more subtle kind, which college teachers have, or can have, on the occupational outlooks of their students.

Groups in Business

Of all the groups studied, those in business stand out as by far the least attracted toward federal employment. Consider these scores based on scale ratings on the ten-step occupational ladder:

Groups in Business	N	Present Occupation	Same Occupation but for the Federal Government	Difference: "Federal" Minus "Present"
Executives	(281)	8.1	5.5	−2.6
Natural Scientists	(83)	8.0	5.9	−2.1
Social Scientists	(73)	8.0	5.3	−2.7
Engineers	(89)	8.1	5.6	−2.5

From these findings, there is little reason to doubt that in general these elite business groups react negatively to the idea of federal service for themselves. Further evidence comes from the answers to the question about the family's reactions to switching to federal employment. From 39 to 58 percent of the business respondents state unequivocally that their families would see this as a downward movement on the occupational ladder.

A third graphic indicator of the lack of pull toward federal employment comes in the ratings assigned to the appeal of working for the government, especially when it is compared with the appeal of private business. It is useful to match the scores of the natural and social scientists and engineers in business with those of their counterparts in colleges (Table 5-5). While the absolute attraction of federal work is low in both sectors, it is considerably lower among the business groups. When this pattern is coupled with the much higher appeal which private business has for the business groups, the resulting difference scores are exceedingly

TABLE 5-5. *Occupational Appeal of Federal Government vs. Large Private Business Among Scientists and Engineers in Colleges and Business*[a]

Special College and Business Groups	Average Number Answering	Appeal of Working for		Difference: "Federal" Minus "Business"
		Large Private Business Firm	Federal Government	
Natural Scientists				
College	(118)	4.1	4.7	+0.6
Business	(84)	6.7	3.9	−2.8
Social Scientists				
College	(105)	4.1	5.1	+1.0
Business	(70)	7.1	4.0	−3.1
Engineers				
College	(87)	5.1	4.3	−0.8
Business	(90)	7.6	3.1	−4.5

[a] "Appeal" statements are quoted in the footnote to Table 5-3.

large and to the net disadvantage of government among the business groups.[9] But among the counterpart college groups the differences are much smaller and, in two instances, reveal an advantage for government.

Because of the limited size of the samples, further analyses of the business natural and social scientists and engineers were few and for the most part provided few noticeable variations. Further work with the larger sample of business executives, however, demonstrated a tendency for certain types of executives to exhibit the least relative attraction to the federal service: the more well-to-do; Protestants less than Catholics, and Catholics less than Jews; Republicans less than Democrats and Independents. Age makes only a slight and inconsistent difference in the attitudes of executives toward federal employment appeal. Finally, level

[9] The difference score for business executives (not shown in the table) is also large and in the unfavorable direction (− 3.8).

of educational attainment within this well-educated population shows no consistent relationship to appeal scores.[10]

The Student Population

Knowing the degree of attraction that current student groups feel toward the federal service is obviously important in terms of the future labor pool from which the government will draw its personnel. It is especially important in respect to the more highly qualified segments of each student population, but before considering the variations within any given population, we will examine aspects of the appeal measures for the three groups in general. One of the measures is a modification of one used in the adult populations: since students are not yet in the work force, they were asked where they *expected* to start on the 10-step, self-anchoring occupational ladder, and where they thought they would be on the ladder if they started with the federal government instead of some other enterprise.

The results obtained from these ratings are distinctly similar to those found by educational level within the general work force. Federal employment appears, relative to where current students expect to start out, more attractive to those of lower educational rank than to those with higher attainments. The sharp division in estimates comes between the high school students (juniors and seniors) and the college seniors. College seniors and graduate students tend to resemble each other with respect to the net appeal of federal service. Here are the mean ratings on the ten-point scale:

	N	Expect To Be at Start	Same Occupation at Start, but for the Federal Government	Difference: "Federal" Minus "Start"
High School Juniors and Seniors	(359)	5.5	5.6	+0.1
College Seniors	(404)	6.3	5.3	−1.0
Graduate Students	(382)	6.8	5.7	−1.1

[10] The only direct evidence that the best-educated executives are the least attracted toward federal work appeared when they were asked to predict family reactions to their becoming federal employees: 37 percent of the least educated (no college) reported "down the ladder," but 60 percent of the best educated (college and some postgraduate work) also gave that reply.

It is coincidental that the 0.1 net advantage given federal employment by present high schoolers is exactly the same as that of the high school incompletes of the general work force; nevertheless, some such parallel is certainly in accord with theoretical expectations. Similarly, the results for college seniors and graduate students, while less negative in absolute terms than the results found among highly educated respondents in presently employed populations, are still much more in accord with them than are the high school student results. In many respects the federal government encounters the same dilemma here as elsewhere—the more educated and ostensibly more qualified a person is, the less positive is his view of federal work.

A second measure, identical to one used for all other populations, is less certain in its support of the educational hierarchy model. When students are asked to rate the statement, "All things considered, working for the federal government appeals to me," there is a statistically significant though not large difference according to groups: high school students, 5.6; college seniors, 5.2; and graduate students, 5.0. This conforms with the results on the first measure, though the differences are not nearly so dramatic as those found in the general work force. However, educational level among students is also negatively related to the appeal of working for a large business, and the ratings run about the same as those assigned government. Thus, in contrast to the general employed public, student educational level makes virtually no difference in the comparative appeal of government vs. large private employment (the difference scores being 0.0, +0.1, and +0.2 for high school, college, and graduate students, respectively).

The equality between government and private appeal for the high school students is not surprising, inasmuch as this pattern resembles that found among the less-educated people in the general work force. The stand-off for college seniors and graduate students seems to result primarily from the fact that neither large business nor government is very attractive to either of these populations. For example, well over two fifths of both college seniors and graduate students expect to go into teaching as an occupation. (This is what they say they expect to do; how many will actually do so is another matter.) In this regard it is significant that the comparative appeal ratings of these two groups approximate those of the teaching populations more closely than they do the ratings of the business groups or the upper educational echelons of the general employed public.

A third indicator of federal employment appeal stems from a question which had no parallel in the questions for the adult populations: "Returning now to when you start out, did you have in mind starting out working for the federal government—that is, the United States government?" The answers ran as follows:

	N	Yes	No	Nothing Particular in Mind
High School Juniors and Seniors	(359)	19%	71%	10%
College Seniors	(404)	16	80	4
Graduate Students	(383)	17	80	3

As the figures indicate, slightly under one fifth of each student population say that they are indeed thinking of federal employment as a possibility. These percentages of affirmative replies may seem high—and certainly the government does not need, nor is it likely to receive, such a high number of novitiates. It should be noted, however, that the question does not specify actual plans for entering federal service, but only whether such employment is being thought about. Thus a "yes" reply signifies merely that the student has not excluded the government as his potential first employer.

Nevertheless, the findings do suggest that there is a potential pool of federal employees, who, if they are qualified and could be tapped, would more than satisfy the government's needs at these respective levels of attainment. Inasmuch as the more customary pattern is for a drop off in federal appeal as the educational ladder is ascended, the fact that the proportion positively inclined is about the same at each educational stage is, from the government's standpoint, a positive sign. It is true that we do not know just how serious or durable the intentions behind the affirmative replies are. But those favorably disposed toward federal employment according to this measure also evince positive attraction when asked related questions—and this is particularly true of the college seniors and graduate students. Compared to the nonfavorably disposed students, the positive ones would expect to start higher on the occupational ladder if they did start with the government; they also rate the absolute and comparative appeal of government vs. private employment much higher.

To get at more latent feelings about federal employment a follow-up question was asked of all students who said they were not entertaining the notion of federal service: "Suppose your first occupation was with the

United States government. Would this be better or worse from your point of view?" Here is the distribution of replies:

	N	Better	Worse	No Difference
High School Juniors and Seniors	(289)	38%	29%	32%
College Seniors	(337)	12	55	33
Graduate Students	(317)	9	61	30

Notice the more common configuration that prevails in these figures. There is little question that high school juniors and seniors express a greater degree of attraction toward, and less repulsion from, federal work than do college seniors and graduate students. As with the adult populations, it is significant that a sizable proportion of all the students are ostensibly neutral about federal employment. But what is perhaps most impressive about this distribution is the large proportion of college seniors and graduate students who state without question that starting out with the government would be worse from their own point of view. This means that there is a very substantial bloc of students which the government, on the surface at least, has no chance of attracting. Furthermore, the importance of this large segment as a peer group reference for other students who might otherwise be positively inclined should not be ignored. It may be, when hard choices have to be made, that the substantial segment of opinion against government employment would swing the balance against entry into the federal service.

A Closer Look at Students

Just as the general work force contains sharp inner divisions of opinion regarding the attractiveness of a federal vocation, so too do the student populations. However, because of the more homogeneous nature of each student population—particularly the college seniors and graduate students—we find that the inner differences are not so great as those for the larger and more heterogeneous general public.

One consistent difference found within the general employed public is that women look more favorably on federal employment than men do. By and large, the intersex variations are not as great among the student populations; although the sex differences which characterize the views of adult employees toward government work are already operative at the high school stage, they are less marked. Furthermore, they are generally even less marked among graduate students than among the high schoolers and college seniors. Graduate students represent a more homogeneous grouping on several scores than do students at lower levels, and these similarities seem to play down the sex divergencies in regard to federal employment.

Family income is also a sharply discriminating factor in how the general working public views federal employment. Taking the income level of students' parents as the measure, we find evidence that a similar pattern prevails among high school juniors and seniors, but not among college seniors.[11] Illustratively, when high schoolers compare where they expect to start on the occupational ladder with where they feel they would start if working for the government, the difference scores range from +0.3 for students coming from homes with under $4,000 family incomes (N = 38) to −0.3 for those with parents in the $8,500 and over bracket (N = 95). Similarly, the absolute appeal scores of working for the federal establishment run from 6.1 at the low-income extreme down to 5.3 at the high-income end. And if the federal appeal ratings are compared with those for large private business we find that low-income students give government a net advantage of +0.6, while high-income students render a net disadvantage of −0.4. There is, then, little question that high school students reflect by income status the opinion pattern which prevails in the adult working society. The more successful the person or his family, as measured by income, the less is the appeal of federal service.

As noted above, this relationship does not apply to college seniors. At various income levels they place the difference in starting for the government vs. where they expect to begin at about −1.0 on the occupational ladder. The reasons for this uniformity are quite clear. College seniors are a select group in terms of their economic backgrounds; their median family income level stands at slightly over $8,000, with less than one fourth reporting their family incomes as lower than $5,500. Thus most college seniors would be expected to reflect the preferences of upper-income people, when income is controlled, because even the controls put most of them at a fairly high level. It seems likely also that what low-income students there are tend to become socialized in the di-

[11] The data concerning graduate students are not presented because of the diverse definitions of family income as applied to them—especially since nearly one half of them are married.

rection of the segments that have higher incomes, and their expectations of entering higher financial brackets than those from which they emanated would seem likely to pull them toward the type of opinion existent at higher levels. Further confirmation of these suppositions rests in the fact that family income level makes little difference in where college seniors expect to start out on the occupational ladder.

Two variables which were not used in analyzing the general work force are of inherent interest in examining the student populations: academic grade average and—for college seniors and graduate students—college major. High school and college students were divided into three groups according to grade averages of "A," "B," and "C" or lower; because of their generally high academic rankings, graduate students were categorized according to "A" and "B" (or lower) averages only.[12]

For the most part grade average makes for only a slight difference in the appeal of federal employment. Although the better students, compared to the poorer ones, at the high school and college levels say they would be starting out on a higher plane if they began their career with the government, the pattern is offset by the fact that they also expect to begin a little better off in their anticipated sector of employment.

The picture is similar in the ratings applied to the absolute appeal of working for the government. Only among high school juniors and seniors is there much of a difference according to grade average; the better students rate federal appeal slightly higher on the ten-point, agree-disagree scale (Table 5-6). When the federal scores are compared with those on the absolute appeal of a large private business, however, better students in all three populations give net advantages to federal employment. High school and graduate students with lower averages see virtually no difference, but college seniors averaging "C" or lower see private business as emphatically more appealing than government. Thus, compared with large business, the appeal of federal work is likely to be greater among the superior students.

However, as pointed out previously, neither federal nor large business employment is, on the average, a highly desirable alternative for the students, particularly college seniors and graduate school students. Nevertheless, we know that both of these giant employers will compete for and also recruit significant numbers from the student populations.

---

[12] For a discussion of the cautions accompanying the analysis by grade averages, see Chapter 4, section on "Variations by Academic Grades."

An assessment of these findings by grade average suggests that the federal establishment is in a relatively advantageous position. It has as good an opportunity to capitalize on predispositions among the better students as among the poorer ones. From a quality standpoint this is a crucial matter. If, for example, it were shown that the better students, particularly those with "A" averages, were much more averse to federal work than the poorer students, the government's prospects would be dim

TABLE 5-6. *Students' Grade Averages, Related to Occupational Appeal of the Federal Government vs. Large Private Business*[a]

Grade Averages	Average Number Answering	Appeal of Working for		Difference: "Federal" Minus "Business"
		Large Private Business Firm	Federal Government	
High School Juniors and Seniors				
A	(51)	5.3	5.9	+0.6
B	(142)	5.7	5.6	−0.1
C and below	(160)	5.6	5.4	−0.2
College Seniors				
A	(88)	4.7	5.0	+0.3
B	(202)	4.8	5.3	+0.5
C and below	(106)	6.0	4.9	−1.1
Graduate Students				
A	(154)	4.6	4.9	+0.3
B and below	(205)	5.2	5.1	−0.1

[a] "Appeal" statements are quoted in the footnote to Table 5-3.

for attracting the kind of high-level talent which will be increasingly in demand. But high school students of all grade average levels see no loss in starting with the government, and, even though college seniors and graduate students at all levels are inclined to think that they would be disadvantaged by starting their careers with the government, the superior students feel no more strongly about this than their less scholarly peers. Furthermore, the better students tend to rate federal employment ahead of working for a large business firm. Other factors being equal, then, the government should do fairly well among the brighter students— although one cannot count on such factors as the inducements offered prospective employees and the alternatives which are available being equal.

We have seen that among high school juniors and seniors the "A" and "B" students (as well as those lower than that) think they would be doing just as well starting careers with the government as where they actually intend to start. The fact that students who earn these grades are usually the ones who will later matriculate at colleges suggests that this may be the stage where the government can do the most to reinforce the relatively positive predispositions of brighter students who will eventually become the skilled and trained talent of the future.[13]

In considering the college seniors and graduate school students according to their college majors, we chose those in the fields of engineering, social sciences, and natural sciences—partly because these are fields from which the government will have to draw a significant share of its high-level personnel, and partly because we could compare students in these major fields with their adult counterparts in the business and college populations.[14]

One pattern is particularly apparent in examining the differential appeal of the federal service according to this variable. A close look at Table 5-7 reveals that both undergraduate and graduate engineering majors are the least enamored of federal employment. They give the lowest ratings to starting out with the government; they see the greatest negative difference between beginning with the government and where they plan to start; they rate the absolute appeal of government work the lowest; and they see the greatest negative difference between the appeal of government and large private enterprise. The variations between the engineers and the other two groups are not always large, but the pattern is consistent. Natural science majors are more favorably inclined toward government than are engineers, and the social science majors are the most positively disposed.

Both federal and private manpower forecasts indicate that engineers and natural scientists will be among the personnel most sought after and in shortest supply in the years to come. It would, therefore, be more encouraging for the government if engineers and natural science majors, rather than the social science group, led the way in evaluating federal employment. Social scientists (and people from other expert fields) will of course also be needed in quantity and in quality by the federal es-

---

[13] A concomitant here is that most high school teachers are also rather favorably disposed toward federal employment.

[14] Caution must be exercised in analyzing and interpreting the tabulations by majors due to the relatively small number of cases involved at some points.

tablishment. But among the students who are aiming at degrees in fields where competition for their services is likely to be most keen, the federal government has a great deal of existing unfavorable predisposition to overcome. This is especially true of the students who will enter the job market as engineers.

TABLE 5-7. *Students' College Majors, Related to Two Measures of the Appeal of Federal Employment*[a]

| Major Subjects | Average Number Answering | Occupational Ladder | | Difference: "Federal" Minus "Start" |
		Expect To Be at Start	Same Occupation at Start, but for Federal Government	
College Seniors				
Engineering	(38)	6.2	4.8	−1.4
Natural sciences	(73)	6.5	5.5	−1.0
Social sciences	(73)	6.0	5.2	−0.8
Graduate Students				
Engineering	(63)	6.8	5.3	−1.5
Natural sciences	(93)	7.1	6.0	−1.1
Social sciences	(75)	6.4	5.5	−0.9

| Major Subjects | Average Number Answering | Appeal of Working for | | Difference: "Federal" Minus "Business" |
		Large Private Business Firm	Federal Government	
College Seniors				
Engineering	(38)	6.7	4.5	−2.2
Natural sciences	(72)	4.8	5.1	+0.3
Social sciences	(73)	4.7	5.8	+1.1
Graduate Students				
Engineering	(63)	5.6	4.7	−0.9
Natural sciences	(92)	5.3	4.9	−0.4
Social sciences	(75)	4.5	5.5	+1.0

[a] Occupational ladder scores are mean ratings on the ten-step self-anchoring occupational scale; the appeal scores are mean ratings on the ten-step agree-disagree scale in relation to two statements (see footnote to Table 5-3).

General Federal Employees

What of the occupational appeal of federal employment as it applies to general federal employees themselves? Offhand, one might say that, since these people are presently members of the federal establishment, they must be rather highly attracted toward and satisfied with such employment. And from the data presented in Chapter 3, we have seen that, over all, they appear to be as satisfied with their jobs as members of the general nonfederal work force are with theirs. However, other findings in Chapter 3—especially by educational level—strongly suggested that personnel on the upper levels of the federal establishment may feel *relatively* less advantaged than counterpart nonfederal personnel. It also seems likely that these upper-echelon people may feel *relatively* less advantaged as federal employees than their lower-level colleagues. These two notions will be tested here by examining, first, the appeal of federal vs. nonfederal employment among various kinds of federal employees, and second, the relative appeal of federal work for federal employees vs. such appeal for comparable groupings in the general employed public.

Among general federal employees, by virtually every measure indicative of educational and occupational attainments, there is a clear hierarchy of responses to the question of where on the occupational ladder they would be if they were pursuing their present line of work, but in the nonfederal sector. There is a step-like gradation in the loss people say they would experience—the higher the level of attainment the smaller the loss expected; by inference, then, the higher the level, the lower the relative appeal of the federal service.

Illustrative of the hierarchical picture is the distribution of ratings according to education and federal grade levels shown in Table 5-8. There is an expected large difference between high-echelon employees and their lower-rank colleagues on where they think they would be if changing to nonfederal employment. But it is of primary significance that high-level employees see themselves as being considerably less hurt by such a switch. This is readily apparent in the progressive movement by the educational breakdown. The other continuum—federal grade hierarchy—involves two subhierarchies as well as postal service employees, but the results parallel those by education. Thus, in the Wage Board subhierarchy, skilled and supervisory personnel see less of a drop than the unskilled and semiskilled. Similarly, there is a clear diminution of expected loss as the General Schedule hierarchy rises; in fact, those at the apex of the hierarchy say they would feel no loss. Distinctly similar patterns prevail according to income and occupational classifications (not shown).

TABLE 5-8. *Education and Federal Grade Level of General Federal Employees, Related to Ratings of Present Occupation vs. Doing the Same Work, but Outside the Federal Government*

Education and Federal Grade	Average Number Answering	Present Occupation	Same Occupation, but Outside the Federal Government	Difference: "Outside" Minus "Present"
General Federal Employees	(927)	7.0	6.1	−0.9
Educational Level				
High school not completed	(188)	6.9	5.7	−1.2
High school completed	(346)	6.8	5.9	−0.9
Some college	(177)	6.8	6.1	−0.7
College graduate	(160)	7.4	7.1	−0.3
Federal Grade Level				
Wage board				
Unskilled and semiskilled	(127)	6.8	5.3	−1.5
Skilled and supervisory	(112)	7.2	6.4	−0.8
Postal service	(101)	6.2	5.5	−0.7
General schedule				
GS 2–4	(174)	6.9	5.9	−1.0
GS 5–7	(168)	7.1	6.5	−0.6
GS 8–11	(142)	7.6	7.1	−0.5
GS 12 and over	(88)	7.7	7.8	+0.1

Not surprisingly, the relative satisfaction associated with federal vs. outside employment is related to other measures reflecting an evaluation of federal work. Thus the relative appeal is much lower among the least satisfied (in absolute terms), those who are planning to leave government employment or are only fairly sure of staying, and those who considered leaving in the recent past.

Very similar results were obtained in response to the question about family reactions to a change to private employment. Almost without exception, as attainment levels rise there is an increase in the proportion of

federal respondents who say their families would view this as a movement up the occupational ladder, or making no difference; by the same
token there is a decrease in the proportion predicting a "down the ladder" reaction. These figures according to occupational income are typical:

Income	N	Up the Ladder	Down the Ladder	No Difference	Don't Know
Under $4,500	(179)	8%	59%	33%	0%
$4,500–5,499	(267)	18	47	34	0
$5,500–6,999	(246)	16	47	36	1
$7,000–9,999	(145)	26	37	37	0
$10,000 and Over	(74)	29	22	46	2

A third measurement of the appeal of federal employment for federal
employees was obtained from the responses to the statement: "All
things considered, working for the federal government appeals to me."
As expected, the mean ratings for this statement run high among nearly
all federal employees—in terms of education, income, occupation, federal grade level, and age. Most scores hover around 8.0 on the ten-point
agree-disagree scale. Hence the high absolute appeal of federal employment transcends various hierarchies. Whatever relative disadvantage
the high-level federal employees may presently feel, the feeling does
not originate from an aversion to federal employment per se. This is an
important point, because it implies that the relative deprivation felt by
upper-level employees is, from their point of view, susceptible to some
solution other than dropping out of the federal work force.

When the appeal scores for federal employment are compared with
those for a large private business, we find that employees at all levels
return a decided and rather uniform edge to the federal sector. Most of
the difference scores show the government with a plus of around 3.5 to
4.0. Thus, when the appeal of government work is compared with the
specific appeal of working for a large private business firm, federal employees do not, in general, exhibit the differential patterning found by
other measures.[15] The most general explanation is that (as the absolute

[15] There are, however, three variables which do set some federal employees apart.
Those planning to leave the federal government (N = 65), those who thought of
leaving within the past five years (N = 188), and those with the lowest level of
present occupational satisfaction (N = 314) all exhibit less pull toward federal work,
both absolutely and in comparison to the appeal of private work. To a certain extent, of course, these are all measurements of appeal phenomena, but the score configuration points toward a confluence of commitment, appeal, and satisfaction. Al-

scores suggest) the prospect of working for a large firm is not a very attractive alternative for most kinds of federal workers.

HAVING DOCUMENTED THE PROPOSITION that in a relative sense the appeal of federal employment is less for the high-level employees in the general government work force than for those of lower rank, let us examine the second proposition, to wit: high-level employees feel relatively less positive about their occupational situation than do their counterparts outside government. Comparing the difference scores emerging from present occupational ratings vs. ratings of doing the same work, but with a change of employer—to the government for the general employed public, to outside the government for federal workers—we find that the federal employees feel they would drop down the occupational ladder about the same degree (-0.9) as do members of the nonfederal work force (-0.6). Contrary to nonfederal workers, men and women in the federal service see about the same difference involved in switching employment sectors, but when there are sex differences they prove consistent with those in the nonfederal group—that is, women look more favorably on government than do men.

When we compare the difference scores according to educational and other levels, we encounter a marked distinction between the two general work forces. The results on the ten-point scale when the scores for present occupation are subtracted from those for a change of employer are as follows:

Educational Levels	N	General Employed Public ("federal" minus "present")	N	General Federal Employees ("outside" minus "present")
High School Not Completed	(324)	+0.1	(188)	−1.2
High School Completed	(503)	−0.4	(346)	−0.9
Some College	(128)	−1.7	(177)	−0.7
College Graduate	(137)	−1.7	(160)	−0.3

though occupational satisfaction levels are correlated with certainty of staying in the federal establishment, there is sufficient deviation to indicate that satisfaction levels and sureness of staying are by no means synonymous.

Obviously the flow of opinion is quite opposite for the two sets of employees. As education rises in the general employed public the relative lack of favor for government employment climbs markedly and is equally high for the two top echelons. In direct contrast, the relative lack of favor for nonfederal employment among federal workers drops almost to the disappearing point as the educational hierarchy ascends. Thus we have strong and reconfirming evidence that the better-educated federal worker finds less occupational satisfaction from and appeal in his employment sector than the nonfederal counterpart does in his. Comparisons of federal and nonfederal employees by such measures as income and occupation reveal similar contrasts in satisfaction and appeal structures.

Answers to the question of how their families would view a change of employers add further confirmation to the disparate patterns prevailing in the two work forces. "Up the ladder" and "down the ladder" figures show that federal employees, over all, perceive less upward mobility and more downward movement in such a change than members of the general employed public do. But a breakdown according to education demonstrates that two opposing internal patterns are again present. As educational achievements rise in the nonfederal public, predictions of gain decline, whereas estimates of loss increase; the opposite pattern prevails among the federal group, where rising education brings more projections of upward movement, and fewer of downward:

| | "Up the Ladder" | | "Down the Ladder" | |
| | General Employed Public (from "present" to "federal") | General Federal Employees (from "present" to "outside") | General Employed Public (from "present" to "federal") | General Federal Employees (from "present" to "outside") |
Educational Levels				
The Groups Over All	39%	18%	21%	46%
High School Not Completed	49	13	15	58
High School Completed	42	16	19	46
Some College	30	20	32	43
College Graduate	17	26	35	28

Notice that the federal employee of slight education, compared with his like number in the nonfederal work force, feels he has much more to lose and less to gain by a switch of employers. But the well-educated federal worker is, if anything, more likely to feel he would gain and less likely to feel he would lose than is his nonfederal counterpart. Again, interpopulation comparisons according to income and occupational analysis produce similar and just as dramatic results.

In sum, it seems evident that the kinds of personnel for whom governmental shortages are likely to be the most acute, in a qualitative sense, are those for whom the relative satisfaction—hence appeal—is the least. This is hardly an encouraging sign. It suggests that the rewards of being a federal employee (rather than a nonfederal employee) are not attuned to the differential distribution of needs, values, and aspirations in the federal work force. In a sense those at the upper echelons are being denied the *relative* rewards which those at the lower levels are experiencing. They are also being denied the *relative* satisfaction which their upper-level counterparts on the outside are enjoying. The retention and morale problems inherent in such a state are obvious. Not so apparent is the effect on potential and new recruits of high quality. If they perceive, as do present high-level employees, that their relative situation will not be decisively on the positive side, they may be dissuaded from federal service.

Special Federal Populations

The findings for the four elite federal groups—executives, natural scientists, social scientists, and engineers—have to a large extent been presaged by the data for the college graduates and upper-echelon employees of the larger sample of general federal workers. Respondents in the four special groups indicate, on the average, little or no difference in their occupational satisfaction were they to switch to a nonfederal employer. Similarly, they are far more likely than the average federal employee to predict that their families would see such a switch as portending a move up the ladder, and far less inclined to cite it as a drop. Again, then, we have evidence that employees in the higher federal echelons are the ones most likely to feel relatively disadvantaged by working for the government rather than doing the same work on the outside.

The certitude of this proposition is further borne out when the special federal groups are compared with their counterparts in business and colleges. Table 5-9 contains two sets of comparisons for groups in these three sectors: the difference scores between present and federal ("out-side" for federal groups) occupational ladder ratings, and the percent-ages indicating family reactions to working for the federal government ("outside" for federal groups).

The pattern evident in both parts of the table is impressive. Taking

TABLE 5-9. *Relative Appeal of Federal (or Outside) Employment vs. Present Employment, and Family Reactions to Working for the Government (or Outside), Among Special Groups in Colleges, Business, and Government*

Special Groups	Average Number Answering[a]	Occupational Scale Ratings: "Federal (Outside)" Minus "Present"	Family Would Feel the Change Was a Move		
			Up the Ladder	Down the Ladder	No Difference
Natural Scientists					
Business	(82)	−2.1	16%	40%	44%
College	(116)	−1.8	12	32	53
Federal	(90)	−0.5	37	23	40
Social Scientists					
Business	(71)	−2.7	6	58	36
College	(100)	−1.7	11	32	57
Federal	(87)	−0.3	24	27	49
Engineers					
Business	(87)	−2.5	11	39	49
College	(84)	−1.5	10	27	64
Federal	(95)	−0.1	29	14	57
Executives					
Business	(278)	−2.6	12	47	40
Federal	(262)	−0.2	31	22	47

[a] Based on averages from questions used for both portions of the table; the number differ-ences involved are slight.

the scale scores first, there is no doubt that the federal specialists indi-cate far less of a sense of loss if going into nonfederal employment than their counterparts do if transferring to federal employment. By contrast, the business and academic groups (particularly the former) all indicate drastic reversals in their occupational satisfaction should they become federal employees. Basically, the same generalizations apply to the re-sponses to the question about family reactions to a change of employer, although the pattern is tempered by the very substantial proportions of all groups, both federal and nonfederal, who reply "no difference." Nevertheless, it is quite clear that, compared with their nonfederal colleagues, the federal groups predict more feeling of upward movement (by being in nonfederal work) and less of downward movement.

The implications of this pattern are important, paralleling as they do the picture presented when the upper echelons of the general federal work force were compared with counterparts in the general employed public. The evidence is persuasive that the pulls of nonfederal employment are likely to be much greater on high-level federal people than vice versa. While the academic or business people who may be tempted to enter the federal service would appear to be few, the latent readiness of their talented colleagues in government to leave that sector is much more common. Hence there is a problem of attraction on the one hand, and a potential morale and retention problem on the other. More significant, of course, is the general climate of opinion reflected by these data and the possible perpetuation of such a climate by these elite groups, both federal and nonfederal.

Summary

1. The appeal of federal employment is lowest among those kinds of employed adults for whom the government's qualitative needs are the greatest and for whom the competition will be keenest in the future. In general, those persons with better education, higher occupational attainments, and more technical skills feel that federal employment would seriously lower their occupational satisfaction. On the other hand, those with less education, lower occupational attainments, and less technical skills feel that government would not seriously hurt their occupational satisfaction, and would, in some cases, raise it.

2. While the appeal of federal employment is lowest among those for whom the needs will be greatest, it is nevertheless true that among even the very highly qualified and occupationally situated, there are substantial numbers of people who are not averse to the idea of working for the government. The appeal varies, however; for example, the business groups are less attracted toward federal employment than the college teachers, and college teachers less than high school teachers.

3. The differential appeal of federal employment is not as clear-cut among future members of the labor force—high school juniors and seniors,

college seniors, and graduate students—as it is among the presently employed groups. College seniors and graduate students feel that federal employment would be less advantageous for them than where they expect to start out occupationally, whereas the high schoolers foresee little difference. However, college and graduate students, like high schoolers, note little difference in the appeal of federal employment vs. one of its main competitors—large private business firms. Furthermore, close to one fifth of the students at each level indicated that they were considering government as their potential employer.

In addition, within each student population the view the better students (by academic grade average) take of federal employment is just as good as, or better than, that of the poorer students. The government seems to be in a particularly advantageous position among the brighter high school pupils, a position heightened by the relatively positive outlook on federal employment held by high school teachers. There also appears to be an ordering of federal appeal based on college major: the engineering majors look least favorably on federal employment, the natural scientists somewhat less unfavorably, and the social scientists the most favorably.

4. The evidence is strong that the occupational satisfaction offered by the federal service is *relatively* lower for the high-level federal employee than for his colleague of lower rank. This is not because high-level personnel are less positive about working for the government as such. Rather, it stems from the fact that the expectations of the people in the lower ranks of the federal service could, in their own opinions, not be matched on the outside. On the other hand, the well-educated and well-placed civil servant would feel relatively little or no deprivation were he to be doing the same work, but in the private sector of employment.

A corollary to this conclusion is that the high-ranking federal employees feel relatively less positive about their occupational situations than do their counterparts outside the government. While upper-level persons in nonfederal work would, in general, feel quite disadvantaged by working for the government, their like numbers in the federal work force would feel little deprivation by a change to nonfederal work. This is particularly apparent when comparing the elite populations in business, colleges, and the government.

Taken together, the two findings indicate that the higher-level federal employees are being denied the relative rewards of the lower-ranking federal employees and the relative satisfaction of their counterparts outside the government.

6

The Image of the Federal Government
As an Employer

WHAT DO PEOPLE OUTSIDE of the federal service see as the probable advantages and disadvantages for themselves if they were to work for the national government? And what do federal employees see as the relative pros and cons of nonfederal employment compared with their own jobs? These two questions are of crucial importance to the recruitment and retention of men and women for the federal service—for the answers to them present, in large degree, the composite image of the government as an employer.

In this chapter we will examine some of the illuminating answers furnished by our respondents to both questions. The answers were elicited by asking all interviewees, after they had replied to the "change of employer" scale question (dealt with in the preceding chapter), to state in their own words "What things would be likely to be better" and "What things would be likely to be worse" about federal (or nonfederal) employment.[1] The respondents were thus invited to make a clear-cut comparison between working for the government and working outside the government, assuming that the specific kind of work they did remained the same. A very few said the character of their work would be so changed by the shift that they could not answer the question. Most, however, made the comparison with ease.

The specific characteristics that people consider to be better and worse in the government are of considerable significance. If the general public feels that a job in the federal service, compared with private em-

[1] Students were asked to rate the occupation they expected to have when they started work, and then to state what things would be better or worse if they worked for the federal government instead.

ployment, provides better pay, greater prestige, more challenging and interesting work, and better opportunities for advancement, one would draw one kind of conclusion about the ability of the federal service to compete for manpower throughout the 1960's. But if people feel that the federal service lags behind nonfederal employment in providing such factors as these, quite a different conclusion about the government's competitive position would be indicated. In assessing the significance for the government of the findings, the relationship of the particular features that a group feels are better or worse in government to the occupational values which are of greatest concern to that group is a crucial point to bear in mind.

The General Employed Public

"It is Civil Service and has a halfway decent pension plan. It's usually steady work." *(Dyesetter in a metal products factory, Oakland, California)*

"It would probably be under Civil Service; and I can see certain problems which would probably curtail the completeness of the job—would curtail the freedom that I now have. Although I have certain policies to follow, I have quite a wide range of freedom—and this I like." *(Director of physical education for the YMCA in a small eastern city)*

These two factors—increased security and fringe benefits versus a loss of autonomy in the work situation—indicate the chief advantage and the chief drawback that people in the general employed public see in government work in comparison with their own jobs. The percentages mentioning these and various other features of federal employment are as follows:[2]

Would Be Better in the Federal Government (N = 1,077)		Would Be Worse in the Federal Government (N = 1,100)	
Security and fringe benefits	42%	Lack of self-determination	22%
Financial reward	26	Bureaucracy	16
Physical environment and working conditions	16	Financial reward	13
Leisure, vacation	10		
Nothing would be better	20	Nothing would be worse	26

[2] In this and subsequent presentations of the percentages mentioning a specific characteristic, the general rule is to list the characteristic if it is cited by a tenth or more of a group's members.

Variations by Education, Income, and Occupational Level

The above figures indicate something of the attitudes in the nonfederal work force as a whole, but they also conceal an important point. Within this group, it is the lower-status individuals, rather than those more advantageously placed in the socioeconomic hierarchy, who are most likely to feel that government employment has a relative advantage in terms of working conditions and pay. Conversely, as one ascends the socioeconomic ladder, the negative factors of lack of self-determination, too much bureaucracy, and poor financial reward loom increasingly large. Note the contrast between the responses of people who failed to finish high school and those who graduated from college:

		Better in Government		Worse in Government		
	N	Good Financial Reward	Working Conditions	Poor Financial Reward	Lack of Self-Determination	Bureaucracy
High School Incompletes	(308)	38%	22%	8%	19%	10%
College Graduates	(135)	16	5	18	29	32

These differences show up even more strongly when the data are analyzed according to the respondents' income level (Table 6-1). For those whose incomes are below the American average, the federal pay scale has considerable appeal, but its attractiveness falls off sharply among those who are earning the highest incomes. The same is true—although to a lesser extent—of the government's edge on working conditions. By contrast, the association of the federal service with greater security and better fringe benefits declines but slightly among the high-income groups. One highly paid business executive probably spoke for a number of his colleagues, however, when he said, "Of course, the federal government does give you a secure position, fringe benefits, and all that; but most of us feel that we can do all right on that score in industry."

On the negative side, complaints about bureaucratic red tape and restrictions on autonomy increase sharply among the high-income people. A supervisor in a Philadelphia chemical plant declared: "They'd have too many papers to fill out. Any time you have to place an order, or something, there's a lot of red tape. Everything has to go through a lot of different channels." Over and over again, variations on this theme were repeated: the government is a vast organizational machine in which the individual is in danger of losing his identity and autonomy.

TABLE 6-1. *Better and Worse Features Seen in Federal Employment, Related to Family Income Level in the General Employed Public*

Better and Worse Features	Income Level			
	Under $4,000	$4,000– $5,499	$5,500– $8,499	$8,500 and over
Likely To Be Better				
High or good financial reward	48%	28%	19%	10%
Security and fringe benefits	45	44	41	37
Working conditions	21	21	14	10
Nothing would be better	12	15	23	31
NUMBER ANSWERING	(223)	(300)	(311)	(201)
Likely To Be Worse				
Poor financial reward	4%	8%	19%	20%
Lack of self-determination	17	17	22	35
Bureaucracy and red tape	11	12	15	27
Nothing would be worse	41	31	21	10
NUMBER ANSWERING	(223)	(305)	(325)	(205)

Given this negative relationship between people's educational and income level and their evaluation of the relative advantages of federal employment, one would expect to find the pattern repeated with respect to occupational level also. In general this is the case. As one moves up the occupational hierarchy from unskilled to skilled laborers and thence eventually to professional and managerial personnel, references to positive features of federal employment decrease and references to negative features increase substantially. Two aspects of the data, however, are worthy of special note. Of all the occupational groups analyzed, clerical employees are the most likely to cite security and fringe benefits as a relative advantage of federal employment. And farmers, at the verbal level at least, are the staunchest individualists. More strongly than any other group, they assert that bureaucratic red tape and restrictions on a person's self-determination would be drawbacks of federal employment.

That the factors which people feel are better or worse in the federal service have a direct relationship to their willingness to work for the government is shown clearly in the ratings for the statement, "All things considered, working for the federal government appeals to me." In the following figures, note the relationship between the low, medium, or high appeal which working for the government has for people and the frequency with which they single out certain advantages in government employment compared with the opportunities outside.

	Appeal of Federal Employment		
Things Likely To Be Better	*Low* (332)	*Medium* (380)	*High* (306)
High or good financial reward	16%	25%	35%
Working conditions	9	18	24
Security and fringe benefits	33	47	47
Nothing would be better	34	17	11

The same general tendency can be discerned in people's replies to the question about what would be worse in the federal service: the weaker the appeal of the federal service, the greater is the feeling that government work would mean less money and autonomy—and more bureaucracy and red tape.

Considered as a whole, these findings should evoke attention—and concern—on the part of those with an interest in obtaining trained men and women for the federal service. Among persons of low socioeconomic status, government employment is often seen as being better than private employment in a number of respects—in the working conditions, in the pay, in the provision of leave and vacation time. It is better, in short, in providing some of the very factors that our earlier analysis of occupational values indicated are of special concern to those with less education, lower incomes, and lower job status. For these groups, the perceived advantages of government employment and their occupational values tend to coincide.

Among the higher-status groups, however, references to most of the commonly mentioned advantages of government employment decline, while emphasis on the disadvantages increases. Moreover, the special stress on lack of self-determination and too much bureaucracy—which is another way of saying there would be too many restrictions on the individual's autonomy in the work situation—underscores the nature of the government's problem among the high-status groups. Self-determination is one of the occupational values of special concern to this kind of person. Among the better-educated, the more highly paid, and those in high-status occupations, there is thus a tendency for the perceived advantages of government employment and their occupational values to be out of phase.

One of the rewards often cited by those in the government, particularly in its upper echelons, is the opportunity to be of public service, and to do worthwhile, important work. As one former high-ranking government official put it, "What . . . would give you greater satisfaction—helping to build the organization that will administer the Marshall Plan or helping to manufacture the best household furniture on the market?"[3] If the chance to do worthwhile, constructive work were generally seen as an advantage of government employment, the appeal of the federal service would be enhanced among high-status members of the population, because this is an occupational value of special concern to these groups. There may be limited circles outside the government where this is an important motivation for government service, but if so, it is a feeling not widely shared by the public at large. In the general work force, opportunities for worthwhile, constructive work are mentioned as an advantage of government employment by 1 percent; among college graduates, the figure is 2 percent.

There remains one factor on which the government is judged to excel private employment by people at all levels of occupation, income, and education—security and fringe benefits. If this were an occupational value of prime concern to people, it should serve as a powerful attraction to government employment. Security is mentioned as an occupational value by some of our respondents, and doubtless it does serve as a factor that encourages some people to enter the federal service. In a period when unemployment looms as a major social problem, the fact that the nation's largest employer is associated with stable, secure work is of no small importance.

Nevertheless, for the federal recruiter, the advantage the government is conceded on security and fringe benefits has an important drawback. Its appeal is likely to be strongest among potential employees for whom the government's recruitment difficulties are least—those with less formal education and training. As a variety of our analyses have demonstrated, concern over the security factor, compared with other occupa-

[3] John J. Corson, "Why Men Work," *Personnel Administration*, Vol. 10 (March 1948), p. 13.

tional values, tends to be greatest among groups with low socioeconomic status. Among the high-level groups, concern tends to decline.

Moreover, in the population as a whole, the feeling that private employment is insecure is not overwhelming. In the general employed public, the scale score registering agreement with the statement, "Employment with the federal government offers a high degree of security" is 7.4 out of a possible 10. But their agreement with the statement "Employment with a large private business offers a high degree of security" is also more than half-way up the scale, at 6.1. And a number of other occupational concerns are mentioned more often than security by people at all income, occupational, and educational levels. In short, the most commonly mentioned advantage of federal employment—security—does not coincide with the chief preoccupations of most people, and especially the more highly qualified, when they consider a job.

For the government, this fact alone illuminates an important aspect of its personnel problem. However, the decline in the relative appeal of government employment among the high-status groups, compared with their present work, is, from the government's standpoint, the more serious problem. Note the people at the two extremes in income level who assert that "Nothing would be better" and "Nothing would be worse" in government employment:

	Under $4,000 (223)	$8,500 and Over (203)
Nothing would be better	12%	31%
Nothing would be worse	41	10

Many low-income respondents are hard pressed to think of any negative features of federal employment. But many high-income people are unable to think of any advantages. If these data have validity, the government should find itself in a reasonably competitive position when it seeks to hire janitors, maintenance workers, or postal workers. But to hire trained research scientists, potential executives, and engineers may sometimes be very difficult indeed.

Variations by Sex

A variety of analyses have indicated that the attraction of the federal service is greater for women than for men. Women's responses concerning what would be better and what would be worse about working for the government provide further confirmation. In the general employed public, women, compared with men, are more likely to feel they would be better paid if they worked for the government (39 vs. 22 percent), and less likely to say that "nothing would be better" about federal employment (13 vs. 22 percent). On the negative side, they are less likely to see the pay (6 vs. 15 percent) and bureaucratic inflexibility (9 vs. 17 percent) as drawbacks of federal work, and more likely (33 vs. 24 percent) to say that "nothing would be worse" in the government. On most other factors, the differences between men and women are negligible.

It may be questioned whether these discrepancies stem from real differences in attitude between men and women, or whether they merely reflect the fact that women are concentrated in the kinds of occupations (of lower or intermediate status) where a generally more favorable view of government employment is common. A number of analyses, the details of which are not reported here, were required to establish the point, but in general it can be said that the differences tend to hold, even when the education, income, occupation, and age of men and women are held constant.

Groups in Education and Business

High School and College Teachers

High school and college teachers tend to resemble college-trained members of the nonfederal work force in their assessment of the relative pros and cons of federal employment, but there are a few salient exceptions. Compared with other college-educated groups in 1960, when interviews with people outside the government were conducted for this study, the teaching profession was not noted for its high pay.[4] And teachers, again compared with other college-educated groups, were more likely to feel they would be better paid if they worked for the federal government. On the other hand, they were less likely to say that security and fringe benefits would be better in the federal service—probably a reflection of the effectiveness of tenure appointment systems and other protective benefits in the teaching profession. Some teachers, especially those in high schools and the natural scientists in colleges, said neces-

---

[4] In 1960 the high school teachers interviewed for this study had a median personal income of $5,600; the figure for the college teachers was $8,300.

sary equipment and facilities would be better in the government. But very few—1 to 3 percent—stated that the opportunity to do worthwhile, constructive work would be better in government than in their present occupation. As data presented in a later chapter will indicate, teachers— especially in the colleges—are more likely than any other group to stress the opportunities for public service and worthwhile work as reasons which might cause a person to enter the federal service. Thus they clearly see such factors as worthy features of government employment, and are in a position to transmit this feeling to those whom they teach. But apparently they also feel that these opportunities are equally available in their job as a teacher.

Teachers are also especially prone to assert that lack of self-determination—inadequate freedom of thought and action on the job—would be a drawback of federal employment. Mention of this factor was frequent among the high school teachers (33 percent); more frequent still among the college teachers (57 percent). Complaints about excessive red tape and bureaucracy are likewise particularly common. On most factors, however, the high school group tends to take a slightly more favorable view of working for the government than the college group.

College Natural and Social Scientists and Engineers

In most respects, these three special college groups resemble the total college teacher population in their assessments of what would be better and what would be worse in the federal service. They are more likely than other college-educated groups to feel that government pay would be better and less likely to concede the federal service the edge on security and fringe benefits. The biggest drawback they see in federal service is lack of self-determination (from 49 percent of the engineers to 57 percent of the natural scientists), with complaints about bureaucracy and red tape (28 to 31 percent) also being common.

Nevertheless, certain differences in attitude can be found—both within the three special groups and between them and college teachers as a whole. Academic engineers and natural scientists are less likely than other college teachers to feel that their pay would be improved in the government. And one in four of the natural scientists says that the government's equipment and facilities would be better, compared with one in ten of the social scientists and engineers. Natural scientists also are more likely (one in ten) than the others to say that opportunities to do the kind of work they were interested in would be enhanced in the federal service, and a number of those who mention this factor pointed out that the extensive equipment and facilities the government provides are a prerequisite for some of the research projects they had in mind.

Engineers also differ significantly from most of the other college teachers. Of all the teachers interviewed, they are the most critical of what the government has to offer. More than one in ten say that, compared with their present occupation, there would be less emphasis on merit in promotions and a loss of drive and initiative in the federal service. And more than a third (36 percent) are unable to think of anything that would be better in federal employment.

Groups in Business

Of all the people interviewed for this study, members of the four special business groups—executives, natural and social scientists, and engineers—are by all odds the most critical of federal employment in comparison with their own jobs. A third of these high-level business employees say that the security and fringe benefits would be better in government, but the number who see other relative advantages in public employment is small. In 1960 the median income of the business groups interviewed was substantially higher than that of their federal counterparts.[5] We find that not one of the business engineers interviewed says his pay would be better in the government; one in three says it would be worse. Most of the groups are also more likely than other groups to see other drawbacks in the federal service: lack of self-determination (31 to 53 percent); bureaucracy and red tape (35 to 50 percent); a lack of em-

---

[5] In 1960 the median occupational income reported by the natural scientists, social scientists, engineers, and executives in business and the federal government interviewed for this study were: federal executives, $12,000, business executives, $14,200; federal natural scientists, $9,600, business natural scientists, $12,800; federal social scientists, $10,600, business social scientists, $14,700; and federal engineers, $10,300, business engineers, $14,800. In recent years, studies designed to make precise comparisons of the pay for similar groups inside and outside the federal service have been sufficiently common that it should be emphasized that this study is not one of them. The figures in this footnote are tabled merely to show that the pay scales for our high-level federal sample groups were, in fact, substantially behind the pay for our special business samples at the time the interviews were conducted.

phasis on merit in promotion (9 to 14 percent); a possible loss of drive and initiative by those who did join the government (15 to 22 percent); and inadequate opportunities for self-advancement (10 to 18 percent). This static conception of the government's operations and personnel procedures is widespread. As a 36-year-old advertising manager for an Ohio electronics firm put it, "The seniority system of advancement is not for me. I feel I can progress faster on ability than on longevity."

These top-level business employees also constitute the only nonfederal group wherein a substantial number of respondents alluded to another potential drawback of federal employment: that there would be too many political pressures involved in the job.[6] This is, however, by no means a pervasive fear of the business community. The mentions of it range from 8 to 14 percent—with social scientists citing it the most often and the natural scientists the least.

Nevertheless, for some the concern is very real. The advertising manager of a New York company said, "There would be harassment by congressional committees and newspapers." And some clearly resent the responsiveness of the federal bureaucracy to other elements in the political system. The labor-relations manager of a Chicago food processing concern declared: "The objectives of the organization would be apt to be more political than genuine. You would be subject to a lot of external pressures which would of necessity have to influence the course the department would follow. You wouldn't be free to manage. For instance, the placing of a munitions plant would reflect as much the clout of the local politician as the scientific value of a strategic location."

Still other evidence emphasizes the lack of enthusiasm with which many high-level business employees evaluate the prospects of working for the federal government. Many cannot think of anything that would be better in the federal service; very few are unable to think of things that would be worse. Moreover, just as engineering teachers in the colleges are the most negative of the academic groups toward federal employment, business engineers are the most negative of the groups in business: 44 percent of them see no way in which the government could improve upon their present position, and only 2 percent see no draw-

[6] Probably one reason for this special concern among businessmen is that most people in the other groups do not see themselves in high-level managerial positions— where "political pressure" might be felt most directly—if they were to work for the government.

backs to federal employment. In competing for executive, engineering, and scientific talent among employees who are already in the business world, the government faces formidable obstacles.

These findings underscore the enormous stake the government has in the early attraction, retention, and training of potential managerial and technical talent for the federal service. Unless it succeeds in revitalizing its appeal among the groups with special training or experience in industry, it will need to depend primarily on the talent it develops within the federal service to staff and direct a major portion of its operations. Given the prevailing attitude among members of the special business groups now, it will be very hard to persuade many of them to shift to government work at mid-career.

The Student Population

The major source of early recruits for the federal service is, of course, the nation's student population. Consequently, the attitudes of this group take on special importance. The chief advantages and disadvantages students see when they compare the government with nonfederal employment are summarized in Table 6-2. A number of points emerge from the data:

> In general, high school students are the most favorable and graduate students are the least favorable toward what the government has to offer.
> College seniors' views are closer to the graduate students' than to the views of the high school population.
> Security and fringe benefits are the most commonly mentioned advantages of government employment in all three student groups.
> The pay and self-advancement opportunities in government look best to the high school students; their attraction is less for college seniors and graduate students.
> But college and graduate students see opportunities for interesting and enjoyable work in the government more often than the high schoolers.
> And the equipment and the facilities the government provides have a special appeal for graduate students.

The general employed public, we have seen, does not perceive the opportunity to be of service and to do work that is worthwhile as a relative advantage of government work compared with private employment.

TABLE 6-2. *Views of the Student Groups on Better and Worse Features of Federal Employment, Compared with Private Employment*[a]

Better in Federal Government		Worse in Federal Government	
High School Juniors and Seniors			
(N=347)		(N=347)	
Security, fringe benefits	45%	Poor financial reward	19%
Financial reward	32	Lack of self-determination	18
Self-advancement	18	Lack of self-advancement	14
Self-development	12	Nothing would be worse	20
Working conditions	11		
Nothing would be better	6		
College Seniors			
(N=394)		(N=397)	
Security, fringe benefits	43%	Lack of self-determination	28%
Financial reward	20	Poor financial reward	26
Interesting, enjoyable work	16	Bureaucracy, red tape	22
Self-advancement	15	Lack of self-advancement	17
Self-development	11	Lack of emphasis on merit in	
Worthwhile work	10	promotion	13
Nothing would be better	10	Nothing would be worse	4
Graduate Students			
(N=376)		(N=380)	
Security, fringe benefits	38%	Lack of self-determination	33%
Financial reward	17	Bureaucracy, red tape	29
Interesting, enjoyable work	15	Poor financial reward	25
Equipment and facilities	12	Lack of self-advancement	13
Nothing would be better	17	Lack of emphasis on merit in	
		promotion	13
		Lack of incentive	11
		Nothing would be worse	8

[a] Entries indicate the percentage of the total number of respondents who cited a particular factor as being better or worse in the government. Except for the categories "Nothing would be better" and "Nothing would be worse," only factors mentioned by 10 percent or more of the respondents are listed in this table.

A significant number of the nation's students, however, clearly do. Of the college seniors, one in ten (the highest percentage in any group interviewed) mentioned the opportunity for worthwhile service as an attraction of federal employment. Among high school students the proportion was almost as large. Many were motivated in part by a feeling of patriotism. A college senior majoring in engineering said: "It is always possible, too, that what you are doing you are doing for the welfare of the nation." And a college girl from Massachusetts declared: "I know this sounds foolish, but you are working for your country; and I think it's patriotic to work for your government." When students ask themselves what they can do for their country, some of them feel that entering the federal service is one way to make a contribution.

The biggest drawback college seniors and graduate students see in government employment is restriction on autonomy (lack of self-determination). This criticism is often accompanied by the closely related complaint about excessive bureaucracy and red tape. A graduate student in psychology summarized his view: "It's a vast organizational set-up, a big bureaucracy where individuality is lost and personal ideas have to be had on your own time. Most of it is busy-work and a lot of red tape, with all that signing and cosigning of papers before any action can be taken." The college groups' ideas of other potential drawbacks are indicated in the following complaints: adequate opportunities for self-advancement would be lacking; there would not be enough emphasis on merit—as opposed to seniority—in promotion; and (among graduate students) government employment might result in a lack of incentive and a loss of drive for the individual. Thus, among college and graduate students, the underlying theme of criticism concerns hampering restrictions on one's freedom of action in the job, cumbersome procedures, and inadequate opportunities and rewards for the truly able person who wants to get ahead.

What are the implications of these attitudes for the federal service? Despite certain obvious negative features, the findings as a whole point to the fairly substantial attractiveness of federal employment to high school students—and to the probable success of government recruitment programs designed to appeal to students at this level of education. They also suggest that government work has positive features that appeal to college seniors and graduate students also. Yet some of the negative feelings among the college groups are so substantial as to constitute a major obstacle to attempts by the federal service to attract college-trained men and women.

More detailed analyses reveal still other aspects of the way students view the federal government as an employer. In assessing both the positive and the negative features of federal employment, girls at all three student levels are clearly more favorably inclined than boys. This finding is not surprising, given the fact that in the general work force, also, women are more favorable to government service than men. But it does suggest that the difference in the way males and females regard federal employment in our society comes at a fairly early stage in the individual's development, and well before most people actually enter the labor force.

Students' academic grade averages are also associated with their various perceptions of government employment, as we have seen earlier. In regard to better and worse features of the federal service, perhaps most outstanding among the high school group is the extent to which the "A" students stress the opportunities for service in the government (22 percent of them vs. 5 and 8 percent of the "B" and "C" students). Among college students, those with the lower averages tend to put more emphasis on the government's security and fringe benefits. In the graduate student population, differences between "A" students and the others are slight; there is, however, a hint that the "A" students place slightly greater emphasis on the opportunity to do work that is worthwhile, while those with lower averages stress the security of government employment more often.

One difference in outlook according to academic averages is revealed most clearly among the college seniors, although it is also echoed in the other two groups. When the potential drawbacks of government service are being assessed, the seniors whose instructors have apparently lumped them in the "Gentlemen C" category tend to differ in their concerns from their fellows who carry off the academic laurels. The "C" students place special stress on poor pay, limited opportunities for advancement, lack of emphasis on merit as a criterion for promotion—all aspects of "getting ahead" or gaining material rewards. The "A" seniors place relatively greater emphasis on lack of self-determination, the existence of poor personal relations, and excessive bureaucracy—categories that indicate concern about the ego-enhancing and the less material aspects of a job.

In Chapter 4 we noted that somewhat opposing clusters of values tended to be emphasized by "A" students at one extreme and "C" students at the other. It now appears that each group of students (according to grade level) tends to single out as negative factors in government those features which are of most concern to them as occupational values. Thus, within the student populations, at least two different sets of values are often found wanting in the government: the "C" students are worried about not making enough money or "getting ahead"; the "A" students are worried about the restrictions on autonomy which are of special concern to students with the most impressive academic records.

General Federal Employees

"I think there would be money advantages on the outside. They're more liberal in their budgeting and working capital. Here that's the end; regardless of what you can do the pay rate is set. Private industry is not restricted as we are here. They can allow an increase in pay." *(Automotive parts and machine inspector, Arsenal Tank Division of the U. S. Army)*

"Your job won't be as steady or stable, I should say. The benefits with the government are better. I get about 26 days now—no company lets you get that much vacation. Also, they wouldn't pay you for sick leave like we get with the government." *(Clerk in the U. S. Post Office, Philadelphia, Pennsylvania)*

When general federal employees contemplate the better and worse features of working outside the government, two considerations overshadow all the rest. The pay would be better; the security and fringe benefits would be worse. To these factors some government workers add two more advantages of private employment—working conditions and opportunities for self-advancement—and three more disadvantages—poor financial reward, inferior working conditions, and less leisure and vacation time. Thus, in the general federal work force as a whole, the pay and working conditions on the outside are commonly seen as both better and worse than in the government. However, these apparently contradictory views usually represent the opinions of different kinds of people.

The perceived advantages of the federal service vs. the opportunities outside, deteriorate among the higher-status federal groups, just as they do in general in the nonfederal population. Among civil servants on the middle and upper levels, the number mentioning various advantages of nonfederal employment tends to increase, and the number mentioning disadvantages tends to drop. Only in the highest echelons, for example, are there substantial numbers of people who cite greater self-determination and less bureaucracy as likely advantages of nonfederal employment. Government workers on the lower levels are relatively unconcerned about such matters.

There are, to be sure, exceptions to this general finding. The achievement of a top-level job in the federal hierarchy apparently causes the occupant to take a relatively benign view of the government's promotion system. Middle-level employees (in terms of income or occupational level) are more likely to rate the advancement opportunities better outside the government than are their superiors. And at nearly all income and GS levels there is agreement that security and fringe benefits would be less advantageous on the outside, as well as working conditions.

The main lesson of the data, however, is this. People both inside and outside the government tend to agree on the relative advantages and disadvantages of federal employment vis-à-vis the opportunities in the nonfederal sector. There is widespread agreement that the government provides more stable employment and better fringe benefits. Many people at the lower occupational, income, and educational levels also feel the government provides better pay. But the upper-level groups—both inside and outside the government—are more likely to feel that private employment has the edge on such factors as pay, opportunities for advancement, and self-determination in the job.

Yet if the broad contours of attitude among federal and nonfederal employees are the same, the specific elevations of the ridges and valleys within each group are also important. There is a marked difference on the question of pay, for example. Professional and managerial people in the government feel much more acutely than their counterparts outside that federal salaries are lagging behind. About one in seven (14 percent) of the privately employed group say their pay would be worse in government, but over half (52 percent) of federal professional and managerial employees say their income would be improved by switching to private employment. (These interviews were conducted in 1960 and early 1961, before the 1962 legislation in which the government committed itself to the principle of providing pay levels comparable to those in private enterprise for most federal employees.[7] It is clear that, in

---

[7] The 1962 pay legislation, it should be noted, fell short of including for many of the government's middle- and upper-level employees a large enough pay raise to bring their compensation into line with the compensation outside the federal service. It also conceded that it would not be feasible to equate the salary of the government's top career employees (GS 16 through 18, or their equivalent) with the compensation of people with comparable job responsibilities in business.

1960-61, upper-level federal employees were keenly aware of the gap between the pay in government and the pay outside for people at their occupational level.)

In other important respects, however, upper-level federal employees see less of a disadvantage for the government compared with private employment than do their counterparts on the outside. Less than one in ten (9 percent) of the professional and managerial people in the federal service say they would have greater self-determination in private employment. But a third (32 percent) of the professional and managerial personnel outside the government say autonomy would be curbed in the federal service. Again, about one in ten (11 percent) of these high-level employees in government say they would encounter less bureaucracy if they switched to private employment. But one in five (22 percent) of the privately employed professional and managerial people say bureaucratic factors would be worse in government. This difference in attitude between upper-level employees in government and in private employment is profoundly important, for it helps explain the ability of the federal service to retain many of its people who are at the top echelons.

Other evidence also indicates that, on the whole, federal employees on whatever level are not a discontented lot. After rating their own jobs on the ten-point ladder scale, federal employees were asked (as were nonfederal employees) what things about their occupation kept them from placing it higher on the ladder, and what kinds of things kept them from placing it lower.[8] In this way they were encouraged to single out what they saw as the specific strong points and weak points about their jobs. Their most common replies were these:

---

[8] The questions asked of most respondents were: "Returning to the present, that is, to the rating marked here in red which you gave your present occupation—what *kinds of things* about your present occupation kept you from placing it higher on the ladder?" Then: "What *kinds of things* about it kept you from placing it lower?" Respondents who rated their job at one on the ten-point ladder scale, in addition to being asked the first of the two preceding questions, were then asked: "What *kinds of things* caused you to place it at the bottom?" Respondents who rated their job at one thus gave two sets of negative responses about their own job. Respondents who rated their job at ten on the ten-point ladder scale were asked: "What *kinds of things* about your present occupation caused you to place it at the top?" They were then asked, "What kinds of things about it kept you from placing it lower?" Respondents who rated their job at ten thus gave two sets of positive responses about their own job.

Factors That Kept Federal Employees from Rating Their Job Lower (N = 925)		*Factors That Kept Federal Employees from Rating Their Job Higher* (N = 814)	
Interest in the job	41%	Poor pay	24%
Enjoy good personal relations with co-workers	28	Poor superior, supervisor	17
Security and fringe benefits	25	Poor physical environment and working conditions	17 17
Good physical environment and working conditions	23	Poor opportunity for self-advancement	16
Good pay	23	Insufficient equipment or facilities	12
Good superior, supervisor	16		
Doing job trained for, that fits capacities	14		
Self-determination in the job	12		
General sense of fulfillment, goals are being met	12		
Variety	10		
Leisure, vacation time	10		

Other factors, mentioned by smaller numbers of government workers, reveal other pluses and minuses federal employees see in their own jobs:

Factors That Kept Federal Employees from Rating Their Job Lower (N = 925)		*Factors That Kept Federal Employees from Rating Their Job Higher* (N = 814)	
Opportunity for self-expression, creativity	9%	Poor personal relations with co-workers	8%
Responsibility and authority	8	Not doing job am trained for, that fits my capacities	7
Challenging work	7	Lack of self-determination	7
Opportunity for self-advancement	7	Not enough variety, too much routine	7
Worthwhile, constructive work	7		

As these responses suggest, federal employees have their share of gripes about their jobs, but they can think of many positive aspects also. And significant numbers find such factors as autonomy, variety, opportunities for self-expression and creativity, challenging work, a sense of doing something that is worthwhile and constructive, interesting work—all these, and more, in their job as a federal employee.

Positive features such as these are mentioned most often by those on the upper levels. There is, however, evidence that the most highly educated federal civil servants, compared with their counterparts outside, are less likely to see certain positive qualities in their own job. We have already seen this tendency in the way college graduates in and outside of government rate their own jobs on a 10-point scale (7.4 among college graduates in the federal service vs. 8.0 among those outside). Here, apparently, are some of the reasons why. Note the differences in the frequency with which the two college-trained groups cite certain negative factors that kept them from rating their jobs higher than they did:

Negative Aspects of Own Job	Federally Employed College Graduates (N = 151)	Nonfederally Employed College Graduates (N = 100)
Poor supervisor	13%	2%
Insufficient equipment or facilities	19	4
Lack of self-advancement	18	4
Lack of self-determination	17	9

Note also these differences in the way the two groups mentioned certain positive aspects of their own jobs:

Positive Aspects of Own Job	Federally Employed College Graduates (N = 159)	Nonfederally Employed College Graduates (N = 135)
Worthwhile, constructive work	11%	23%
Doing work trained for, that fits my capacities	13	21
General sense of fulfillment	12	17

These figures, however, give only part of the picture. Another part—and one more encouraging for the government—is indicated by the following figures on other job aspects:

Positive Aspects of Own Job	Federally Employed College Graduates (N = 159)	Nonfederally Employed College Graduates (N = 135)
Security, fringe benefits	19%	7%
Good supervisor	16	7
Opportunities for self-development, self-expression, and creativity	15	9
Challenging work	18	11
Good working conditions	21	13

Federal employment is often associated with security and good working conditions, but much less often (especially by people outside the federal service) with challenging work and opportunities for self-development, self-expression, and creativity. Yet, as the above figures show, when the college graduate groups in the two general work forces assess the positive aspects of their own jobs, it is the respondents in the federal service rather than those in private employment who more often say that they find these ego-rewarding factors in their work. This fact underscores the positive feelings many upper-level federal employees have toward their job.

Yet despite this very real measure of job satisfaction on the part of those who are in the federal service, the general pattern is clear. The government's position vis-à-vis private employment deteriorates on such vital matters as pay, job autonomy, absence of bureaucracy, and opportunities for advancement as one goes up the socioeconomic scale. Among its higher level employees, in short, the government's relative appeal tends to be least on some of the factors that are of most concern to people at that level.

Through the hundreds of interviews with people both inside and outside the government, an underlying theme can be detected. In many people's minds, there is a picture of a federal personnel system that serves to provide a floor for those on the bottom rungs of the socioeconomic ladder, while restricting the opportunities for those at the top. A laborer in Des Moines, Iowa, working for the government with a rating of GS 3, said of private employment: "The pay scale would be lower. I don't think I'd have as good sick leave and vacation benefits. Janitor work out of civil service would not pay a living wage. I'd have to go back to my old job of butchering for a meat packing plant and that's bad for my health." But the chief of the Personnel Division in a Veterans Administration hospital declared: "What would be better on the outside? I'd have the flexibility to come up with a job offer to fit the requirements of the highly qualified applicant we really want to hire. We're hemmed in on what we can offer the professional people here. And in most private industry there's no top of the grade where you're stuck and can't get more raises."

Variations by Sex

Like their counterparts on the outside, women in the federal service compare public employment with private employment more favorably than do men. This difference is most pronounced when financial considerations arise. The government's women employees are much less likely to feel they would be better paid outside the federal service (24 vs. 45 percent), and considerably more likely to feel the pay would be worse (31 vs. 14 percent). They are also more likely to concede the government an edge on leisure and vacation time. The men, however, do lead the women on stressing the presence of better working conditions in government. When such factors as income, education, or occupational status are held constant, the same distinctions between the sexes prevail.

Special Federal Populations

The members of the four elite groups in the federal service—the executives, natural and social scientists, and engineers—differ considerably from the "typical" government worker in their assessment of the relative advantages and disadvantages of a job outside the government. In the general sample of federal employees, many people feel that nothing would be better on the outside, but nearly all of the employees in the special groups can find both pros and cons of switching to nonfederal employment to single out. The main factors they cited, and the range in the percentages of the groups mentioning them, are as follows:[9]

Would Be Better Outside Government		*Would Be Worse Outside Government*	
Financial reward	58%–75%	Security and fringe benefits	42%–62%
Self-determination	10–25	Self-determination	9–30
Less bureaucracy	10–22	Too much pressure or tension	10–27
Equipment, facilities	10–19	Leisure, vacation time	6–19
Self-advancement	9–17	Physical environment, work-	
Physical environment, work-		ing conditions	7–15
ing conditions	10–16		
Nothing would be better	3– 8	Nothing would be worse	3– 5

[9] N's for "better": executives, 264; natural scientists, 89; social scientists, 87; engineers, 96. N's for "worse": executives, 265; natural scientists, 90; social scientists, 86; engineers, 96.

The familiar factor of security and fringe benefits is most commonly mentioned by these groups as a potential loss if they leave the federal service. The belief that there would be greater self-determination, less bureaucracy, and better advancement opportunities in private employment also is strong. But note particularly the figures on financial reward. Despite the technical difficulties in making such comparisons, the extent to which in recent years salaries for upper-level government employees have lagged behind the pay in industry for people with comparable job responsibilities has been well documented.[10] As we noted earlier, when the top federal groups were interviewed in 1960-61, they were well aware of this discrepancy. Thus we find that the proportions of federal executives, social scientists, and engineers who feel they would be better paid on the outside are enormous. Among federal natural scientists the feeling is strongest of all: 8 percent say their pay would be worse outside the government; 75 percent say it would be improved.

Some of the members of the special groups feel that there might be poorer working conditions and less leisure time on the outside. And sizable numbers are worried by a problem that is seldom mentioned by the typical federal employee: that there would be too much pressure or tension outside the government. This looms as a drawback to about a tenth of the federal executives and social scientists, and to 18 percent of the engineers and 27 percent of the natural scientists.

That this misgiving is most common among the groups with special technical skills is significant, for certainly the type of people who spoke of it are not those who want easy work. Many, particularly the specialists in various technical fields, feel that in industry they would not have the freedom or the time to do what they regarded as a good job. These were some typical comments. A young physicist with the U. S. Bureau of Standards in Colorado: "Probably the biggest drawback in private industry would be that you are always pushing towards a schedule. In research work you can't do that and do really good work. However, industry tries this and it makes a lot of pressure." An economist with the U. S. Department of Agriculture in Washington: "There's prob-

[10] *Revision of Major Federal Statutory Salary Systems,* Hearings Before the House Committee on Post Office and Civil Service, on Bills to Revise Major Statutory Salary Systems of the Federal Government, and for Other Purposes, 87th Cong., 2d sess. (1962), p. 8. A later survey, released in early 1963, found that the compensation of top-level business employees had edged somewhat higher since the previous study. (See *The Washington Post,* Feb. 27, 1963, p. C 1.)

ably a more rigid time schedule for accomplishing a certain amount of work out in industry." A government entomologist in Maryland: "More pressure; one must constantly come up with something that benefits them directly."

Some of these high-level employees see still another possible disadvantage outside the government. As we have seen, substantial numbers of government scientists, engineers, and executives feel they would have greater self-determination outside the government, but there are also many who feel that they would encounter greater restrictions on autonomy in private employment. Note the differences among the groups on this point:

| | Self-Determination | |
	Better Outside Government	Worse Outside Government
Executives	24%	9%
Social Scientists	25	17
Engineers	10	18
Natural Scientists	14	30

These discrepancies among the four groups as to the degree of freedom they would have in a job outside the government should be pondered with care. Self-determination, of course, is a broad category. It ranges all the way from the college professor's cherished academic freedom to the desire of the factory employee for a little more flexibility in his work hours. Only when the content of their comments is analyzed in detail does the basis for the considerable variation become clear.

The bulk of the complaints about self-determination by federal executives focus on the elaborate "base-touching" that is necessary in government before they can act. A high-ranking official in the U. S. Department of Labor said: "You might have more latitude in making decisions outside the government. You would not have to go through as many lines or channels as you do here." And a GS 15 in another large department declared: "There would not be a necessity for a large amount of paper work, progress reports, letters, and documents supporting our moves before we make the move. You would have more independence in your operation and decisions."

By and large the executives, when they speak of self-determination, are thinking in terms of the generalized exercise of power—often for the advancement of programs of broad scope. As one moves to the high-level federal groups who are concentrating more on some technical specialty—the social scientists, the engineers, and especially the natural scientists—the balance shifts in the evaluations of the degree of autonomy provided by government and business. In large part, this is because these technical specialists are most concerned about a kind of autonomy that differs from the federal executives' idea of autonomy. Many members of the three groups emphasize their freedom to pursue their own specialty, very often their ability to follow their own particular research interests. They are concerned, in short, with their opportunities for the specialized exercise of their technical training, and many scientists and engineers who are in the federal service feel that their opportunities to do this are better in the government than on the outside.

Some feel, for instance, that the scope of operations outside the government might be more limited, thus preventing them from realizing their own interests. A young biologist with the U. S. Fish and Wildlife Service, doing field and laboratory research throughout the Great Lakes region, said: "The work [outside government] would be more routine and monotonous. The geographic area in which I do my work would be much more restricted."

But the most common theme was that the dominance of the profit motive in industry meant that one would be restricted to doing research on projects that would "pay off." The following comments are typical on this point. A development engineer in the aerodynamics section in a federal weapons system installation: "I think that the job would be much more confining, much more limited in its scope; it would be restricted to the product the organization was trying to sell." A geologist with the U. S. Geological Survey: "I wouldn't be able to pursue things that interested me scientifically, as I would be restricted to doing that which would make profits for the company." A government research social scientist: "Your research work [in private industry] has to be aimed at an immediate profit, or else you cannot explore certain areas of work."

Still other comments mirror some of the attitudes members of these high-level groups have toward their own job. Some found their work satisfying because of the basic purposes the work was designed to achieve. A high-ranking official involved in research on productivity and technological development for the U. S. Bureau of Labor Statistics said of private employment: "The job content might be more limited—limited goals doing research for a large corporation would not give me the kind of satisfaction which I get now out of doing the broader economic research which, to a large extent, is done only by the government." The replies to the questions about what kept them from rating their job higher or lower on the ten-point scale throw further light on the way many of these top-level federal employees regard their own jobs. The responses of one of the groups—the federal executives—are as follows:[11]

Factors That Kept Federal Executives from Rating Their Job Lower (N = 272)		Factors That Kept Federal Executives from Rating Their Job Higher (N = 242)	
Interest in the job	36%	Lack of self-determination	26%
Have responsibility and authority, power to make decisions	30	Poor financial reward	17
		Poor superior, supervisor	16
Good personal relations with co-workers	29	Lack of responsibility, authority, and power to make decisions	15
Self-determination	21	Insufficient facilities or equipment	14
Challenging work	20		
Work is worthwhile, constructive	20		
Financial reward	20		
Have opportunities for self-development, self-expression, and creativity	15		
General sense of fulfillment, goals are being met	15		
Have variety in the work	13		
Sense of accomplishment	12		
Doing work that fits my capacities, am trained for	12		
Security and fringe benefits	11		
Physical environment and working conditions	11		
Good superior, supervisor	11		
Opportunities for self-advancement	10		

As has been shown earlier, top-echelon federal employees are somewhat less satisfied with their own jobs, compared with similar top-level

[11] The other special groups—natural scientists, social scientists, and engineers—differ somewhat from the executives in the frequency with which they mention particular positive and negative features of their own jobs. But like the executives, large numbers cite a variety of positive aspects of government work.

groups outside the federal service and relative to lower-level employees in the government. In addition, for many top-level government workers the relative appeal of outside employment is strong. Yet, as the figures presented above attest, federal executives also see many virtues in their present jobs. All in all, their account of the positive features makes an impressive list. It underscores the very real measure of satisfaction that these high-level government employees have found in their work in the federal service.

Summary

1. Better security and fringe benefits is the chief advantage, and less self-determination and increased bureaucracy and red tape are the chief disadvantages that members of the general employed public most commonly see in federal employment compared with their own jobs.

2. The government's relative position tends to deteriorate among the higher-status members of the general employed public and among the elite nonfederal groups. In general, references to relative advantages other than security in government tend to decline as one ascends the socioeconomic ladder, while references to alleged drawbacks of government work increase.

3. Top-level business people draw an especially unfavorable comparison of federal employment with their own jobs. Large numbers of them feel that the pay, self-determination, and bureaucracy would be worse in the federal service. Appreciable portions of the business groups also see a loss of drive and initiative and inadequate opportunities for self-advancement as relative drawbacks of federal employment.

4. Students, on the other hand, take a more favorable view of working for the government. Many emphasize the opportunities in the federal government for interesting, enjoyable work, for self-advancement and self-development, for using good equipment and facilities, and—more than any other group interviewed—for being involved in worthwhile, constructive activities that are of service to others. References to negative features of government work increase among the college and graduate students, leaving the high schoolers as the student group which, over all, sees the most relative advantage in federal employment.

5. When federal employees themselves compare working outside the

federal service with their present jobs, a loss of security and fringe benefits is the most common relative drawback they see. Among general federal employees, better pay, working conditions, and advancement opportunities are the most commonly mentioned advantages of outside employment.

6. The relative position of the federal service, compared with the opportunities outside, tends to deteriorate among the higher-status federal groups, just as it does in the high-level nonfederal populations. The percentages of people in the elite federal groups who feel they would be better paid if they were to shift to outside employment are enormous.

7. On the other hand, both the general federal employees and the elite groups in the federal service see many positive features in their present jobs. Among the top groups, these include opportunities for challenging work, self-determination, self-development, worthwhile service, a sense of accomplishment, and other factors that are of prime concern to people at their level of experience and training.

8. The extent to which upper-level federal employees find these values in federal employment indicates that there is a discrepancy between the way they perceive federal employment and the way comparable high-level groups outside the federal service perceive it.

7

The Federal Government As an Employer:
Some Comparisons with Private Business

IN THIS CHAPTER we shall examine how people evaluate federal employment on certain specific characteristics, and how they compare it with private business employment on these characteristics. We obtained the evaluations and comparisons from five pairs of categorical statements which were among the fifty-five scale-sort items respondents rated on the ten-step, agree-disagree scale. The statements dealt with five aspects of employment, as follows (each pair being here telescoped into one statement):[1]

> For a young man of ability, his best chance for being *really successful* lies in working for the federal government (for a large private business corporation).
> A person who works for the federal government (for a large private business) generally has a good chance to get ahead.
> A young man of ability who starts work in the federal civil service (in a large private business) has a good chance of ending up in one of the top-level jobs.
> Employment with the federal government (with a large private business) offers a high degree of security.
> Most jobs in the federal government (in private business) are routine and monotonous.

The relevance of these specific items to more generalized attitudes toward government employment and employees is shown in the data of Table 7-1; individuals who have a more favorable attitude toward civil

---

[1] In the interviews, the ten statements appeared on cards in random order among other cards for the forty-five other statements: see Item 17 of the basic questionnaire in the Appendix.

TABLE 7-1. *The General Employed Public's Evaluation of Civil Servants and the Appeal of Federal Employment, Related to Ratings of Evaluative Statements About Federal Employment*

Evaluative Statements	Evaluation of Civil Servants[a]			Appeal of Federal Employment[b]		
	Low	Medium	High	Low	Medium	High
"Most jobs in the federal government are routine and monotonous"	5.3	4.9	4.4	5.2	5.1	4.3
"Employment with the federal government offers a high degree of security"	6.6	7.4	8.2	6.4	7.4	8.3
"A person who works for the federal government generally has a good chance to get ahead"	5.6	6.3	7.7	5.3	6.6	7.5
"For a young man of ability, his best chance for being *really successful* lies in working for the federal government"	3.7	4.2	5.3	2.9	4.7	5.7
AVERAGE NUMBER ANSWERING	(341)	(393)	(310)	(357)	(391)	(315)

[a] The evaluation of civil service employees was derived by combining the scale-sort ratings respondents gave "Federal civil service employees in general" on "honesty," "ability," and "interest in serving the public."

[b] The appeal of federal employment is based on responses to the scale-sort item, "All things considered, working for the federal government appeals to me."

servants and who report that the idea of working for the government appeals to them most strongly also tend to rate the government highest on chances for success, opportunities for getting ahead, and the security it provides. They are also least likely to agree with the statement that most jobs in the federal service are routine and monotonous. In the pages that follow, highlights of the way people rate the government and private business on each of the five characteristics are presented.

Security Factors

A variety of analyses have indicated that most people equate government employment with security. The data obtained by the scale-sort items are entirely unequivocal in strongly confirming these findings. In every group, federal and nonfederal alike, ratings of federal employment on security are not only very high in absolute terms, but also significantly higher than the ratings given to large business on security. Among the nonfederal populations, the differences in favor of the federal government range from 1.0 to 2.7 points on the ten-point scale—with the elite groups tending to give the government an even bigger edge over business than the general public does. Within the general employed public, however, the magnitude of the advantage given the government varies little according to the respondent's education, income, or occupational level.

Federal employee groups give the government an even bigger lead over business on security. Here the difference scores in favor of the government range from 3 to nearly 4 scale points. In part, these enormous discrepancies occur because federal employees regard the federal service as somewhat more secure than the nonfederal populations do, but in larger part they occur because of the lower average ratings government workers assign to large private business employment. Compared with people who are actually working outside the government, federal employees—particularly women—take a markedly more pessimistic view of the security and stability of work in private enterprise. Note how the government and private business are rated on security by the general employed public, the general sample of federal employees, and by men and women within each group:[2]

| | General Employed Public | | | General Federal Employees | | |
	Federal Government	Private Business	Difference: "Government" Minus "Business"	Federal Government	Private Business	Difference: "Government" Minus "Business"
Men	7.3	6.1	+1.2	8.1	4.9	+3.2
Women	7.5	5.8	+1.7	8.3	4.4	+3.9
Total	7.4	6.1	+1.3	8.1	4.8	+3.3

Routine and Monotony

The data on the amount of routine and monotony people commonly associate with work in the federal government and in business can also

[2] N's for general employed public: men, 835; women, 252. N's for general federal employees: men, 648; women, 283. In this and subsquent presentations of scale ratings in this chapter. N's are an average figure based on the numbers of people who rated business and government on the factor or factors tabled.

be summarized briefly for all of the groups interviewed. These findings are of particular interest because at the beginning of the study we hypothesized, on the basis of limited developmental work, that federal employment tended to be regarded as more routine and monotonous than nonfederal work. The scale results indicate that to some extent this hypothesis is correct, but not overwhelmingly so.

For the most part, scores on routine and monotony are low (ranging from 3.5 to 5.0) for both types of work and differ but little for either type. There is a slight tendency for the nonfederal groups to consider government employment as somewhat more routine and monotonous, and the evidence is positive that this tendency is related to educational level. The mean ratings given the government and business on routine and monotony by members of the general employed public with varying amounts of formal education are as follows:

Amount of Formal Schooling	N	Federal Government	Private Business	Difference: "Government" Minus "Business"
High School Not Completed	(304)	4.9	5.2	−0.3
High School Completed	(495)	4.6	4.5	+0.1
Some College	(123)	5.3	4.2	+1.1
College Graduate	(135)	5.6	4.6	+1.0

In the student groups a similar relationship between comparisons of government and business employment on this factor and educational level can be discerned. College seniors and graduate school students are more likely than the high school students to feel that government work is more monotonous than business employment. But of all the nonfederal populations, the business groups are the most inclined to rate federal employment as routine and monotonous in comparison with private business employment. This is especially true of the executives and engineers, who place the government about 2 scale points higher than business on the factor.

Federal employees are less likely than nonfederal groups to give the government a bad comparative rating on routine and monotony: among all the federal groups the ratings of government and business are approximately equal, and what differences there are are generally either not significant or of borderline significance. There is, however, a faint suggestion that federal employees who attended or graduated from college, compared with the less-educated, feel that federal employment is somewhat more monotonous than private employment.

The Three Aspects of "Success"

The three other characteristics on which evaluations of federal and business employment were obtained—chances for getting ahead; chances for reaching a top-level job; and chances for being "really successful"— are three distinct aspects of the amount of opportunity the two types of employment provide. The idea of getting ahead or of reaching a top-level job focuses on the individual's chances for advancement within his employing organization; the idea of achieving "real success" is a more global concept, and the ratings of the concept may involve judgments about the status and attraction of federal and business employment in American society as a whole. Since there was substantial variation in the way different groups evaluated these three aspects of opportunity, the replies are considered here group by group.

General Employed Public

Both the federal government and private business are judged moderately high by members of the general work force on chances offered an individual to get ahead and to reach a top-level job. The opportunities for getting ahead are considered about equal, but the government is seen as lagging slightly behind in providing a chance to get to the top. The discrepancy on "real success," however, is large—with the government being ranked substantially below business on this factor. The following mean scores (average number rating being 1,087) on the ten-point scale reveal the general picture:

Characteristic Rated by General Employed Public	Federal Government	Private Business	Difference: "Government" Minus "Business"
Chance To Get Ahead	6.5	6.4	+0.1
Chance To Reach a Top-Level Job	6.4	7.0	−0.6
Chance for "Real Success"	4.4	5.4	−1.0

Variations by Education, Income, and Occupational Level. As has been indicated, the belief that federal employment rates high on security is widely shared throughout all segments of the general public. But the evaluations of government on our three opportunity-oriented notions contrast sharply with this homogeneity in outlook. We find, for example, that the least-educated (those who failed to finish high school) rate the federal service highest on the chances it provides to "get ahead"; among the more highly educated groups, the government's rating drops off substantially. In contrast, the ratings given private business vary only slightly by educational level. Consequently, while the least-educated are likely to see the federal government as a better avenue than business for getting ahead, among the college graduates the balance shifts the other way, as can be seen in the following figures:

Amount of Formal Schooling	N	Good Chance To Get Ahead in Federal Government	in Private Business	Difference: "Government" Minus "Business"
High School Not Completed	(304)	7.2	6.8	+0.4
High School Completed	(495)	6.5	6.2	+0.3
Some College	(123)	5.6	6.0	−0.4
College Graduate	(135)	5.3	6.4	−1.1

A similar pattern prevails when members of the general work force are asked to compare the government and a business corporation on opportunities offered for reaching one of the top jobs or for achieving real success. And the same tendencies are seen when all three opportunity aspects are related to ascending income and occupational levels.

These scale-sort ratings are entirely consistent with findings based on responses to open-end questions. They are also disturbing in their implications for the recruiting needs of the federal government. High-status individuals tend to evaluate large private business on the opportunities it provides—for getting ahead, for reaching the top, or for achieving "real success"—about as favorably as do those whose social status is lower. Positive evaluations of the government on these factors, however, drop off substantially as one ascends the socioeconomic ladder. Thus, among the high-status groups, not only do favorable ratings of government employment tend to decline in an absolute sense, but the government's position also declines in comparison with one of its principal competitors in the job market—large private business.[3]

[3] Other factors also are related to the way people compare federal and large busi-

Variations by Sex. Women compare the government with large business employment more favorably than do men. In evaluating the federal service, their attitudes are not greatly different from men's, but any differences point consistently in the same direction: women rate the government higher than the men do on all three of the opportunity aspects.

There is also little difference between the sexes in their ratings of large business employment, but what differences there are suggest that women are less, rather than more, favorably disposed than men. Thus, women give the government a lead over the business corporation on chances to get ahead—which men do not—and they consider government and business virtually equal in opportunities for reaching one of the top jobs—which again men do not. On chances for "real success," they rate government below business (−0.7), but not to the degree that men do (−1.1).

Further analyses (the details of which are reported in the *Source Book,* Chapter 15) indicate that this more favorable predisposition of women toward federal employment persists at various educational and age levels. By income level, there is relatively little intersex difference for employees with low family incomes (under $5,500); however, women with larger family incomes are more favorable to the government than are comparable men, largely because men with larger incomes tend to evaluate federal employment lower than do those with smaller incomes. Occupationally, the biggest difference in favor of the government is between men and women in the clerical field. Women in clerical jobs rate the government well ahead of large businesses—both on opportunities for getting ahead and on the chances for "real success."

Groups in Education and Business

High School and College Teachers. High school teachers rate the government and large business about equal on opportunities for getting ahead and for reaching a top-level job, but they rate government lower

---

ness employment on the opportunities they offer for "real success." There is a slight tendency for the government's relative position to decline among older people. And an analysis based on the respondent's place of residence indicates that people in small towns (population 1,000 to 9,999) rate the government best on this factor in comparison with private business. These and other relationships are traced in some detail in the *Source Book,* Chap 15.

than business as a route to "real success." In general, the college teachers
echo these views; although they place both the government and the corporation lower than the high school teachers do as routes to "real success," they share the disposition to give business the edge over government on this factor. The views of the college natural and social scientists
and engineers differ only slightly from the attitudes of the college
teacher population as a whole.

Groups in Business. As we have seen, the business groups, compared
with other groups, take an unusually harsh view of federal employment,
and this is found again in their comparisons of it with private business
on all three aspects of opportunity. Consider, for example, the attitudes of business executives. They see much better opportunity for advancement in business than in government, and they rate the business
corporation far ahead of the federal service as an avenue to "real success"—rating it higher in this respect than any other group except the
business engineers:

Characteristic Rated by Business Executives (N = 272)	Federal Government	Private Business	"Government" Minus "Business"
Chance To Get Ahead	5.0	6.9	−1.9
Chance To Reach a Top-Level Job	5.5	7.2	−1.7
Chance for "Real Success"	3.0	5.9	−2.9

On the whole, the other special groups in business—the natural and
social scientists and engineers—share this view, but among the four groups
the engineers are the most critical.

These high-level groups in business reflect an attitude that, to some
extent, is shared by other elite groups in American society: large private business is associated with such dynamic factors as getting ahead,
reaching the top, and achieving outstanding success. On the other hand,
as has been noted, the government is rated high on a purportedly less
dynamic, or even static factor—the provision of security—and is seen as
lagging behind the business world in providing outlets for the more dynamic motivations a potential employee may have. There can be no
doubt that this broad patterning of attitudes lessens the appeal of federal employment for the elite groups in our society.

The Student Population

A variety of analyses in earlier chapters have suggested that the idea of working for the government is regarded with considerable favor by many of the nation's high school students. The scale ratings on the three opportunity factors reveal still another aspect of this generally favorable attitude. High school students compare federal employment relatively favorably with working for a large private business. They rate the government almost as high as the business corporation as a route to "real success," and equal to business on opportunities for getting ahead; they rank it somewhat below business on chances for an individual to reach a top-level job, but here, too, the difference is not large.

Among the college seniors and graduate school students, by contrast, the government comes out less well. With their added age and years of schooling, these two groups are less sanguine than the high schoolers about the chances for getting ahead and reaching a top job in either government or business; nevertheless, they rate business somewhat ahead of the government on both factors. They also feel that the business corporation ranks substantially ahead of government as a route to "real success."

To reveal additional nuances of attitude within the different student populations, a lengthy series of supplementary analyses were conducted, the detailed results of which are reported in the *Source Book,* Chapter 20. A few of the highlights of these probings are as follows:

Differences in attitude are small between female and male students, and between students with high grades and those with low grades.

High school students from low-income families give the government the edge over large private business on the opportunities for getting ahead and for "real success."

College seniors as a group compare the government less favorably with business on these factors; but within the college senior population, those from low-income families tend to rate the government best in comparison with the business world.

Among college and graduate students, those who are majoring in engineering tend to compare the government least favorably with business on the opportunities for advancement and success. The government comes out best in this comparison among social science majors.

As one would expect, students at all levels of education who are thinking of working for the government compare government work with business work more favorably than those who are not.

General Federal Employees

The way people who actually work for the government compare the federal service with business employment has been a topic of special interest throughout this study. If federal and nonfederal employees differ from each other in the way they *compare* the two kinds of employment, this is because they differ in their perceptions of government work, or in their perceptions of business work—or some combination of the two. By looking at the *absolute* ratings federal and nonfederal workers give to the two kinds of employment, one can determine where the major differences in perceptions occur. The responses of the general federal sample—when compared with those of the nonfederal work force—reveal some of these contrasts in attitude.

General federal employees differ definitely and unequivocally from the general public by giving the government better comparative ratings on all three aspects of opportunity. They rate the government noticeably higher than private business on the chances for getting ahead, and virtually equal with business on the opportunities for reaching a top-level job. The general public does neither of these things. Federal workers do agree with the general work force in ranking the business corporation somewhat above federal employment as a route to "real success," but they give the corporation less of an edge than people outside government do.

Characteristic Rated	General Federal Employees (N=930)			General Employed Public (N=1,087)		
	Federal Government	Private Business	Difference: "Government" Minus "Business"	Federal Government	Private Business	Difference: "Government" Minus "Business"
Chance To Get Ahead	6.7	6.1	+.6	6.5	6.4	+0.1
Chance To Reach a Top-Level Job	7.0	7.1	−.1	6.4	7.0	−0.6
Chance for "Real Success"	4.4	5.0	−.6	4.4	5.4	−1.0

Variations by Education, Income, and Occupational Level. As we have seen, favorable evaluations by the general employed public of federal employment tend to decline among the groups with higher socioeconomic status. A similar tendency can be discerned within the general federal population. Compared with the less-educated federal employees, the more highly educated government workers rate the government less high on opportunities for "real success" and on chances for ending up in a top job. The ratings federal employees give the government on these factors are also inversely related to the level of their federal grade, income, and occupation.

There is, however, a difference to be noted. Among federal employees, unlike the general public, the ratings given private business on two of the opportunity-oriented factors—chances for "real success" and for reaching one of the top jobs—also drop with increasing educational and occupational status. As a consequence, among federal workers on the higher educational and occupational levels there is no uniform pattern for the government's position relative to business to deteriorate. Instead, there appears to be some tendency for federal employees at both the top and the bottom of the educational hierarchy to compare the federal service most favorably with business. This relationship shows up most clearly on the "getting ahead" and "getting to the top" factors, and is less marked on the opportunities for "real success." The responses of federal employees with varying degrees of education reveal the general pattern:[4]

Characteristics by Educational Level	Federal Government	Private Business	Difference: "Government" Minus "Business"
Chance To Get Ahead			
High school not completed	7.2	6.2	+1.0
High school completed	6.6	6.2	+0.4
Some college	6.2	6.3	−0.1
College graduate	6.7	5.6	+1.1
Chance To Reach a Top-Level Job			
High school not completed	7.9	7.6	+0.3
High school completed	7.0	7.1	−0.1
Some college	6.2	6.9	−0.7
College graduate	6.5	6.3	+0.2
Chance for "Real Success"			
High school not completed	5.7	5.4	+0.3
High school completed	4.1	5.1	−1.0
Some college	4.2	4.9	−0.7
College graduate	3.6	4.3	−0.7

[4] Average N's throughout are: high school not completed, 182; high school completed, 353; some college, 179; and college graduate, 162.

This finding is both interesting and of considerable importance for the government. The government's position relative to private business tends to decline as one moves from the least-educated federal employees up to those with "some college." But among the college graduates this trend reverses itself—or, for "real success," is halted; compared with business, the government is regarded as favorably as it is by those in the middle educational levels—or more favorably. One consequence, of course, is that college graduates in the federal service draw a more favorable comparison of government with business than do highly educated people on the outside. For highly qualified individuals, actual experience in the government apparently makes certain aspects of the federal service look more, rather than less, attractive than some of the opportunities outside.

To sum up, the government's position *relative* to private business does not deteriorate among top-level federal employees in the way it does among comparable high-level people outside of government. However, in an *absolute* sense there is a tendency for the luster of the federal service to diminish among the upper-level people in its employ.

Other Differences Within the General Federal Service. More detailed probings of the data reveal other nuances of attitudes within the federal service. On the whole, variations by age and length of employment are not great, although older government workers are somewhat more inclined than younger ones to feel that a person has a good chance of reaching the top of the federal hierarchy. The differences between the scale ratings given by men and women are very slight. So too are the differences between ratings given by government workers who are based in Washington and those in the field—on all but one of the five factors analyzed in this chapter. On one factor, however, the heady atmosphere in Washington appears to make a difference to the government's white-collar workers.

On the upper levels, white-collar workers are more optimistic about the chances for getting ahead in the federal service if they are based in Washington than if they are in the field. But Washington area white-collar workers on the lower levels—perhaps intimidated by the concentration of top-ranking men of affairs in the capital—are less optimistic about advancement opportunities than their equivalents in the field. Thus, Washington area respondents who are GS 8's or above assign a higher rating than their field counterparts to the statement that a person who works for the federal government generally has a good chance to get ahead (7.3 vs. 6.5); those in grades GS 2 to 7 rate the government lower than do comparable field personnel (6.2 vs. 6.7).

As one might expect, people who are thinking of leaving the government judge it more harshly than do those who feel sure that they will not leave. The number of relevant cases in our general federal sample is small (58), but on all three opportunity factors the people who are planning to leave rate the government lower than do those who are not.[5] Compared with those who plan to stay, they also attribute more routine and monotony to federal work and rate the government lower on security and fringe benefits. However, the differences between the two types of employees are smallest on the routine and security statements, and greatest on the statements having to do with advancement and success. Thus it appears that federal workers who say they are planning to leave are particularly inclined to stress their disappointment about the opportunities for advancement in government.

One other finding is worthy of note—the special way federally employed Negroes view the opportunities in government service compared with opportunities outside. On all three aspects of opportunity, Negroes compare federal employment with business employment decidedly more favorably than do their white colleagues. These differences by race hold also when the data are controlled for occupational income. At this point, however, another question suggests itself. Do Negroes make this more favorable comparison because they tend to rate federal employment higher, or because they rate private business lower? Primarily it is the latter, as these figures show:

Characteristic Rated	White Federal Employees (N=749)			Negro Federal Employees (N=173)		
	Federal Government	Private Business	Difference: "Government" Minus "Business"	Federal Government	Private Business	Difference: "Government" Minus "Business"
Chance To Get Ahead	6.7	6.3	+0.4	6.7	5.3	+1.4
Chance for "Real Success"	4.3	5.2	−0.9	4.8	4.5	+0.3

[5] Federal employees who have thought about leaving at some time in the past also rate the government less well than do people who have never thought of leaving. This tendency is traced in some detail in the *Source Book*, Chap. 17.

That Negroes in the federal service actually rate the government slightly ahead of private business as an avenue to "real success" sets this group apart from any other major group analyzed for this study. In the rhetoric of public debate the government's role in leading the way in providing job opportunities for Negro citizens has been emphasized repeatedly in recent years. From these figures it is clear that Negroes recognize the government as a good employment opportunity—better, in fact, in this respect than private business.

Federal Executives, Natural and Social Scientists, and Engineers

From some of our probings of the attitudes of the general federal sample, the impression grows that many high-level federal employees take a more favorable view of the opportunity aspects of government compared with business than do groups with similar training and qualifications who are not working for the government. A look at the scale placements made by the four special federal groups provides added evidence of this tendency. On the whole, the executives feel that the government compares well with private business on these matters. Their comparison is decidedly more favorable toward government than that of the business executives, and somewhat more favorable than that of any other high-level nonfederal group.

Having reached the upper echelons of the federal hierarchy themselves, the executives rate the government fairly high on the chances it offers for getting to the top and for getting ahead; on both factors, they also rate government ahead of private business, whereas high-level nonfederal groups tend to give business the edge over government. Federal executives also feel that the government's relative disadvantage on the chances for "real success" is not nearly as great as their counterparts in the business world do, but they still rate the government almost a full scale point below private business on this factor:

Characteristics Rated by Federal Executives (N = 271)	Federal Government	Private Business	Difference: "Government" Minus "Business"
Chance To Get Ahead	7.2	6.1	+1.1
Chance To Reach a Top-Level Job	7.6	6.9	+0.7
Chance for "Real Success"	3.8	4.7	−0.9

Within the federal executive population, some interesting differences in attitude can be found. Two examples, based on executives' age and length of service may be cited. Compared with their opposites, the younger executives and those who have been in the government a shorter time (and hence presumably have made unusually rapid progress into the executive group) are a bit more optimistic about the possibilities for getting ahead, reaching a top-level job, and attaining "real success" in the government. Here are the figures on the chance for "real success":

Characteristic Rated by Federal Executives	Age			Government Employment		
	Under 40	40–49	50 and Older	Under 10 Years	10–19 Years	20 Years and Over
Chance for "Real Success" in Federal Government	4.2	3.8	3.7	4.1	3.9	3.7
Chance for "Real Success" in Private Business	4.2	4.5	5.0	4.4	4.5	4.8
Difference: "Government" Minus "Business"	0.0	−0.7	−1.3	−0.3	−0.6	−1.1
(N)	(38)	(113)	(121)	(34)	(105)	(133)

Over all, the attitudes of the natural scientists, social scientists, and engineers in government work differ only slightly from the views of the executives. They, too, tend to rate the government better than private business on opportunities for getting ahead and for reaching one of the top jobs, while ranking it slightly lower on the chance for "real success." The engineers are the primary exception to this general pattern; they rate government just about even with private business on opportunities for rising to the top. The social scientists, on the other hand, give the government a fairly big advantage (1.1 scale points) on this factor.

Within the engineer and social scientist groups, there is a slight tendency for those who are younger, those who have been with the government a shorter time, and those on the lower federal grade levels to see the government less favorably than their opposites. This is especially true when comparisons with private business employment are drawn on these points, and much less true when federal employment alone is being considered. The largest differences occur among the engineers. A variety of analyses have indicated that engineers outside the federal establishment are particularly critical of the lack of opportunity government employment affords. It also appears that engineers who work for the government, especially the younger ones, are more disenchanted about the opportunities in federal employment than are any other of the special groups in our sample.

Still another difference in outlook is found among the natural scientists. There are very few differences according to age, length of employment, and grade level, but when they do occur we find the younger scientists and those who are less experienced and of lower federal grade level assigning higher scores to government employment—both absolutely and in comparison with private business. The small samples involved preclude making general statements with surety, but the data at least suggest that the government's newer crop of natural scientists are more positive about federal employment.

To sum up, federal executives, natural and social scientists, and, to a lesser degree, engineers give their employer generally favorable marks on the opportunities for getting ahead and for getting to the top. This is profoundly important for the government. It means that these high-level employees feel considerable satisfaction about the advancement opportunities in government. On the other hand, they still give the business corporation a slight advantage over the government as a route to "real success"—a fact that should be noted with care by all who are concerned with the quality and effectiveness of the public service.

Opportunities for Advancement and "Real Success" in Business and the Federal Service

One major feature of these findings calls for additional comment. As we have seen, the government invariably comes out worse when people are asked whether a "young man of ability" will find "his best chance for being *really successful*" in working for the federal government or working for a large private business corporation. On this the scores are unequivocal. In every federal and nonfederal group interviewed, the government is placed below the large business corporation as a route to outstanding success.

Precisely what people had in mind when they made these ratings, however, is not so unequivocal. Two significant variables may be involved here. The first is the factor of "chance," embodied in that part of the statement which says "his best chance." People may rate the government relatively lower on "real success" because they see the *"chances"* for getting ahead or reaching the top as less in the federal service than in private business. On the other hand, there is the second factor—"real success"—embodied in that part of the statement which says "for being *really successful.*" Respondents may perhaps feel that *chances* for getting ahead or reaching the top are about equal in federal and business employment, but that the upper levels of federal employment are not as well endowed with the ingredients of *"real success"* as are the top echelons of the business world.

It is unlikely that either explanation is exclusively true. But the question remains—which of them played a greater role in a respondent's judgment that, compared with business, federal employment offers less chance for a young man of ability to be really successful? We can get at least a partial answer to this question by considering the scale ratings on "real success" in relation to the way federal and business employment were rated on the two "chance" factors.

As has been shown, on the chances for getting ahead, most nonfederal groups rate the federal government and private business about equal. Only the general employed public's college graduates and the special business groups clearly feel that the federal service lags behind business in this respect, and even here the differences favoring business, substantial as they are, are considerably smaller than the differences favoring business on the "real success" factor. Thus it appears that not one of the nonfederal groups rates the government below private business as an avenue to "real success" simply because the chances for promotion and for getting ahead in the government are seen as being poorer.

Among federal employees, the findings are even more clear cut. All of the federal populations rate government employment higher than business employment on opportunity to get ahead. The differences are not always large; they are, however, consistent from group to group and mostly large enough to be significant. This pattern is directly contrary to what should be found if federal employees rate federal employment lower on the chance for "real success" because they see federal employment as relatively lacking in opportunity to get ahead. Thus it appears that federal employees tend to rate federal employment lower on the chances for "real success" *in spite of* their feeling that the government provides equal or better opportunities for getting ahead.

There remains, however, another possibility. Perhaps people feel the government lags behind private business on one particular aspect of opportunity—the chance to get to the top. That is, people may believe that private employment offers a better chance than the federal service for "real success," not because they see its promotional opportunity in general as being better, but because they see in it greater access to top-level jobs.

Among nearly all of the nonfederal groups, business is, in fact, rated ahead of the government in this respect. But generally the difference scores in favor of the corporation are very small, and some are not even of borderline significance. Only for the college-trained in the general employed public and for the various groups in business and industry are the differences sufficiently large to show unequivocally that the business corporation is rated higher than the federal service on this aspect of opportunity. Thus, for some groups, differences in estimates of the chances for getting to the top in business and the government may be responsible for some of the much higher ratings given to private business on the chances for "real success," but it is unlikely that more than a part of the higher scores may be accounted for in this way.

This indication applies with even greater force to the federal populations. Although the difference scores are not large, nearly all of the federal groups rate the government equal to or better than the corporation on the chances for getting to the top of the organization. Yet, as we have seen, the groups also tend to rate the federal service somewhat below the business corporation as an avenue to "real success." Apparently the *nature* of the top jobs in the government, rather than the *opportunities for getting to the top,* compare less favorably with what the business world has to offer.

It appears then that the ratings on "real success" cannot be fully accounted for by perceived differences in either promotional opportunity or the chances of winding up in one of the top-level jobs. By inference, one may conclude that many people feel that the top echelons of the business world, compared to the federal service, provide more of what they define as "real success." It is possible, of course, that for some of the nonfederal populations the combination of the two "opportunity" factors may account for a considerable amount of the advantage accorded large business on chances for "real success." But for most of the nonfederal populations and all of the federal populations, it seems likely that certain other unstated elements of "real success" are perceived as lacking, relatively speaking, in federal employment.

Summary

We have traced the scale ratings given by various groups to government and business employment in some detail. It remains to summarize some of the principal findings.

1. The following general differences in emphasis among various groups are to be found:

Women compare the government with private business more favorably than do men.

Federal employees are more favorable to government than people outside the government.

High school students are more favorable than college and graduate students.

Among people outside the government, respondents of lower socioeconomic status are more favorable than those of higher status.

Among federal employees, the tendency for the government's comparative position to decline with increasing socioeconomic status is also present but much less pronounced.

The executives, natural scientists, social scientists, and engineers in business are particularly critical of government employment.

Aside from the security factor, high school and college teachers tend to rate private business and the government about even on all of the factors except "real success." On this success factor, the government is rated lower.

2. The federal government is given the edge over business employment on security by every group interviewed. Federal employees give the government an even bigger lead than the nonfederal populations do, largely because government workers are markedly more pessimistic about the amount of security private business provides than are people who do not work for the government.

3. To the modest extent that there is a tendency to stereotype government work as more routine and monotonous than business employment, it occurs primarily among the more highly educated nonfederal populations and among the special groups in business. In this respect, the business groups are the most critical of federal employment.

4. Most groups outside the federal service rate the government and business about equal on the chances they offer their employees for getting ahead. There is, however, some tendency for the balance to shift to

the disadvantage of the government among nonfederal respondents on the higher educational and occupational levels. By contrast, federal employees themselves take a more sanguine view of the advancement opportunities in the federal service. Every federal group gives the government the edge over business on the chances for getting ahead.

5. Most groups are reasonably optimistic about the chance a young man of ability has of ending up in a top-level job in either the large business corporation or the federal service. Most nonfederal groups give the business corporation a slight edge over the government on the factor; the comparative advantage for the business corporation becomes marked only among the more highly educated members of the general employed public and in the special business groups. On this factor, also, federal employees differ in their attitudes from people outside the government. Nearly all types of federal employees rate the government equal to or better than the business corporation on the chances for reaching a top job, and the comparison does not shift to the disadvantage of the government among high-status respondents.

6. Groups outside the federal service rate the government relatively low on the chance it provides a young man of ability for "real success." Their scale ratings of large private business on this factor tend to be higher. In addition, the government's comparative position grows worse among the high-status groups, with the special business groups comparing the government with the corporation the most unfavorably of all. Nearly all the federal populations share this feeling that private business exceeds the government in the opportunities for "real success." Nevertheless, federal employees tend to give business less of an edge than do comparable people outside the government. And, unlike the situation in the general employed public, the government's comparative position does not deteriorate among the more highly situated federal respondents even though the absolute scores given the government do decline.

7. In all groups, the government is compared with business less favorably on the opportunities it offers for real success than it is on the chances for getting ahead or for reaching one of the top-level jobs. Many people feel the opportunities for moving up the organizational ladder are about as good in the government as in business. But apparently many of them also feel that the top itself in government provides fewer opportunities for "real success" than do the top echelons of the business world.

8

Further Views About the Federal Service

THE IMAGE OF FEDERAL EMPLOYMENT consists of many subimages. In this chapter we direct our attention to three of these which presumably play important roles in the over-all picture of the federal service.

1. Preferred parts of the service: To what extent do people see certain parts of the government as better to work for than others? Are there specific parts they would prefer? Why?

2. Sex differentiation: Is government employment seen as being more suitable for men or for women? If so, why?

3. Monetary rewards: Do people have accurate knowledge of the upper reaches of the federal salary structure? Do they feel the top salaries are too low or too high?

Awareness of
Selective Employment Opportunities

The relative attractiveness of certain parts of the government is conditioned both by information about them and by the evaluations made of them. To the extent that people express the feeling that they would prefer some parts more than others, we may say that the image of employment opportunities in the federal service is pluralistic, rather than monolithic. But the reverse is not necessarily true. Failure to discriminate may be due, not to a monolithic view, but to lack of preference.

The question put to the nonfederal populations was, "Suppose a person in your line of work did go to work for the United States government. Are there any particular branches or parts that would be better

TABLE 8-1. *Extent to Which Nonfederal Employees See Certain Parts of the Government As Preferable to Others*[a]

Nonfederal Employee Groups	Number Answering	"Yes"	"No"	"Don't Know"
General Employed Public	(1,140)	39%	20%	42%
By sex				
Men	(875)	43	20	37
Women	(265)	24	19	58
By educational level				
High school not completed	(330)	29	19	53
High school completed	(513)	36	23	41
Some college	(128)	50	16	34
College graduate	(139)	60	14	26
Groups in Education				
High school teachers	(282)	60	16	24
College teachers	(466)	78	7	15
Natural scientists	(118)	77	8	15
Social scientists	(104)	79	9	12
Engineers	(87)	71	9	20
Groups in Business				
Executives	(287)	50	16	34
Natural scientists	(85)	81	7	12
Social scientists	(73)	74	12	14
Engineers	(90)	63	20	17

[a] Based on replies to the question: "Suppose a person in your line of work did go to work for the United States government. Are there any particular branches or parts that would be better to be in than others, from your point of view?"

to be in than others, from your point of view?"[1] About two fifths of the members of the general employed public say that certain parts of the government would be better for someone in their line of work (Table 8-1). A nearly identical proportion confess to not knowing, and one fifth say no part would be better than any other.

That less than one half of the nonfederal working public differentiated among the various parts of government may seem to confirm the general notion that a great deal of ignorance exists about federal employment. Notice, however, that men do better in this respect than women. Even more significant is the sharp rise in positive replies ac-

[1] Students were not asked this question because most of them were not at the time in the work force. Federal employees were asked a parallel question, the results of which are discussed in Chapter 9.

cording to educational level. This pattern is echoed in the responses of the highly educated groups in education and business, where solid majorities reply positively. Quite clearly, the more highly educated the person is, the more likely it is that he can and will distinguish certain segments of the federal service which he feels would be better for him.

It is perhaps ironical that such positive responses are highest among the kinds of people who, generally speaking, are least disposed toward federal employment, and lowest among those most favorably inclined. Thus women and the less-educated respondents take a more positive view of federal work, as shown earlier, but exhibit the least tendency to choose particular parts of the government which might be best for them. Conversely, men and the better-educated respondents are less favorably inclined toward government but more inclined to exhibit a preference.

A major reason for this is that the sheer amount of information input is obviously greater for the better-educated. Their exposure to the federal apparatus through formal education, post-formal learning (mass media, for example), and occupational encounters is likely to be considerably higher than that of the less-educated. Whether the highly educated and trained people would like to work for the government is somewhat moot in this connection; the main point is that they have enough information to feel that, assuming they did become federal employees, some parts would be better for them than others.

A second reason is that specialized occupational endeavors are more common among people who are better educated and occupationally situated. It is not too surprising that people whose work or training are not highly specialized do not make a distinction as to preferred parts of the government. In addition to lacking information, they may also operate on the assumption, quite justified, that many parts of the government would have need for their rather general skills. Thus the laborer or clerical typist, both of whom are unlikely to come from upper educational levels, probably feel there is no particular advantage to being in one segment than any other. By the same token, women—who come disproportionately from the clerical and unskilled and semiskilled occupations —are also inclined to feel that their services could be used in a variety of places. This kind of thinking can also prevail among more elite groups, however. Business executives—and it is significant in this regard that they have the lowest percentage among the college and business groups—might justifiably feel that their general administrative skills could be applied with equal benefit in almost any sector of the government. Therefore, those who make no statements of preference should not necessarily be regarded as ignorant of the various components of government work, although it is quite clear that many, especially among the less-educated, know next to nothing about the components.

While education and occupational specialization are rather directly related to awareness of what segments of the federal establishment would be better, it is nevertheless true that a core of about 20 to 40 percent of the groups in colleges and business (excluding business executives) claimed an inability to make such distinctions. Since they are engaged in specialized pursuits requiring considerable training, the argument that they see themselves as being able to fit in most anywhere in the federal service appears to be inapplicable here. Rather, a vacuum of information seems to be operative in their cases. This is particularly likely since their replies were more often "don't know" rather than an outright "no." When substantial portions of these highly select people do not make a judgment about certain parts of the government, we may suspect that they are not sharply attuned to the specialized outlets for their talents in the federal service.

Preferred Parts of the Federal Establishment

Given the fact that nonfederal workers in meaningful numbers do see certain parts of the federal establishment as being better than others for them, it becomes a matter of interest to know what these parts are. Respondents who made such a distinction were asked a follow-up question intended to elicit references to specific government departments, agencies, or bureaus: "What particular branches or parts of the government would be better?"

Members of the general employed public mention a great many departments and agencies, but with none being pre-eminent. No Cabinet-level department (or division therein) or independent agency is mentioned by more than 15 percent in this group.[2] The Defense Department (or parts thereof, such as Army, Navy, and Air Force) and the Post Office Department, the two largest employers of federal personnel, receive the most notice.

[2] For more detailed information relating to this section see the *Source Book*, Chap. 10.

While the choices of the general public do not peak in any parts of the government, the picture is otherwise for the special groups in education and business. Although the high school teachers, for example, pay about the same attention as the general public to the Defense Department, they completely eschew the Post Office Department, and indicate a preference for the State Department and the Department of Health, Education, and Welfare (HEW).

Distinctions are even more apparent among the college teachers. In general, this group avoids the Post Office Department, and gives slightly less notice than the general public to the Defense Department. But, like the high school teachers, substantial numbers of them (about one fourth in each case) select State and HEW; lesser numbers (around 10 percent in each case) select the Departments of Commerce, Agriculture, and Interior, and various foreign technical programs.

For the business executives, Defense, State, Commerce, and Treasury are the most popular segments.

Predictably, the more specialized his enterprise, the more likely the nonfederal employee will be to single out certain parts of the government as being better for someone in his line of work. This is borne out when we look at the preferences of the natural scientists, social scientists, and engineers among college teachers and in business and industry. One result of this tendency is that all government departments, except Treasury, Post Office, and Justice, receive moderate attention from at least one of the three categories of specialists from the campus and from business firms. Also included are a flock of miscellaneous independent agencies, cited in all by over one tenth of each group of specialists.

But the diversity within these groups of natural and social scientists and engineers is considerable. In the college and business groups the engineers single out parts of the Defense Department more often than do the social and natural scientists, with the Navy and the Corps of Engineers receiving the most attention. Along with natural scientists, engineers are also more drawn toward programs in the Department of Interior. On the other hand, engineers express virtually no interest in HEW. Social scientists, by contrast, are more attracted than natural scientists and engineers to parts of the State Department (over one fifth mention it) and the Labor Department. Natural scientists stand apart from the other two groupings in their interest in the Agriculture Department. Even where all three groups of specialists show an affinity for a certain department, there may be considerable particularization within that department. Consider, for example, these figures referring to the Commerce Department:

	N	Bureau of Standards	Other Specific Divisions	Not Further Specified
College				
Natural scientists	(91)	18%	0%	2%
Social scientists	(82)	0	4	10
Engineers	(62)	11	3	2
Business				
Natural scientists	(69)	12	1	1
Social scientists	(54)	0	4	13
Engineers	(57)	5	7	5

Natural scientists and engineers, especially the former, are more prone than the social scientists to think of a specific part of the Commerce Department—most often the Bureau of Standards. It seems reasonable to suppose that the clear identification of a special division or unit within a department provides a better target for attraction, favorable disposition toward, and potential employment than does a more global and less differentiated view of a department as a whole.

Reasons for Preferring Certain Parts

Why did those nonfederal employees who would prefer certain parts of the government make the choices they did? The two most plausible reasons are in fact the ones most frequently advanced. Both tell us little about the specific nature of the reasons for preferring certain parts. One is the argument that the work performed in the segment of government designated would be interesting, enjoyable, and satisfying because it is the kind of work the employee wants and likes to do. Percentages mentioning this in the various groups ranged from about 20 to 50 percent. Here are some examples of the interest and enjoyment rationale:

"Because it's what interests me. A person doesn't mind work if it's something he's interested in." (*Skilled laborer who designated an Army Ordnance Depot*)

"Because I'd like it. I want to eventually work in security markets." (*Retail manager; nominated business statistics in Agriculture or Commerce Department*)

"I think it would be interesting to work with foreign people." *(College graduate who preferred the Foreign Service)*

The second reason (noted by 45 to 65 percent) is that the work fits the person's training, capacities, and abilities. The "suitability" statements ran in this vein:

"Because I'm familiar with the type of work they do. I know the people and like them. I know what they're doing and understand their objectives." *(College teacher of agriculture; designated several relevant segments of government)*

" 'Cause that's all I know. Like I said, I ain't got another trade. I don't know nothing else—that's reason enough." *(Poorly educated semiskilled laborer)*

"I have knowledge in doing the work, and the experience in it too. I have been there and worked for them." *(Lawyer, had spent some time with the Interstate Commerce Commission and the Justice Department)*

People simply prefer those parts of government where they could transfer their present skills and where they could presumably derive the same satisfaction from their work as they now do. (Members of the business groups, however, were especially likely to emphasize suitability more than interest.) Few people seem inclined to mention something new or venturesome in government service—they would continue along their present pursuits with the only difference being their employment under government aegis. What is most significant about these two general explanations is that they show that people expressing a preference do see how their interests and abilities could be fitted into the federal service and thus do not foresee a radical disjuncture.

There are, however, more specific reasons why certain parts are singled out. The following reasons are advanced by at least 5 percent of the general employed public:

High or good financial reward (12%)
Security, stability, protection, fringe benefits (12%)
Self-advancement and progress—getting ahead (8%)
Self-development, self-expression, and creativity (7%)
Doing work that is significant for others (7%)
Favorable active personal relations (5%)
Work that is worthwhile, useful, constructive (5%)

The less-educated general employees stress the monetary and security aspects more than the better-educated do. On the other hand, the latter are more struck by the chance of doing work that has significance for others, and by the opportunities for active personal relations—the chance to interact with stimulating and interesting people. In general, the lower the educational level, the more the reasons appear to be justifications for federal employment at large rather than any particular part of the service.

For the most part, the special groups in education and business ignore the monetary rewards, security aspects, and advancement possibilities as reasons for preferring one part of the government to another. They do, however, refer to a variety of other reasons, many of which are closely articulated with the specific segments designated. In contrast to the general population, for example, some of the special groups prefer certain segments because of the high standards called for in terms of the skills demanded and the progressive nature of the work being done. Social scientists and engineers in colleges (18 percent of each) and natural scientists in business (22 percent) are especially likely to note this feature. There is also moderate attention devoted to the self-development and self-expression advantages, to doing useful work and work that is significant to others, and having rewarding active personal relations with others at work. None of the latter reasons are mentioned by more than 20 percent of any group, with about 10 percent being most common.

The results of the questions dealing with awareness, preferences, and rationale are sobering—primarily because of the distribution of information and attitudes among the people surveyed. From the government's viewpoint it would be comforting to say that one of the reasons the more elite portions of the nonfederal public are less attracted toward government work is that they simply do not know of the opportunities the federal service can offer them. The data do not fully support this, however.

Awareness and concrete information are greatest among these people, and least among those most positively oriented toward federal work. Furthermore, the reasons the elite groups give for preferring one part or activity to another are more directly related to the outlets they cite. As shown in various parts of this study, even these groups have some critical gaps in their supply of information about federal work, but they are in general fairly well informed and discriminating about specific potential areas of opportunity.

Is the Federal Service Better for Men or Women?

Under the prevailing norms in our society, certain jobs and work activities are usually set aside for men, with others commonly reserved for
women and still others accessible to either sex. Thus most secretaries are
women, most mechanics are men, while great numbers of both men and
women are teachers (although the system works so that incumbents at
the pinnacle of the teaching profession—college professors—are more
usually men, while women are in the majority at the elementary level).
Because some occupations and some enterprises are more often associated
with one sex rather than the other, it becomes a matter of some moment
to know if the federal government is viewed as a place better for men
or for women, since the critical shortages in federal personnel are most
common and likely to persist in fields traditionally occupied by men.

To get at least a partial answer to what we wished to discover, the
following inquiry was directed to all the populations, both federal and
nonfederal: "On the whole, who would be most likely to be satisfied with
civil service employment—men or women?" Alternative responses were
"men," "women," "no difference," and "don't know."

One of the most significant findings is that about one third to over one
half of the people in each of the various groups say "no difference" or
"don't know." Members of the general employed public were more inclined not to make a judgment than were general federal employees.
(51 vs. 37 percent). Quite clearly, the question of whether men or
women would be happier in the civil service is not a relevant one for
great numbers of people. In essence they are saying that either could be
happy (or unhappy) in the civil service. Any patterning found among
those people who do make a choice between men and women must be
put into this over-all context.

From nearly one half to about two thirds of the respondents in each
of the populations did make a choice as to whether federal employment
would be better for one of the sexes, and the distribution of these judgments is far from uniform. Let us deal first with the two general populations (Table 8-2). In the general public almost twice as many people
say the federal service would be better for men than say better for women.
Quite the reverse applies among general federal employees, who give

TABLE 8-2. *Judgments of Whether Civil Service Employment Is More Satisfying to Men or to Women*

Nonfederal and Federal Employee Groups	Number Answering	"Men"	"Women"	"No Difference"	"Don't Know"
General Employed Public	(1,139)	31%	18%	33%	18%
By sex					
Men	(873)	31	19	33	17
Women	(266)	30	15	31	24
By educational level					
High school not completed	(329)	34	7	32	26
High school completed	(512)	32	18	33	16
Some college	(129)	30	28	29	13
College graduate	(139)	16	37	33	13
General Federal Employees	(947)	24	39	30	7
By sex					
Men	(661)	27	35	30	8
Women	(286)	16	52	29	3
By educational level					
High school not completed	(192)	26	28	36	10
High school completed	(356)	27	40	28	5
Some college	(180)	20	50	24	5
College graduate	(163)	22	41	30	7

the edge to women by a ratio of over 1½ to 1. Within the nonfederal work force the sex of the respondent makes virtually no difference in this judgment—both favor men. But in the federal group, men give a slight edge to women, and women see the civil service as more satisfactory for their own sex by a ratio of over 3 to 1.

Even more striking is the difference by educational level within the two general populations. In the nonfederal work force the higher an employee's educational attainment, the less likely he is to see the civil service as better for men and, by a greater margin, the more likely to see it as better for women. Thus the high school incompletes say *men* by a 5 to 1 ratio, whereas college graduates designate *women* by more than a 2 to 1 margin. In the federal work force educational level makes virtually no difference in the extent to which men are designated, but employees with a high school diploma or better choose women far more often than do the high school incompletes. The upshot is that the high school incompletes divide evenly between naming men and women, but those at higher levels name women much more often than men.

It is obvious, then, that educational attainment is directly related to a feminine depiction of the federal service. Thus we would expect the special populations to reflect this tendency as well, and for the most part the data bear this notion out. The present high school student group is almost evenly split between designating men and women. But the college seniors and graduate students designate women much more often, as do the college teachers and groups in business. Only high school teachers depart from this norm, with about equal designations being given to each sex. Among the special federal populations the picture is mixed. Executives and social scientists fit the pattern, with more choices of women; natural scientists and engineers divide about equally. But the important point is that in no instance among any federal or nonfederal group at the higher educational and occupational levels do the proportions saying men exceed those nominating women; in most instances the picture is just the opposite.

In sum, we may say that moderate to high proportions of the respondents made no distinction as to whether men or women would be more satisfied in the civil service. Where they do make choices the image is likely to be masculine or "neuter" among people at the lower educational and occupational levels, but feminine at the higher echelons.

Given the presence of manifold opportunities for both men and women in the federal service, it is not surprising that so many people do not make a judgment as to whether men or women would find greater satisfaction in federal service. This indicates fairly wide acceptance of the premise that occupational satisfaction in the federal service is not contingent upon sex differences. Additionally there seems to be a tacit recognition that a considerable measure of equal opportunity for women prevails in government. From the government's standpoint, however, it is discomforting to see that, among the substantial numbers of nonfederal respondents who do make a choice, those of the higher socioeconomic echelons designate women more often than men.

It is surely among the occupational categories in these echelons, populated predominantly by males, that the quality shortages now exist and are likely to persist. Yet these people are the ones who opine most often that women would like the civil service better, hardly a favorable omen for attracting men of this stripe into the civil service. We must also remember that it is among these groups that the relative appeal of federal employment is lowest. By inference it appears that one of the reasons, in addition to those explicitly singled out, is that many of them view federal employment as offering the kinds of rewards more suitable to women than men. Furthermore, the fact that federal employees themselves more often designate women than men suggests that those who "should know" share this view of higher satisfaction being probable for women.

Reasons for the Answers

There are a number of conceivable reasons why people make the kinds of judgments they do about who would be most satisfied in the federal service. Unfortunately, only one somewhat inadequate follow-up question was asked: "Why do you say that?" However, enough was learned from the answers to enable us to make a few generalizations about what respondents had in mind when they said that men or women would be more satisfied or that there would be no difference in terms of satisfaction.[3]

A large number of the people who said "no difference" explain their answers by saying that there are so many kinds of jobs and opportunities available in federal employment that it is impossible to make a judgment as to whether men or women would be more satisfied. Another type of reply, somewhat less common, is an expression of the feeling that in general men and women want about the same things from their jobs; thus the distinction being asked for simply could not be made. There is also considerable opinion that while men and women might want different things from their work, federal civil service employment offers some features that men like especially well and some things that women like especially well. Since these factors are likely to balance out for men and women there would be no real reason for feeling that one would probably be more satisfied than the other. A final major reason is that the security provisions of federal employment were seen as being good for both sexes.

A sizable majority of those who said they think civil service employment would be more satisfying for men advance two reasons which are related to the feeling that federal employment offers an especially high

---

[3] People replying "don't know" were not asked the follow-up question. A more detailed account of the distribution of responses is found in the *Source Book,* Chap. 10.

degree of occupational security. Thus, in the various nonfederal and federal populations, from 25 percent to over 75 percent of those choosing men express the feeling that since men value occupational security more highly than do women they are thus more apt to be satisfied with federal employment.

From 40 to 90 percent of them convey this same idea somewhat differently, saying that in general men are more often the real breadwinners and that a job is a more central aspect of a man's life than of a woman's. Therefore, men are more apt to be satisfied by what federal employment has to offer simply because work and earning a livelihood are more important to them. At the same time there is a recognition that federal employment is conducive to meeting this function because of its stability. Other reasons offered with moderate frequency by most groups, and particularly common among federal employees, included the feelings that men would have a chance to move ahead and satisfy their ambitions and that there are a great many job opportunities for men in the civil service.

Of those who think that women are most apt to be satisfied with federal employment, roughly one fourth to one third in the various nonfederal groups say that the level of pay in the civil service is sufficiently high to satisfy women but not high enough to satisfy men to the same extent. Interestingly, this reason is even more pervasive among some federal groups: two fifths of general federal employees and one half of federal executives give this argument. The second major reason, given by one fifth to two fifths of the people in the various groups, is that women are more likely than men to be satisfied with the kind of routine and clerical type work which they see as being characteristic of federal employment. A third reason is that the work offers the kind of clean, safe, and nontiring work which is supposedly valued more by women than men.

These three judgments are rooted in the common perception—especially prevalent among the upper educational and occupation groups— that civil service employment is characterized by relatively low pay, routine, monotonous, and clerical-type work, and generally good, safe, and nontiring working conditions. A fourth prime reason shows the ubiquity of the security image of the civil service: the security factor, having been advanced as a reason for not only men alone but both sexes to prefer civil service, is also used to explain why women alone would be most satisfied.

Views on Federal Salaries

The provision of salaries that would be adequate to attract top-level people to the federal service has been a continuing problem for the American government. We sought to learn something about public knowledge of and attitudes toward federal salaries by asking all respondents the following two questions: (1) "What is the top salary per year in the United States Civil Service—that is, not the salaries of elected and appointed officials, but the highest salary anyone in the regular United States Civil Service can get?" (2) "What do you think the highest salary per year *should be* for people who hold the top-level jobs in the United States Civil Service?"

When we examine the respondents' estimates of present top salaries, the main showing is that there is a gross amount of ignorance on this point. At the time of the interviews the top federal salary figure was $18,500 annually.[4] Since it seemed unreasonable to insist that the correct answer to the question must be $18,500, we accepted any estimate within the $17,000 to $19,999 range as "correct." Using this criterion we found that accurate answers are rare among the nonfederal populations; the range is from 1 percent (high school students) to 26 percent (natural and social scientists in business). Lack of knowledge is also apparent in the large proportion of both the general public (29 percent) and the high school students (24 percent) who cannot even make a guess about the top salary. Predictably, there are more correct estimates among the federal groups, though only 29 percent of the general federal work force gives figures in this range, vs. 60 percent or more of those in the special federal groups who did likewise.

But the fact that accurate approximations are much more the exception than the rule does not indicate the direction of the estimating errors. Counting figures of $20,000 or higher as overestimating and figures below $17,000 as underestimating, we find that the general tendency of respondents is to underestimate, in some instances drastically. Thus only 16 percent of the general employed public overapproximate, compared

[4] This was the figure for the top of the Classification Act schedule (GS 18), although a few salaries for professional and scientific research and development personnel went slightly higher.

with 52 percent that underapproximate. Among students the figures for underestimates and overestimates are, for high schoolers, 63 and 12 percent; college seniors, 62 and 21 percent; and graduate students, 57 and 24 percent. These latter figures suggest that the ratio of under to over will be more nearly equal among the groups that are better educated and occupationally situated. This is so, but even among the academic and business groups the absolute proportions of people who underestimate range, with one exception, from over one third to over one half.[5]

Surprisingly, low estimates are also quite common among general federal employees, some 41 percent mentioning figures below $17,000. Inasmuch as the four special federal groups have a high proportion of accurate approximations, errors of either type are not nearly so frequent. Nevertheless, low estimates are as common as high ones among the one third of each group estimating inaccurately.

Another way of viewing the top salary approximations is to consider the median figures. Using the medians for the various groups (excluding respondents not making a guess) provides single figures with which to appraise central tendencies and is useful for comparative purposes. The figures are presented in Table 8-3 along with medians for salary "should be" figures and the differences between the two. Considering first the estimates of what the top salary *is*, we see the tendency to underestimate, especially if we take $18,500 rather than the $17,000 to $19,999 range as "correct." It should be noted, however, that underestimation is greatest in the general public—especially among the less-educated—and among high school juniors and seniors. Although the business and academic groups show some underestimation, their medians come considerably closer to the real top. Over all, the underestimation is considerably less among the sort of people who would be in a position to command the better salaries, but is still enough in evidence to suggest that the attractiveness of federal employment may be suffering as a consequence. The median estimates of federal employees are relatively accurate, though even here slight underestimation rather than overestimation is the rule.

The prevailing impressions of what the top salary in the civil service *is* provides an important base with which to compare the estimates of what it *should be*. As was the case with the first estimate, there are a

[5] Social scientists in business are the exception; only 26 percent underestimate, while 45 percent overestimate. This is the only instance where excessive figures were clearly more frequent.

TABLE 8-3. *Median Estimates of What the Top Salary in the United States Civil Service Is and Should Be*

Federal and Nonfederal Groups	Number Answering for[a]		Top Salary Is[b]	Top Salary Should Be[b]	Difference: "Salary Should Be" Minus "Salary Is"
	What Top Salary Is	What Top Should Be			
Nonfederal Populations					
General employed public	(811)	(788)	$10,000	$14,000	+$4,000
By sex					
Men	(657)	(635)	10,500	14,500	+ 4,000
Women	(154)	(153)	8,000	9,500	+ 1,500
By educational level					
High school not completed	(185)	(190)	9,000	10,000	+ 1,000
High school completed	(390)	(379)	9,000	12,000	+ 2,000
Some college	(100)	(95)	12,000	16,000	+ 4,000
College graduate	(115)	(106)	15,000	20,000	+ 5,000
Students					
High school students	(274)	(270)	9,500	11,500	+ 2,000
College seniors	(369)	(334)	14,500	19,500	+ 5,000
Graduate students	(351)	(325)	15,000	19,500	+ 4,500
Groups in education					
High school teachers	(243)	(214)	14,000	17,500	+ 3,500
College teachers	(427)	(361)	16,000	24,000	+ 8,000
Natural scientists	(116)	(105)	15,000	23,000	+ 8,000
Social scientists	(104)	(91)	17,000	23,500	+ 6,500
Engineers	(82)	(74)	17,500	23,500	+ 6,000
Groups in business					
Executives	(261)	(222)	14,500	22,000	+ 7,500
Natural scientists	(78)	(71)	17,500	24,500	+ 7,000
Social scientists	(71)	(60)	18,500	25,000	+ 6,500
Engineers	(85)	(73)	18,000	25,000	+ 7,000
Federal Employee Populations					
General federal employees	(832)	(775)	17,000	20,000	+ 3,000
By sex					
Men	(596)	(555)	17,000	21,000	+ 4,000
Women	(236)	(220)	17,000	19,000	+ 2,000
By educational level					
High school not completed	(141)	(135)	15,000	17,500	+ 2,500
High school completed	(319)	(298)	16,500	19,000	+ 2,500
Some college	(164)	(151)	17,500	24,000	+ 6,500
College graduate	(158)	(149)	18,000	25,000	+ 7,000
Executives	(273)	(253)	18,000	25,000	+ 7,000
Natural scientists	(90)	(82)	18,000	25,000	+ 7,000
Social scientists	(90)	(81)	18,000	25,000	+ 7,000
Engineers	(98)	(92)	18,000	25,000	+ 7,000

[a] Excludes those who did not make an estimate.

[b] Figures rounded to nearest $500. Because of rounding and the clustering of estimates, the combined medians by sex and education level breaks may not equal those of the two general populations.

number of people who say they cannot make the second one; these proportions, in fact, run a little higher for the judgmental question than for the factual inquiry. In general the "don't know" and "cannot guess" replies are less frequent among men, among the groups that are more highly educated and occupationally situated, and among federal vs. nonfederal respondents.

But for those who do make estimates, and this includes a large majority within each population, the direction of the "should be" ceiling parallels that for the "is" ceiling. That is, the estimates run higher at the upper educational and occupational levels, among general federal employees compared with nonfederal employees, and among men vs. women. Median estimates range from $9,600 among women in the general employed public to $25,000 among several groups in business and government.

Median "should be" salaries run considerably higher among general federal workers, compared with the general employed public. Significantly, however, the gap between federal and nonfederal figures is low or nonexistent when the special groups in colleges and business are compared with those in the federal establishment. All estimates are between $22,000 and $25,000. Not shown by the table is the fact that for these high-level groups the most frequently given (modal) figure for the "should be" top is $25,000.

When the median "is" estimates are compared with the median "should be" estimates, the results are truly remarkable. Without exception the "should be" figures exceed the "is." They show a gap between what people believe the top salary is and what they think it ought to be. But the gap is far greater for some groups than others. Thus women and high school incompletes in the general employed public see a difference of only $1,500 and $1,000, respectively. In contrast, all of the special groups in colleges, business, and government show a deficit of at least $6,000 between the perceived reality and the ideal. Quite clearly the biggest jumps in absolute terms are urged by men and, more significantly, the groups that are the more highly educated and better occupationally situated in both the federal and nonfederal populations.

Offhand one would say that these findings demonstrate a strong sentiment for a higher top to civil service salaries. But there is an analytic problem to a conclusion such as this. Should we use the absolute figures or the relative differences as a guide? Either base would yield similar conclusions in the case of the higher educational and occupational groups; their median estimates of actual top salaries, although a bit shy of the real top, are close enough to it so that the discrepancy between reality and perceptions is not drastic. Similarly, these groups show rather substantial agreement that the top should, in most instances, be several thousands of dollars above where it *actually* was in 1961, as well as where they *thought* it was.

The interpretive problem comes from employees in the general employed public, especially those at the lower educational levels. Their "preferred top" is actually a good deal below the existing top. Thus one might argue that there is scant support for a higher top in the general employed public. Furthermore, since this population comes closest to being a representative sample of the American voting public, it might be argued that upping the federal top would be politically unpopular and inexpedient.

However, in viewing the estimates of the general employed public it seems reasonable to consider a *comparative* interpretation of the figures. The $14,000 "should be" figure must be placed in the context of the very unrealistic $10,000 estimate of the actual top. It is logical to suppose that their approximations of the desirable top civil service salaries are thus heavily conditioned by a lack of good information about existing levels. Perhaps even more important as a conditioning factor are their own family incomes, the median figure for which is only $5,500. For an employee at this level, $10,000 may appear to be very high indeed. This supposition is supported by the fact that rising educational level, which is accompanied by higher incomes, produces higher estimates of both "is" and "should be" medians.

If we adopt the point of view that very few people in the general employed public have accurate knowledge of the top salary possibilities in the federal service, and that they make projections of an ideal top based on guesses about the real top and the conditioning factors of their station in life, we arrive at a different conclusion than that which takes the absolute figures as the standard. From this viewpoint what is of chief significance is that the general employed public, on the average, favors an increase of 40 percent in the top salary potential of civil servants—a percentage of increase not dissimilar to that shown by the more elite groups, although the absolute increase in dollar amounts is smaller. Whether the favored increase would hold even if the general employed public had perfect information about the salary structure of the federal service is a matter for conjecture and research, and one on which no sure answer can presently be given. However, it seems probable that if this increased information were accompanied by more accurate knowledge about salary structures in other endeavors (where misinformation is also likely to prevail) the outcome would probably assume the same shape even though the absolute figures would differ.

Implicit in what we say here is the contention that even the general employed public thinks that employees at the upper reaches of the civil service establishment are underpaid. There is no doubt that this is true in both a relative sense and an absolute sense among the more elite groups. It is possible that this attitude prevails because people feel that higher salaries are necessary to attract better people than now fill the upper slots, that those now filling these posts are not adequately compensated, or combinations of these two feelings. In view of the generally high ratings given top-level civil servants on a number of characteristics (see Chapter 10), the first alternative would seem to be less apt than the second. In any event, the sentiment among the better educated and more highly placed is definitely for a higher top in the salary structure. And the preference for a higher top carries with it, of course, the notion that the general pay structure at the upper levels should be elevated.

Summary

1. *Awareness.* Although the appeal of federal employment is higher among the lower-ranking nonfederal groups, it is nevertheless true that their awareness of federal occupational outlets is considerably lower than that of the higher-placed groups, for whom the appeal of federal work is lower. The specific departments and agencies people see as relevant for themselves are associated with their own kinds of occupational pursuits; thus, the more specialized the person's occupation, the more likely he is to see specific segments of the government as being better for him. The two most important reasons for preferring particular segments are the belief that the work would be compatible with the person's interests and that it would suit his capacities and training. In general, the more elite

groups also seize upon some service-oriented and ego-enhancing advantages, while the lower-ranking groups cite the more materialistic advantages.

2. *The Federal Service: More Advantageous for Men or Women?* In all populations, substantial proportions of respondents feel that federal employment is of equal merit for both sexes, a finding which suggests that the government is perceived as offering opportunities and gratifications for all and as not discriminating between the sexes. However, at least half the members of every population feel that federal employment would be better for one sex or the other; and the higher the educational and occupational level, the greater is the feeling that federal employment would be better for women. For example, among people in the general employed public who have not finished high school, those who feel federal employment would be better for men outnumber those who feel it would be better for women by a ratio of 5 to 1. But among college graduates in the general employed public, people who say federal employment would be better for women outnumber those who feel the opposite by more than 2 to 1. General federal employees, especially females, are themselves likely to feel this way. Given the critical manpower needs in areas to be filled by men, the feminine image often held by high-ranking, predominantly male groups is, from a personnel standpoint, hardly a favorable omen.

3. *Salaries.* Ignorance of the federal salary structure is widespread in the general employed public; this is much less true among higher-placed nonfederal groups and the federal populations. In absolute terms, all high-level federal and nonfederal groups feel that the top echelons of the federal salary structure should be elevated over the levels that prevailed in 1961. In addition, in all populations, both special and general, respondents feel that top salaries should be hiked considerably over what they perceived the 1961 highs to be.

9

Some Additional Attitudes
of Federal Employees

To learn more about the civil servant's views of his work world, we asked the federal respondents whether they had ever considered leaving government employment or were considering it now, and why or why not. We also asked them whether they had ever thought that particular kinds of nonfederal employment would be more suitable for them than other kinds, and why. The answers obtained shed additional light on the interplay of occupational satisfaction, occupational values, and the comparative image of the government as an employer.

Present Intentions of Leaving or Staying

Without doubt, the great majority of general federal employees presently plan to remain with the government (Table 9-1). Among the special federal groups, the natural and social scientists and the engineers are slightly less intent on staying, but it is significant that the executives have the highest expectations of remaining—higher even than the general employees. As will be discussed later, this disposition of the executives appears to be related to their long length of service.

How sure are those who plan to continue with the government? The two groups with the highest expectations of staying—general employees and executives—also express the greatest conviction about this intention. Not only do the natural and social scientists and engineers have lower expectations of remaining, but also among those who do plan to remain the certainty is significantly less. For an extreme case of potential disaffection consider the federal engineers: they show the lowest proportions

TABLE 9-1. *Intentions of Federal Employees To Continue with or Leave the Federal Service, and Degree of Certainty of Plans To Continue*[a]

Federal Groups	Number Answering	Plan To Leave	Plan To Continue				Don't Know
			Not Sure	Fairly Sure	Very Sure	Total	
General Employees	(948)	7%	2%	16%	72%	90%	4%
Executives	(273)	3	2	25	69	95	2
Natural Scientists	(92)	10	2	23	59	84	6
Social Scientists	(90)	18	1	30	48	79	3
Engineers	(99)	15	3	29	40	73	12

[a] Based on replies to this question: "Now returning to your present situation, do you plan to continue working for the federal government, or do you think you might leave it?" For those replying "continue" or "leave" a follow-up question asked them how sure they were— "very sure," "fairly sure," or "not sure."

for planning to continue and of being very sure of continuing, and next to the highest proportion for presently planning to leave.

Since 90 percent of the general federal employees interviewed expect to continue with the government, it is unlikely that large-scale variations in these intentions will occur according to most standard classifications. Sex, occupation, education, income, and federal grade level account for only minute differences in intentions. But two interrelated variables—age and length of service—are more highly associated with such intentions. Here is the distribution of replies by age brackets:

	N	Plan To Continue	Plan To Leave	Don't Know
Under 33	(150)	73%	16%	11%
33–39	(196)	89	9	2
40–48	(300)	92	5	3
49 and Older	(296)	96	3	1

The profile by length of employment is quite similar.[1] Although large majorities in each age and length of service category plan to continue, there is little doubt that such expectations increase directly with older age and longer service. By the same token, plans to leave and uncertainty of plans show a progressive drop as age and length of employ-

[1] The biggest jump in plans to continue occurs at the five-year mark (according to the groupings used); 78 percent of those with less than five years' experience and 90 percent of those with five to ten years' experience expect to continue.

ment climb. Younger and recently employed males are particularly less disposed toward remaining.

The firmness of intentions to continue varies little by sex or according to such standard hierarchies as education, income, occupation, and grade level. Employees with twenty or more years of service do have stronger convictions than those with fewer years, but age and degree of job satisfaction are even more strongly related to surety of intentions. Thus 72 percent of those under 33 years vs. 87 percent of those over 48 are very sure of staying. And while 71 percent of the least satisfied are very sure of continuing, the figure is surpassed by the 90 percent of the highly satisfied who share the same conviction.

Age and length of service are also important factors in determining whether personnel in the four special populations plan to stay with the government. In Table 9-2, this is demonstrated by length of service. Quite clearly, government service of a decade or more increases the likelihood that executives and professionals intend no employer change. This relationship helps explain why executives have the greatest predilection for remaining. As Table 9-2 indicates, nearly 90 percent of them have

TABLE 9-2. *Intentions of the Special Federal Groups To Continue with or Leave the Federal Service, Related to Length of Employment*

Length of Service	Number Answering	Plan To Continue	Plan To Leave	Don't Know
Executives				
Under 10 years	(34)	71%	15%	15%
10–19 years	(105)	100	0	0
20 years or more	(134)	98	2	1
Natural Scientists				
Under 10 years	(41)	73	15	12
10 years or more	(51)	92	6	2
Social Scientists				
Under 10 years	(37)	62	32	5
10 years or more	(53)	91	8	2
Engineers				
Under 10 years	(49)	55	26	18
10 years or more	(50)	90	4	6

been federal employees for more than ten years. Longevity of service is also associated with the certainty of remaining in government; for example, among the engineers and social scientists, two fifths of those with less than ten years service are very sure of staying, but more than three fifths of their longer-employed colleagues express the same certainty.

We set ten years of service as the main dividing line for purposes of analyzing these four special groups. It may be, however, that the most critical period of personal decisions about remaining with the government comes some time before that—say at the seven- or eight-year mark. At any rate, use of the ten-year mark reveals the weight that length of service (and the ramifications thereof) brings to bear on this question. The odds are very high that an employee who has served at least ten years and is at least 40 years old foresees a continuation of federal employment and is more sure of this than his less-experienced and younger fellow worker.

Summing up, it is clear that those who *are* thinking about leaving and/or those who are least sure of staying are most often (1) specialized personnel—the natural and social scientists and engineers—and (2) the younger and newer employees in both the general and the special populations.[2] Thus, the potential disaffection emanates most commonly from the ranks of those (with the exception of veteran executives) for whom governmental shortages are likely to be the most critical and those with the most years of service yet remaining.

Reasons for Staying with the Government

Why do most federal employees—at all levels—foresee continued federal careers? The reasons given illustrate the retentive strength of federal employment in that they show the occupational values which federal workers desire and feel are being maximized in their jobs.

Before considering these reasons, it will be helpful to look briefly at the 7 percent of general employees saying that they plan to sever their work ties.[3] These people most frequently point out their dissatisfaction with the economic rewards, self-advancement and progress, and self-

[2] The positive relation between occupational satisfaction and surety of continuing seems to be partly a function of the generally lower satisfaction of younger and newer employees.

[3] All respondents, after they had indicated whether they planned to leave or to continue in federal employment, were asked, "Why? What are the main things that make you feel that way?"

TABLE 9-3. *Reasons Given by Federal Employees for Expecting To Continue with the Federal Service*

Reasons Given	General Employees	Execu-tives	Natural Scientists	Social Scientists	Engineers
Security[a]	70%	61%	52%	46%	60%
Not further specified	14	8	10	7	7
Job security	20	11	10	6	13
Financial security	5	2	4	2	1
Retirement security	42	47	34	32	38
Other protective benefits (sick leave, insurance, etc.)	23	10	10	13	25
Length of service and experience	31	44	29	25	25
Lack of other job opportunities	13	15	9	24	13
Interest, enjoyment, satisfaction	27	45	46	59	44
High or good financial reward	19	17	27	15	13
Self-advancement and progress	11	16	18	21	14
Good physical environment, working conditions	11	4	9	6	4
Good relations with people at work	9	11	17	13	4
Vacation, leave, time off	18	6	9	7	13
NUMBER ANSWERING	(850)	(256)	(77)	(68)	(72)

[a] Percentages in this category represent respondents who mention security in at least one respect.

determination to be found in federal service as work-related reasons for planning a departure. Significantly, three of the common negative impressions which (as discussed in Chapter 6) the nonfederal populations hold about federal employment—inadequate salaries, insufficient opportunity to move upward, and restraints on personal autonomy—are echoed in these statements.

Turning now to the reasons people submit for continuing as federal employees (Table 9-3), we find that the most popular one is the security (stability, protection, and fringe benefits) afforded by the government. This is especially true for the general federal employees and only slightly less so for the executives and engineers. And although security is less dominant among the natural and social scientists, it is nevertheless of signal importance to them also. Not only is this value pervasive in comparison to other values; it is also large in absolute terms, being mentioned by three fifths of the general employees, executives, and engineers.[4]

Retirement benefits are easily the most salient aspects of security,

[4] In addition to emphasizing some aspect of security more often, the general employees also tended to specify more than one of the security factors more frequently than did the high-level groups.

with other protective benefits being a distant second. (Sick leave provisions constitute the major element of "protective benefit" references.) The only component to show a systematic difference among the groupings is job security, which is stressed more strongly by general employees than by the four special populations.

The following verbatim comments give an idea of the qualitative content and variety involved in the inordinate emphasis placed on security.

> "I've had all my experience with the government, and I do like the annual leave and sick leave benefits." *(35-year-old mail clerk)*
>
> "I have a few years with the government, and the job is rather secure, and I'm working toward retirement. I have ten years and I can't quit now, and those are the only reasons." *(GS 7 computer operator in the Navy Department)*
>
> "For one thing, I have been with the federal government so many years I wouldn't want to lose my pension at this stage of the game." *(Clerical supervisor, with twenty years of service)*
>
> "I want security. I want to work continuously, full-time employment. I want to keep the privileges of leave and security of insurance for my family." *(Widowed mother, a GS 3 clerk with less than five years of government service)*
>
> "Security. [What do you mean?] I'm in a groove—my age. If I should die the retirement plan would take care of my family. You're fairly secure in your work as there are no strikes." *(41-year-old GS 10 investigator for the Treasury Department)*
>
> "The job security, that's the whole thing right there. I have veteran's rights that help me to avoid certain 'rifs,' reductions in force that is; I think with these rights it's better for my family and me. I have been with the government eight and a half years; that makes me permanent. Puts me in a category only topped by the disabled veteran category." *(27-year-old Air Force expediter, without a high school diploma)*

Two other explanations for staying in the government are allied to the security factors. Many people point to the sheer extended length of time they have been with the government and the position of seniority attained. The main content of the statements is the general feeling of the employees that they have so much invested in federal employment that they cannot "afford" to leave—a feeling that suggests some inertia. And it is the executives, with their long average tenures, who most often invoked this reason. The other explanation, voiced by fewer people, was that they would not be able to obtain jobs elsewhere if they left the government. This would be either because of the *lack* of qualifications or (less often) the *presence* of peculiar qualifications and interests which could not be applied or satisfied elsewhere than in the federal service. As a 50-year-old transportation supervisor noted, "When a fellow my age tries to get a job outside, they turn their backs to you."

We said that these rationales of length of service and lack of other opportunities are linked to the reason of security. Like the security factors, they are only tangentially associated with the particular kind of work being done and the satisfactions inherent in the work itself. They are actually engendered by preoccupation with the extrinsic, material rewards of security and with the material benefits accruing through long service.[5] Taken together, references to security, length of employment, and lack of other opportunities account for more than one half of all major reasons advanced by general employees, executives, and engineers, and for approximately two fifths of the reasons offered by the social and natural scientists.

However, it would be misleading to disregard the importance of several other reasons for remaining a civil servant. One of these—the interest, enjoyment, satisfaction, and pleasure found in the work—is the second-ranking reason among all groupings save the social scientists, for whom it is the first. Significantly, this explanation is more common for all four special groups than for general employees. As we have noted before, a reason of this type lacks specificity about the characteristics that make the work interesting, enjoyable, and so on. Yet, in the present context, the response does represent a psychic involvement and commitment to the work—in distinction, for example, to the concern for security and related matters. Such feelings stem from the intrinsic, nonmaterial rewards found in the job. This involvement is evident in the following comments:

"Main thing is because I love the job that I have right now. [Anything else?] Once I love a job, I wouldn't want to go to a job where I'm not sure how it would turn out." (*52-year-old naturalized citizen, supply data clerk in the Army Department*)

"I'm satisfied with the work I do here, and the arrangements I have made. I debated a long time before I decided to leave teaching and work here." (*Married woman, a claims representative for Health, Education, and Welfare Department*)

[5] Another argument, infrequently advanced, provides a further hint of the emphasis on the desire for security. Around 5 percent of both general and special employees specifically indicate that they are wary or fearful of changing jobs, that they do not want to upset the status quo.

"Because of my enjoyment in my chosen field." *(GS 11 chemist, super-visor in the Interior Department)*

"I'm contented and have no feeling of making a change. [What are the main things that make you feel that way?] Well, there'd be no point in my leaving. My work is what I like." *(Accountant in the Treasury Department; rated her job at "10" on the occupational ladder)*

Other features that act to keep federal employees on the job include high or good remuneration and opportunities for advancement and progress.[6] Small to moderate numbers of general and elite employees also mention a good physical environment, satisfactory personal relations, and the vacations, leave, and time off available in the government. General employees tend to emphasize the physical environment and time off provisions more than other respondents. The engineers stand out for particularly low emphasis on personal relations (4 percent).

That federal employees possess a wide and intensive repertory of values was shown earlier (Chapter 4); not many of these values, however, are mentioned as reasons for staying with the government. Does this mean that such values are of concern and importance in the abstract but not in a concrete situation? We believe not, for the data suggest that the saliency of some values becomes subordinate to such others as security, interest in the work, financial reward, time off, self-advancement, working conditions, and personal relations when the issue is posed in terms of the few major factors operating to retain the employee.

The differences between the general employees and the four elite groups in the reasons they give suggest that differences may also be found among various classes of general employees. While the importance attached to physical environment and to personal relations is rather uniformly distributed throughout the general federal population, several other reasons received unequal attention from various groups within the general employee population.

Citations of the interest and enjoyment derived from the work as a reason for staying increase with rising education: from 21 percent for high school incompletes to 38 percent for college graduates. This reason also climbs, not surprisingly, with rising occupational satisfaction: from 16 percent for the less-satisfied to 40 percent for those highly satisfied with their present jobs. Postal employees attach significantly less importance to this motive than people in other federal grade categories; their

---

[6] Significantly, natural scientists—for whom special salary exemptions have been made—lead all groups in explaining their intentions to stay in terms of monetary rewards.

figure of 18 percent is doubled by the 37 percent of the GS 12 and over echelon. These findings are consistent with the showing that the four elite groups emphasize interest and enjoyment more than the general federal employees do.

The data for financial reward as an explanation contain one seeming paradox: employees with the very lowest incomes mention money as a reason for staying about twice as often as people of other income levels—31 vs. around 15 percent. The paradox is probably explained by differences in expectations. Given the limited present and potential earning power of people in the low-income group, their actual incomes are more likely to compare rather favorably with their expectations.

Women, younger workers, and employees with less than ten years of service in the government also place somewhat greater weight on satisfactory monetary returns. And younger and newer workers prove much more inclined than their older and more experienced colleagues to speak favorably of the advancement opportunities of government work. It appears that the federal government's hold on an employee in his first few years of service lies partially in the attractions of economic reward and self-advancement. But these attractions diminish in relative importance with advancing age and service time.

In sum, the blend of forces operating to retain the federal employee is complex in nature and varied according to the employee's station in life and time in service. Two facts, however, are particularly compelling. First, we cannot gainsay the importance of security and security-related concerns as retentive forces. Without these plusses, from the employee's standpoint, it is doubtful whether the government would be retaining its employees in present proportions. Second, statements about finding the work interesting, satisfying, and so on, vague as they are, and those dealing with satisfactory personal relations indicate that certain intrinsic, nonmaterial, nonphysical aspects of the job are persuasive retaining factors, especially among upper-level personnel.

Past Intentions of Leaving Federal Employment

As we have seen, relatively few of the federal employees interviewed have decisive plans for leaving the service at present. Among the many who plan to stay, it could be surmised that a considerable number had thought of leaving in the past, then decided to stay. Several of our questions were directed at gaining a clearer notion of the extensiveness of these past considerations, the reasons for them, and why the decision not to leave was made.

Of present federal employees, about four in every ten (39 percent) have considered leaving their government work in the past. However, these past thoughts of leaving are unevenly distributed throughout the general federal employee population. Although men and women differ little in their present intentions, men are more likely than women to have thought of leaving in the past (42 vs. 30 percent). And the higher the education, income, or grade level, the longer the time of service, and the lower the job satisfaction, the more likely it is that the employee has considered severing his ties in the past. By grade level, for example, the range is from 28 percent at the GS 2 to 4 brackets, to 57 percent at the GS 12 and higher. These results are not unexpected, inasmuch as the longer an employee has been with one employer and the higher his qualifications, the more he has probably been exposed to the pull of other jobs and the more frequently he has been in demand. On the other hand, the lower his job satisfaction the more he will have considered other employment in order to raise his level of satisfaction.

The importance of these findings lies partially in projecting future trends for recent and incoming recruits. Under present circumstances, it seems probable that new employees will follow the prevailing pattern of differential temptation during their federal work careers. Evolving personnel strategies to cope with these eventualities is a major task confronting the federal government as an employer.

Reasons for Past Thoughts of Leaving

The employees who had formerly considered cutting their ties with the federal service were asked, "What were the main things that caused you to think fairly seriously about leaving the federal government?" As one way of viewing the explanations, we determined their sources—that is, whether a reason emanated from negative aspects of the government job, from occupational opportunities outside government, or from personal and domestic or other matters unrelated to work, per se. Here we are mainly concerned with the work-related sources, since they comprise the overwhelming majority of those mentioned.

Sources involving negative features of one's job are typified by these statements:

"Monotony of work; couldn't get along with my supervisor. In general I was fed up with everything." *(Blue-collar worker with over ten years of government service)*

"I was doing mechanical work, and I felt my body was breaking down. I put in for a better job. I passed my civil service exam, but they would not give me the job. So I thought I would quit, for there was no reason for them not giving me the other job, since I passed the test for the exam, and the test never said whether they wanted a male or female. So I was pretty mad about it." *(35-year-old woman, a file clerk in the Air Force Department)*

"The fact that I was not getting salary advancement. It seemed to me that I was at a dead end. From the work I was doing I could not get any papers out due to the multitude of assignments. One must get papers out to get recognition and salary raises." *(Chemist in the Commerce Department)*

References to outside opportunities, either specific or general, usually ran in this vein:

"I had an opportunity to go into business for myself." *(Engineer who changed his mind fourteen years ago)*

"At the time I could have gotten a better job with better pay and a few more opportunities for advancement." *(Warehouseman who made his decision within last two years)*

"A job teaching in a university opened up." *(GS 15 seismologist with graduate training)*

The relative importance of these two sources is a significant matter. In no instance among the general or special employee groups do aspects of nonfederal work opportunities provide the major source of the reason for leaving. On the whole, federal employees are as apt (or more apt) to think of leaving because of something disagreeable about their work as they are to be tempted by greener pastures elsewhere. Allusions to negative features of one's job outweigh favorably inclined statements about outside chances by a ratio of 7 to 4 among general employees, 3 to 1 among natural scientists, and 2 to 1 among engineers. Clearly, irritation with one's own occupational world proved more salient among these groups as a motive for contemplated departure. The executives and social scientists, however, cite reasons emanating from internal and external sources in about equal proportion. That interplay between the two sources often comes to pass is explicitly recognized by those workers (around 20 percent of both general and special employee groups) who spoke of both negative aspects and outside pulls.

Looking further at the general employees, we find that they vary only slightly in their sources of reasons according to most socioeconomic classifications.[7] However, the less time a person has been with the government, the more recent his thoughts of leaving, and the lower he rates his present job, the more likely he is to dwell on the negative aspects of the job, and the less prone to mention outside possibilities.

To a great extent people giving these differently couched statements fall into two camps. Those addressing themselves to negative features of their job probably began to think of leaving as a consequence of these disturbing elements. On the other hand, the employees who speak of extra-governmental employment were probably spurred into entertaining thoughts of leaving by real or potential outside opportunities. Subtle as this distinction may be, it is nevertheless compelling. In the first instance the employees are more characterized by disenchantment, in the second by enticement. The first instance is much more a reflection on the government as an employer, and by and large the government is more beset by it than by the latter.

But what was it, *specifically*, about the negative features of the government job or the positive nature of the outside opportunity which made the employee ponder leaving? Whether the explanations, in effect, were aspersions on federal employment or praises of nonfederal employment, the *relative* disadvantage lies with federal employment. For instance, one employee might complain, "My working conditions were bad," while another might say, "The outside job I was offered was in a cleaner building." In either case federal work is being viewed as relatively worse with respect to working conditions. For the most part we may think of these reasons as occupational values which the employee felt were not being adequately realized in his current job.

Only three reasons are advanced by more than 10 percent of the general and (for the most part) the special federal employees (Table 9-4). Significantly, the two most prominent reasons, money and advancement, both relate to "getting ahead" and improving one's lot. Feelings about the government's relative performance on these two counts easily constitute the major substantive causes of past inclinations to leave.[8] This

[7] There is, however, some indication that men, the GS 8 to 11 bracket, and the middle-income groups were more attracted than others by the pull of outside chances, and that clerical personnel, especially the lower echelons, were less affected by such possibilities.

[8] Throughout this discussion it should be remembered that these are reasons expressed by people who thought of leaving, not by employees who actually did.

TABLE 9-4. *Major Reasons for Thinking of Leaving the Federal Service*

Federal Groups	Number Answering	Seen as Poor Inside Government or Good Outside		
		Financial Reward	Self-advancement and Progress	Relations with Supervisors
General Employees	(377)	31%	25%	14%
Executives	(170)	39	26	15
Natural Scientists	(47)	38	34	11
Social Scientists	(43)	28	28	12
Engineers	(51)	33	29	12

parallels the earlier finding in this chapter which indicated that considerations of economic reward and of self-advancement were the main work-related motives of people who are *presently* planning to quit the government; all three reasons (financial reward, self-advancement and progress, and relations with supervisors) also parallel the leading negative features seen by federal employees in their present jobs (Chapter 7).

While the general and elite employee populations do not differ markedly in the emphasis assigned these three characteristics, there are some important contrasts within the general population as a whole. Predictably, men are more motivated than women by a concern over income, but the situation is reversed when it comes to relations with supervisors. Professional and managerial workers seize upon self-advancement somewhat more often and on relations with supervisors a little less often than do people of other occupational status. The more recently the employee pondered a separation, the greater is his emphasis on self-advancement and his relations with the boss, but the less his concern about monetary rewards. Tying in with this relationship, there is a strong hint that the less sure a person is of presently staying, the more significance he attaches to self-advancement.

Reasons for Deciding To Remain

Most of the employees who reported they had thought of leaving eventually decided to stay; a few of them left the government for a period, only to return later. All of them were asked this question: "What

were the main things that caused you to stay in the federal government?"
Again, one way of looking at the replies is in terms of the sources of the
reasons. These were of three major types.

Some employees point toward *internal* sources, of which there are
two varieties. They might cite a real or potential improvement of their
federal job, as in these comments:

> "With no effort on my part I was placed in a better position, better grade,
> and from then on I went up." *(52-year-old professional in the Treasury
> Department)*
>
> "Things got better. [What do you mean?] I got a promotion and ac-
> quired more responsible work, more interesting work." *(State Department
> veteran)*

Alternatively, they might say they had reconsidered and re-evaluated
their job, with the ultimate realization that the job was satisfactory after
all. Notice this method of reducing dissatisfaction in the following remarks:

> "We were in the throes of a depression. Employment by the government
> was more certain than private employment and salaries were commensurate
> with private employment." *(GS 11 engineer in the Army Department)*
>
> ". . . then my wife and I talked it over and we decided that with the
> pension and sick time and your annual leave coming in things would be
> better." *(Long-time Navy employee who was initially disappointed with
> government employment)*
>
> "I talked it over with the Deputy Regional Director and he told me to
> think it over. I did, and decided to stay." *(Mail clerk for U.S. Civil Service
> Commission)*

Factors *external* to the federal environment are a second major source
of reasons. One subtype is simply that the outside opportunities fell
through for one reason or another:

> "I couldn't get located outside of government. I made applications, but
> all I had was government experience, and I couldn't even get an interview
> for a prospective job in industry." *(GS 14 who, at the time, feared he was
> going to be released because of reduction in force—"riffed")*
>
> "I never did get a job in private industry. I just didn't get around to it.
> Even then there was an accent on your age. If you were over thirty-five,
> they—in private industry—didn't consider you so fast." *(College graduate
> who was in his early forties when he considered leaving the government)*

On the other hand, the employee may have re-evaluated and reappraised
his external employment opportunity:

"I think that the main thing was I hated to start all over again. I would have had to start at the bottom of the ladder. Every new place has a new routine; I would have to learn all over again." (*Medical secretary in the Veterans Administration*)

"The company went on strike and I would have had to wait almost a year for my equipment. Veterans coming out of service were opening up fly-by-night businesses, taking the farmers' money and not giving them what was promised, and spoiling it for those who were trying to carry out a good honest business. I finally decided it was too much to fight against, and stayed where I was in the government." (*Assistant branch chief, now rates his job at the top of the occupation ladder*)

Finally, various *nonwork sources* may have prompted the decision. These usually involve personal and domestic matters, as in the case of the husband who explained simply, "My wife objected," and the man who said, "I had just signed a contract with a builder for a house and it was impossible to go at that time."

The general sources pertaining to intragovernmental (internal) matters weighed more heavily upon the employees than did those dealing with outside employment (external). Improvement of the job and general reconsideration of the job are each noted by one third to one half of the general and the special employee groups. Thus, while federal employees are most inclined to think of *quitting* their employer because of internal *negative* aspects (as shown above), they are also most often persuaded to *stay* by *positive* internal aspects reflecting changes in or re-evaluation of their job. And the internal aspects are commonly more persuasive than the external.

However, there is a marked difference in the relative attention given these two internal sources by the general employees vs. the four special groups. The special groups most often decided to stay as a result of an actual or anticipated betterment of their current job. By contrast, the general employees more often rationalized their contemporary situation; after a second look they decided they were really not doing too badly. Not surprisingly, this is more true of the less-educated general employees.[9]

When we consider the substantive explanations for past decisions to remain in government, we find that, if a reason deals with occupational values or characteristics, the employee typically broaches it as follows: "My pay went up, so I stayed," or "The job on the outside did not pay

[9] Other analyses revealed that improvement of the job (vs. re-evaluation) was noted more often by employees who thought of leaving over five years ago and by those most satisfied with their present jobs.

enough." In either instance the *relative* advantage is with government employment. In both cases, he is signifying the relative favorableness of income in his government job as the cause for staying.

Four reasons bearing directly on occupational values were advanced by over one tenth of the general employees and the executives, natural and social scientists, and engineers: interest and enjoyment in the work; self-advancement and progress; security; and financial remuneration. Other reasons given by 5 to 10 percent of the groups included doing work that fits one's capacities, long service career, and the location of the work.

Standing unquestionably as the most popular value-oriented reason among the general employees is the cluster of security factors. While the four special groupings are less inclined toward security as a value, at least one fifth of them (with the exception of natural scientists) do stress it. Earlier we saw that the security theme was the predominant reason for *present* plans to continue with the government; thus it appears that security has been a key retaining force over a lengthy span of time.

Over all, among the general employees the ordering of the four major occupational value reasons for remaining in the government clearly peaks in the security theme. The elite populations tend to have a more balanced complex of reasons, with interest, financial return, and self-advancement being of more equal concern.

There are a few points of special interest about the reasons offered by the general employees. Financial considerations are given about equal emphasis throughout various strata, but security aspects assume more importance among men, less-educated workers, nonprofessional and nonmanagerial personnel—especially postal employees—people over 33, and people who are least satisfied with their present jobs. Employees whose reasons were guided more by thoughts of self-advancement and progress come disproportionately from the other end of the scale: the better-educated, the professionals and managers, the more affluent and the occupants of higher grade levels, and people with medium and high levels of job satisfaction. These same groups also emphasize more than others the interest and enjoyment of the work—a value which the postal employees are noticeably unlikely to single out.

Preferable Kinds of
Nonfederal Employment, and Why

Since the bulk of employment in the United States lies outside the public sector, it is logical to expect many federal employees to be aware of nonfederal employment opportunities. As noted above, a moderately high proportion of federal employees have actually considered outside opportunities in the past; and these outside opportunities probably serve as one reference point around which they evaluate their present jobs. Consequently, all federal employees were asked: "Suppose a person in your line of work did go to work outside the federal government? Are there any particular kinds of employment or business that would be better to be in than others?" Those who answered in the affirmative were then asked:[10] "What particular kinds of employment would be better?" Replies were allocated as follows:[11]

Federal Groups	N	Business and Industry[12]	Professional Firm or Private Practice	College or University
General Employees	(559)	74%	20%	2%
Executives	(230)	77	22	5
Natural Scientists	(75)	53	33	32
Social Scientists	(74)	60	35	31
Engineers	(85)	68	34	2

While business and industry is the sector most commonly nominated by all groups, the general employees and executives are more inclined this way than the natural and social scientists and engineers. Similarly, the latter three groups single out professional firms and private practice more often. The greatest intergroup variation is the fact that almost one third of the natural and social scientists identify colleges and universities as good sites for them, whereas negligible numbers in the other

[10] The elite groups exceeded the general federal group in this respect: over 80 percent of the elite groups gave affirmative answers, vs. 57 percent of the general population.

[11] Figures do not total 100 percent for the general employees because the percentage for "miscellaneous" has not been tabled. Among the special groups, figures exceed 100 percent owing to multiple replies.

[12] When a specific type of business or industry was indicated, large firms predominated.

groups do so. Having the necessary qualifications for an academic position (increasingly the Ph.D.) is the most likely reason for this deviation of natural and social scientists from other employees. So in addition to the potential pulling power the business-industrial and professional worlds have for them, natural and social scientists may also be attracted to the campus.

Considering the general employees only, men, somewhat more than women, are disposed toward business and industry, but women prefer professional outlets more than men do. By educational level, the college graduates prove less enamored of business and industry, but 40 percent of them are drawn to professional enterprises.

The respondents who identified specific kinds of nonfederal employment as being better for them were asked, "Why do you think that?" Of the eight main reasons advanced, two predominate. Most common among general employees, executives, and engineers, and also fairly common among the natural and social scientists, is the thought that certain kinds of work would be better suited to their capacities and training than other kinds. The second predominant reason—that the work named would be interesting, enjoyable, or satisfying—is cited more often by the natural and social scientists and engineers than the general employees and executives. Although this value is, like suitability, unspecific, those who cite it are apparently implying that a necessary condition for preferring some parts of nonfederal employment to others is a basic interest in the work.

Other, and more specific, justifications for preferred parts of private employment are named by small to moderate percentages. The most frequent of these reasons among the general employees is high or good financial reward. On the others cited—security provisions, existence of high work standards, favorable active personal relations, and opportunities for self-development, self-expression, and creativity—there are no large-scale, systematic differences between the general and special employees.

Perhaps the major point to be made about this profile of the reasons offered for a hypothetical preference of certain types of nonfederal employment is that it does not reflect adversely on the employee's satisfaction with and evaluation of his own position as a federal employee. The two dominant reasons—suitability to one's capacities and the interest of the work—are minimal conditions which most people would want regardless of type of employment.[13] Other factors of a more specific nature are not (with the possible exception of financial reward) mentioned often enough to constitute any severe criticism, by inference, of government employment. At the same time, the fact that a large share of federal employees, especially the better-educated and those in the elite occupational echelons, are definitely aware of nonfederal alternatives and are able to see how these jobs would fit their own capacities suggests that federal employees have independent yardsticks and alternatives by which they evaluate their present employer.

Summary

1. The vast majority of federal employees presently intend to continue with the federal government. However, those who are thinking of leaving and/or are least sure of staying are most often the specialized, high-ranking personnel (except for veteran executives), and younger and newer employees. Thus the retention problems occur in the groups for whom the needs are likely to be most critical now and in the future. Similarly, past thoughts of leaving the federal establishment occurred much more frequently among the higher-placed and better-educated employees.

2. There is little question that a prime factor (in most cases the key factor) in retaining federal employees of all types, at present and in the past, is the security they see in federal employment. However, federal employees do have other reasons for remaining with their employer, and among the better-educated not the least of these is the feeling that their employment is something they truly enjoy and from which they derive inner satisfaction.

3. Complaints about their employment stiuation, rather than the allure of outside employment, is the more frequent source of past doubts about remaining a federal employee. Hence, it is probable that the disaffections experienced by the government stem more from failings of its own than from the enticements of outside employment. The three major substantive reasons for considering leaving were the relative disadvantage of federal

[13] Supporting this contention is the fact that these two reasons were also the two main ones offered by nonfederal employees when explaining why some types of federal work would be preferable to others. However, better financial reward looms larger for federal than nonfederal employees.

employment in regard to financial reward, self-advancement and progress, and relations with supervisors.

4. Federal employees who considered leaving in the past were most often led to stay by factors relevant to their present jobs, rather than by factors on the outside. However, the better-educated and occupationally situated people cite some definite or anticipated improvement in their jobs, whereas the lower-placed more often rationalized that they were not doing so badly after all. Thus, the employees who are more in demand were apparently able to extract visible improvements. The four major substantive reasons for deciding to stay with the government were: security (especially among general employees); self-advancement and progress; financial reward; and interest and enjoyment in the work.

5. Although business and industry are the main possible alternatives that federal employees visualize for themselves outside government employment, it is significant that the natural and social scientists also see, as alternatives, universities and (along with the engineers) professional and private-practice outlets as well. Similarly, the better-educated general federal employees express an interest in professional possibilities as well as business. The interest and suitability of the work cited are the major reasons given for preferring specific opportunities outside the federal service.

10

The Image of the Federal Employee

OUR PERCEPTIONS OF THE SORT OF PEOPLE who are engaged in a given type of employment play a large role in shaping our image of that employment. What we think of the profession of teaching, for example, is based to an important degree on the stereotypes we have made for ourselves about teachers. One of the aims of this study was to obtain as precise a notion as possible of the images that come to people's minds at the mention of "federal civil servants." To the extent that these pictures embody qualities which are generally admired, respected, and sought after in an occupational setting, they can be said to exert a positive effect on the image of the federal service as a place of employment. To the extent that the perceived qualities are not admired, respected, and sought after, the effect can be said to be negative.

What, then, are the generally held images of the federal employee? Do they include the ubiquitous bureaucrat so often depicted in political cartoons? Or the faithful postman plodding through rain or snow on his rounds, and the government clerk endlessly and haphazardly shuffling papers?

One way of getting at the picture was to ask all of our respondents this open-end question: "Now let's think about one particular kind of person in the Federal government. If you were to describe your general idea of a United States civil service employee, what sort of a person would that be?"[1] The range and quality of descriptions elicited by the query are of interest and significance in and of themselves, and provide

[1] At first glance this may appear to be a poor question, since there are, of course, all varieties of people in government work. Most people, however, do have generalized evaluative pictures. Some do not. Since the purpose of this question was to determine both the degree and content of generalization or stereotyping attached to the image of the federal employee, even the persons who rejected the idea of generalizing supplied us with valuable and relevant information.

the basis for some provocative group-by-group analysis. But how does the image of the civil servant stack up against that of his counterpart in the business sector of private employment? If we know that, we have another important measure with which to evaluate the civil servant's image. Therefore, a further question was put to the interviewees: "Turning away from government people for a moment, how about a person employed by a large private business or industry? If you were to describe your general idea of such a person, what would that be?"

Stereotyping and Over-All Tone of Descriptions

Four fifths or more of the respondents in all populations were willing to generalize about the civil servant, although respondents at higher educational and occupational levels proved a little less willing than others. The inclination to generalize about the employee of a large private business was slightly less, and this reticence again was most prevalent among the people with better education and more favorable occupational situations. Thus, there is an implication that more people, particularly those at the upper socioeconomic levels, perceived homogeneity in the federal sphere than in the private business sector.

What is the general tenor of the federal employee stereotype? And how does it compare with that of the large business employee? One way to assess this general disposition was to classify the *entire* description given by the interviewee in one of four ways: clearly favorable; unfavorable; about equally balanced between favorable and unfavorable (ambivalent); or neither clearly favorable nor unfavorable (ambiguous).[2]

The flavor of the favorable and unfavorable modes of descriptions are demonstrated by a few statements from the interview schedules. Here are three examples of favorable descriptions:

[2] By favorable characteristics we mean those which are generally revered and esteemed in our society; by unfavorable, those which ordinarily have a low rank in the American scheme of values; and by "not clear" those about which there is sufficient ambiguity in our society to prevent a clear labeling.

The rules of thumb used for such classifications are by no means infallible, although consistent rules were used in the coding operations and intercoder agreement was rather high. Because of the lack of precise standards, however, a conservative approach was taken in classifying the descriptions. That is, the components had to be *clearly* favorable, unfavorable, or ambivalent before being classified in that fashion. If doubt existed about the entire response it was considered ambiguous and "not clear."

"In most jobs they're meeting the public, so they'd be cordial persons. As a rule, they can be considered honest. They have a good reputation. If they have a responsible job, they usually have earned it."

"It would be someone who wants to work and get a better job. They would have to be smart and keep up with things, because you have to pass a test to get into civil service. If I was younger and had more education I would sure like it, but I am too old now to study and get all those new ideas into my head."

"A good, honest person; educated and able to do what he's supposed to do."

Now consider the decidedly different tone of these unfavorable remarks:

"Well, I don't believe they work hard. I know when it snows or the weather is a little bad they don't even get up to go to work. They have that sick leave; I never understood why they get that sick leave—vacations yes, but not sick leave. That's all I know. I guess they have a pretty snappy life—easy. When they don't want to go to work they just take off sick leave."

"A person with not too high intelligence. Someone looking for security. Not too sure they can stand on their own ability. Someone who wants something for nothing."

"A jerkwater bum. Has an 'in' with a politician. No ambition, no goals, lazy, no confidence."

Most of the over-all descriptions could be classified as either favorable, unfavorable, or ambiguous. Very few were ambivalent. From one fifth to two fifths of the interviewees in all groups gave essentially ambiguous descriptions. This finding is not unimportant, for it indicates that substantial numbers of people are relatively "neutral" about federal employees. Presumably, then, their impressions of the civil servant would not drastically affect their feelings toward the government as a place to work.

Far greater proportions of the interviewees, however, offered clearly favorable or unfavorable portrayals. Table 10-1 shows the distribution of these, as applied to both civil servants and employees of large business by all the populations studied. There are some remarkable disparities present in the general tenor of replies about the civil servant.

Most respondents in the general employed public, among high school students, and in the federal employee populations express more approbation than disapprobation of civil servants. But it is equally clear that some groups have a much less positive view than others. In general, the familiar pattern according to sex and education and in the special groups which we have learned prevails in the evaluation of federal employ-

TABLE 10-1. *A Comparison of Favorable and Unfavorable Over-All Tones of Respondents' Descriptions of Federal Civil Servants and Large Private Business Employees*

Nonfederal and Federal Populations	Average Number Answering[a]	Favorable		Unfavorable	
		Civil Service Employees	Large Business Employees	Civil Service Employees	Large Business Employees
Nonfederal Populations					
General employed public	(1,140)	51%	56%	10%	4%
By sex					
Men	(875)	48	56	11	4
Women	(266)	59	57	8	4
By educational level					
High school not completed	(331)	60	56	3	2
High school completed	(512)	52	57	9	5
Some college	(129)	42	61	16	5
College graduate	(139)	30	54	27	6
Students					
High school students	(358)	63	60	7	4
College seniors	(400)	33	49	24	12
Graduate students	(378)	26	34	32	13
Groups in education					
High school teachers	(278)	49	51	13	5
College teachers	(467)	30	34	24	9
Natural scientists	(119)	30	29	21	11
Social scientists	(104)	26	30	24	16
Engineers	(86)	24	43	29	5
Groups in business					
Executives	(282)	20	58	39	5
Natural scientists	(84)	20	41	31	2
Social scientists	(72)	15	46	37	4
Engineers	(88)	12	37	46	4
Federal Employee Populations					
General federal employees	(916)	66	50	6	6
By sex					
Men	(636)	64	48	6	6
Women	(280)	70	57	7	5
By educational level					
High school not completed	(184)	72	51	3	7
High school completed	(346)	66	52	7	6
Some college	(175)	61	55	9	5
College graduate	(156)	62	36	5	4
Executives	(266)	70	48	8	11
Natural scientists	(92)	59	34	8	14
Social scientists	(88)	56	41	16	13
Engineers	(91)	55	37	9	8

[a] This is an average of respondents replying to the two applicable questions. The two sets of numbers were quite close to each other.

210

ment also prevails in the evaluation of federal employees. Women are some-what more prone to give favorable descriptions than are men; there is a sharp decline of favorable depictions and a sharp rise in unfavorable ones as educational level rises; a similar relationship with education appears in the student population; college teachers are about evenly divided be-tween those with favorable and unfavorable impressions of federal em-ployees; high school teachers' responses are very much on the positive side; and of all the groups interviewed, the special groups in business are the most critical of federal employees.

When federal employees themselves describe the federal civil servant they are more charitable. However, it is worth noting that, except for federal executives, the upper educational and occupational level federal employees yield somewhat fewer favorable replies than the lower-ranked employees.

When we compare the nonfederal populations' descriptions of civil servants with their descriptions of large business employees, we find that the civil servant comes out on the short end. In not one of the non-federal populations does the proportion of favorable characterizations of the civil servant *clearly* exceed the proportion of favorable characteriza-tions of the business employee. The best ratio achieved is a rough equality of percentages—a pattern found among women and the less-educated em-ployees in the general work force, and among high school students and high school and college teachers. But many of the groups that are highly educated and well situated occupationally put civil servants at a disad-vantage; the most extreme examples of this occur among the business group respondents: only 13 to 21 percent give favorable descriptions of the fed-eral employee, compared with a range of from 37 to 58 percent for the business employee.

A comparison of the favorably oriented descriptions, however, reveals only a part of the advantage accorded the business employee. As Table 10-1 shows, a second and more discriminating factor is that in each non-federal population the proportions of *unfavorable* descriptions of fed-eral workers are almost invariably and markedly higher than those as-signed to large business workers. Thus even the groups wherein there was only a slight difference in the ratio of favorable replies put civil serv-ants at a disadvantage on the unfavorable measure. These two factors together—fewer positive and more negative portrayals of federal em-ployees vis-à-vis business employees—document a generally less advantageous picture of the civil servant among virtually all the nonfederal groups. The configuration is particularly sharp at the higher educational and occupational levels. Consequently, among the kinds of people the government is likely to need the most, from a quality standpoint, the image held of federal employees is the least positive, both in absolute terms and in comparison to the prevailing image about people who work for a key competitor of government—large business and industry.

The federal groups are less likely to be unfavorably inclined toward the civil servant. But there is an interesting variation here: they are also not much disposed to portray the business worker in an unfavorable light, in contrast to the nonfederal respondents' tendency to portray civil servants unfavorably.

The Civil Servant Described

Knowing the over-all tone of feelings about the civil servant supplies us with some valuable general information about the image of civil servants in American society. But it is important to know what the specific components of this image are, how the components differ among various groups, and how they compare with those attributed to the worker in business and industry.

General Employed Public

The range of characteristics attributed to civil servants by respondents in the general employed public is extensive. (Table 10-2 presents those mentioned by 5 percent or more.) But only one trait was singled out by as many as one fourth of the interviewees—that the civil servant has good personal character. This quality was described in a number of ways; the following quotes from the interviews are typical:

> "I think honest beyond reproach."
> "It would be a man of honesty and integrity, one you could depend upon to keep secrets of our government."
> "Very finest type—high moral character."

The frequency with which this response appears belies the notion that there is any substantial concern about the integrity of the nation's fed-

TABLE 10-2. *Major Characteristics Attributed to Civil Service Employees by the General Employed Public*

Characteristics	Percent of Respondents Mentioning
Good personal character (honest, ethical, high integrity, etc.)	28%
Capable of doing the work because of ability, training, background, qualifications	16
Good worker (works hard and willingly; efficient, dependable)	15
Agreeable personality (friendly, nice, neat, personable)	15
Security conscious (wants security, rates security high, places security above advancement)	13
Educational level above average	12
Mental ability above average	9
Not very ambitious (not aggressive or competitive, little drive or effort to get ahead, succeed)	8
Serves or wants to serve others (help, benefit others; dedicated to, interested in, serving others)	5
Sincere and conscientious worker—*tries* to work well	5
Poor or mediocre worker	5
NUMBER ANSWERING	1,142

eral work force, especially since there were virtually no attributions of low or bad personal character.

Possibly most striking among the figures shown in Table 10-2 is the meager 5 per cent of the general employed public that cites the civil servant as being service-oriented. This is significant, since the opportunity to serve the public is often held out as one of the distinguishing features of the federal service.

When the general public's picture of federal employees is refined according to educational level, some marked variations are seen. Although such major attributes as excellent personal character, good worker, and capability are perceived in about equal measure by people at various educational levels, several less frequently cited, but very significant, characteristics show interesting differences. One of the strongest examples is the positive relationship between educational level and the perception of civil servants as security conscious. The range of such responses climbs from 5 percent among high school incompletes to 27 percent among college graduates.

Other features which the better-educated respondents stress more are related to these perceptions of security consciousness. Thus, as educational level rises, people are more likely to portray civil servants as lacking ambition (from 1 percent among high school incompletes to 26 percent among college graduates); as liking, or adaptable to, routine work (0 to 9 percent); as noncreative, dull, and unimaginative (0 to 6 percent); and as poor or mediocre workers (2 to 12 percent). All of these characteristics would usually be considered "unflattering" in our society, and it is significant that such responses run universally higher among the better-educated.

When the image of the civil servant is analyzed according to the perceptions of men and women, we find that men, somewhat more often than women, see the civil servant as security conscious and also as lacking ambition. Aside from these modest differences, however, the picture of the civil servant varies hardly at all between men and women. Whatever may be the relative attraction of federal employment for men vs. women—and, as we have seen earlier, it is greater for women—the difference apparently does not reside in any gross contrast in the characterizations of the civil servant.

When we examine how the civil servant fares against the employee of a large business in the estimation of the general public, we find that he achieves a standoff with respect to many major attributes. Approximately equal elements of agreeable personality, work capability, good work habits, high mental ability, and above-average education are imputed to both types of employees. But in the two sets of descriptions there are four important divergencies:

Attributes	Civil Service Employees	Large Business Employees
Good personal character	28%	13%
Security conscious	13	2
Not very ambitious	8	1
Ambitious, high initiative	4	23

As might be expected, these differences in picturing the two types of employees become more exaggerated as the educational hierarchy ascends.[3]

---

[3] Interestingly, variations by education were considerably less in describing the large business employee. This is one reason why the differences in the images of the two types of employees are more marked among the upper educational strata. One

Groups in Education and Business

To a considerable extent the elite groups in education and business depict the civil servant in much the same fashion as do the better-educated respondents in the general employed public. There are, however, some nuances peculiar to individual groups. High school teachers are somewhat more disposed than like-educated members of the general public to invest the civil servant with several positive kinds of characteristics. In addition, whereas college graduates in the general employed public attribute service orientation to both federal and business employees in about the same low degree (4 and 3 percent respectively), the high school teachers give a distinct edge to the civil servant in this respect (13 vs. 2 percent).

College teachers in general, and college natural and social scientists and engineers resemble the college graduates of the general public in their characterization of the federal employee. Of the three special groups of college teachers, however, engineers stand out for some particularly adverse portrayals of the civil servant. For example, they are more apt than their colleagues to think of him as security conscious, lacking in ambition and initiative, and a poor or mediocre worker.

It was shown in Table 10-2 that the business groups rendered the least favorable over-all descriptions of civil servants. The substance behind this tone is easily discerned in looking at the components of the image. Compared with other high-level groups, the business groups less often impute generally positive characteristics such as sound personal character, capability, sincerity and conscientiousness, and good work habits. Congruent with this pattern, they more often see such qualities as inordinate concern with security, lack of ambition and initiative, poor or mediocre work habits, and adaptability and affinity for routine work.

It is not surprising that the business respondents also attribute to the large business employee many of the qualities which they see as lacking in the civil servant, while at the same time playing down other features by which they characterize the civil servant. The following percentages

---

relationship was strong and important, however. Ambition and high initiative are increasingly accorded the large business employee, the higher the respondent's educational level; the figures range from 14 percent among the high school incompletes to 32 percent among college graduates.

for 282 executives and 88 engineers indicate the differential view held of the two kinds of workers:[4]

Attributes	Business Executives Characterizing		Business Engineers Characterizing	
	Civil Service Employees	Large Business Employees	Civil Service Employees	Large Business Employees
Ambitious	3%	52%	1%	47%
Materialistic	1	10	2	12
Security conscious	42	6	52	6
Lack of ambition	38	2	40	2
Adaptability to routine	12	0	11	2
Poor worker	18	0	21	0
Noncreative, dull	9	0	10	1

General Federal Employees

How do the characteristics federal employees themselves attribute to the civil servant compare with those set forth by the nonfederal groups? One of the most significant findings about the specific descriptions given by general federal employees is the relatively high degree of agreement the resulting profile shows with the descriptions given by the general employed public.[5] Over all, there is only a moderate discrepancy in the specific components of the image—but when there is, the federal employees more often picture "good" qualities.

By educational level, the federal employees' images differ less than the images of the general nonfederal work force. On only three items is there a noticeable variation. Significantly, the more highly educated federal employees are *more* likely to depict the civil servant as security conscious and not very ambitious, and *less* likely to cite his agreeable personality. (There is also, however, a hint that college graduates perceive more sincerity and work capability in the civil servant.)

Just as the image of the civil servant held by federal employees and the general employed public show a distinct resemblance, so too do the comparative images of civil servants vs. business employees. Where there is a discrepancy between the comparative images held by the two

---

[4] The numbers are the average of respondents on the two germane questions. Differences in number answering the two questions were minute.

[5] The two distributions are compared in detail in the *Source Book*, Chapter 11.

work forces, the federal work force comes up on the side which imputes more positive qualities to the civil servant than to his large business counterpart.

Special Federal Groups

Compared with general federal employees, the special federal groups somewhat more often attribute to the civil servant sincerity, conscientiousness, capability, and service orientation. On the other side of the ledger, they describe him more often as lacking ambition and initiative, and they are less inclined to say that he has an agreeable personality. Thus the special groups perceive positive and negative qualities in the civil servant relatively more often than do federal workers in general.

The comparative images which the special federal groups, vs. the special nonfederal groups, have of civil servants and large business employees are predictable from what has been said thus far. Business and academic groups are more likely than their federal colleagues to see civil servants (compared with business employees) as lacking ambition, being security conscious, having an affinity for routine work, and (in the business groups) possessing poor work habits. Similarly, they give much greater emphasis to the business employee's ambition and initiative. The federal groups see less discrepancy between the two types of employees than their scholarly and business brothers do, and they see the civil servant in the lead with respect to such qualities as service orientation and sincerity on the job.

Student Groups

The image which the three student groups—high school juniors and seniors, college seniors, and graduate students—have of the civil servant follows closely the pattern shown by educational level in the general employed public. The high school students' pattern parallels that shown for high school incompletes and high school graduates; the patterns for college seniors and graduate students more nearly resemble the profiles offered by those in the general public with some college experience and the college graduates. There are also many indications that graduate students resemble college teachers in their views of federal employees.

Evaluations of General Federal Employees
on Five Characteristics

The free-response descriptions of the civil servant give us a notion of what is most salient about the image of the civil servant. There are, however, a number of characteristics of federal employees which may not be salient to some people but are of extreme importance in assessing the quality of a public bureaucracy. Therefore, all interviewees were asked to rate general civil service employees on these five qualities: "honesty," "interest in serving the public," "how well respected they are," "ability," and "drive to get ahead."

The distribution of mean scores is shown in Table 10-3. There is a definite range in the scores assigned for the five characteristics: the highest ratings by all federal and nonfederal populations are given to the honesty of the civil servant, and in absolute terms these ratings are rather high on the ten-point scale—all about 7.0. Coupled with the kinds of answers obtained from the open-end questioning, this evidence suggests that the concepts of a corrupt civil service which were engendered by events of the nineteenth and early twentieth century have largely disappeared. Apparently dishonesty and graft are no longer seen as the hallmarks of the federal service; the reverse is now the case.

Anchoring the lower end of the range of scores assigned by virtually all of the nonfederal groups are the assessments of civil servants on their drive to get ahead. Again the correspondence with the descriptions obtained from the free-response question is strong.

Ratings on interest in serving the public, respect, and ability all occupy intermediate positions between the high of honesty and the low of drive to advance. That these scores tend to fall much closer to the ratings for drive to get ahead than to those for honesty emphasizes again the high standing of federal employees with respect to honesty.

The federal populations differ somewhat from the nonfederal on the assignments of their lowest scores. Among general federal employees the ratings on respect share low billing with drive to get ahead. And the special federal groups rate civil servants the very lowest on the respect accorded. These groups seem to be sensitive about this matter—particularly the natural and social scientists and engineers; their assessments are all well

TABLE 10-3. *Evaluations of General Federal Employees on Five Characteristics*[a]

Nonfederal and Federal Populations	Average Number Answering	Honesty	Interest in Serving the Public	How Well Respected They Are	Ability	Drive To Get Ahead
Nonfederal Populations						
General employed public	(1,093)	7.6	6.8	7.0	6.9	6.6
By educational level						
High school not completed	(308)	7.7	7.1	7.4	7.3	7.1
High school completed	(495)	7.6	6.9	7.1	7.1	6.7
Some college	(124)	7.5	6.3	6.6	6.4	6.1
College graduate	(137)	7.4	5.9	6.2	6.0	5.6
Students						
High school students	(356)	7.7	7.1	7.0	7.2	6.7
College seniors	(401)	7.1	5.9	5.8	6.1	5.6
Graduate students	(379)	7.1	5.7	5.5	5.9	5.3
Groups in education						
High school teachers	(277)	7.5	6.4	6.6	6.5	6.1
College teachers	(464)	7.5	6.2	6.0	6.2	5.7
Natural scientists	(118)	7.7	6.2	6.0	6.2	5.5
Social scientists	(103)	7.5	6.1	5.7	6.1	5.8
Engineers	(87)	7.4	6.0	5.9	5.8	5.5
Groups in business						
Executives	(273)	7.7	5.9	6.0	5.9	5.4
Natural scientists	(84)	7.5	6.1	5.9	5.9	5.2
Social scientists	(70)	7.5	5.5	5.5	5.6	4.6
Engineers	(88)	7.6	5.4	5.6	5.7	4.9
Federal Employee Populations						
General federal employees	(934)	8.3	7.5	7.2	7.5	7.2
By educational level						
High school not completed	(184)	8.3	7.9	7.6	7.8	7.6
High school completed	(354)	8.5	7.7	7.4	7.7	7.3
Some college	(180)	8.0	7.1	6.7	7.0	6.8
College graduate	(162)	8.3	7.3	6.6	7.0	6.7
Executives	(271)	8.7	7.7	6.7	7.4	7.1
Natural scientists	(92)	7.8	6.6	5.6	7.0	6.5
Social scientists	(90)	8.3	7.2	5.8	6.9	6.6
Engineers	(98)	7.9	7.2	6.1	7.0	6.5

[a] Mean ratings on the ten-point, "high-low" scale; the higher the score, the higher the employees are rated on the characteristic.

below those assigned on other characteristics, and compared to their business and academic counterparts they rate federal employees just as low on this characteristic in an absolute sense. This does not necessarily mean that the federal groups themselves lack respect for their fellow employees, although this could be the case. Rather, it suggests that they perceive the public as according the civil servant a comparatively low degree of respect.

On the other characteristics, however, both the general and the special federal employees take a brighter view of civil servants than do their like numbers outside the government, and the differences are significant in a statistical sense. It would be surprising, and from the government's point of view disappointing, if such differences had not been manifested. Again, this finding parallels, in general, the federal-nonfederal contrasts noted in the free-response descriptions of civil servants.

On four of the qualities the evaluations vary significantly by educational and occupational levels and by employment sectors in precisely the manner we have learned to expect. In both the federal and nonfederal populations the ratings drop as educational and occupational status rises. On honesty, however, all groups view the civil servants most favorably and about equally high. Evaluations of federal employees are also strongly related to the occupational appeal of federal employment and to perceptions of federal employment as an avenue to success.

Evaluations of Top-Level Civil Servants and Businessmen on Five Characteristics

The evaluations reported above indicate something of the public's attitudes toward the general run of civil servants. But they do not reveal what the public thinks of the people in the highest echelons of the permanent government service, nor how the public feels high-level civil servants compare with any other top leadership group in American society.

When the ratings given to top-level federal employees are compared to those for general federal employees they are found to be universally and substantially higher among all populations surveyed, with the upgrading distinctly more prevalent in the upper socioeconomic groups. But how does the upper-level civil servant fare against his counterpart in the private business world? Using the same five characteristics, respondents were asked to assess these two higher-echelon groups: "people in the top-level jobs in the federal civil service" and "people in the top-level jobs in private business."

Table 10-4 presents the comparative ratings applied to the two types of top-level personnel. The entries represent the differences in mean ratings on the ten-point scale. The plus sign indicates that the upper-level civil servant is given the advantage, the minus sign, that he is rated lower than his business counterpart.

Even a cursory glance at the table reveals a basic division according to the positive or negative direction of the signs. With only one exception the top-level civil servant is considered the superior person on the attributes of honesty and interest in serving the public. In direct contrast, he is put at a disadvantage on the remaining three charcteristics—how well respected, ability, and drive to get ahead. Although some of the differences are not large, especially for the general public, the basic pattern is persistent and compelling.

This patterning clearly reveals that on the two characteristics which fall within the normative expectations of what top government personnel should be like—honest and service-oriented—they are, in fact, perceived as substantially "better" than top business people. But to dismiss this as not significant for this reason overlooks an important change in the image of top public servants. Not too long ago they were commonly viewed as always having a hand in the till, and more recently as being self-seeking empire builders much more concerned with aggrandizing their own positions than with meeting public needs. It also overlooks the general prestige our society accords the top-level businessman and the intense efforts of public relations experts to picture him as epitomizing American virtues and constantly directing his efforts toward making life better for the society. Our data suggest that the business leader's "halo effect" is imperfect, insofar as he is compared with the civil service leader on these two qualities.

However, when we turn to the other three qualities, the comparative image of the top-level federal employee does not fare so well. On drive to get ahead, the normative expectations attached to business careers clearly give a built-in edge to the businessman. Certainly one of the hallmarks of the business ethic in our society is the emphasis on "getting ahead" and "improving" oneself; the characterization of the businessman as actively oriented toward getting ahead in the world is pervasive—

TABLE 10-4. *Evaluations of Top-Level People in the Federal Service and in Private Business*[a]

	Average Number Answering	Honesty	Interest in Serving the Public	How Well Respected They Are	Ability	Drive To Get Ahead
Nonfederal Populations						
General employed public	(1,093)	+.6	+.4	−.2	−.4	−1.0
By educational level						
High school not completed	(308)	+.5	+.3	+.1	0.0	−.6
High school completed	(495)	+.7	+.4	−.2	−.3	−1.0
Some college	(124)	+.4	+.6	−.4	−.6	−1.4
College graduate	(137)	+.5	+.4	−.9	−1.1	−1.9
Students						
High school students	(356)	+1.0	+1.3	−.1	−.1	−.8
College seniors	(401)	+1.0	+1.5	−.6	−.5	−1.8
Graduate students	(379)	+1.0	+1.5	−.9	−.9	−1.6
Groups in education						
High school teachers	(277)	+.6	+1.0	−.4	−.6	−1.3
College teachers	(464)	+.9	+1.4	−.7	−.4	−1.8
Natural scientists	(118)	+.8	+1.8	−.4	−.5	−1.6
Social scientists	(103)	+.9	+1.9	−.9	−.3	−1.6
Engineers	(87)	+.6	+1.2	−.6	−.7	−1.6
Groups in business						
Executives	(273)	+.1	+.1	−1.1	−1.2	−2.1
Natural scientists	(84)	+.4	+1.3	−.4	−1.0	−2.0
Social scientists	(70)	+.5	+.8	−.9	−.9	−2.2
Engineers	(88)	−.1	+.1	−1.0	−1.3	−1.8
Federal Employee Populations						
General federal employees	(934)	+.9	+.8	−.1	−.3	−.4
By educational level						
High school not completed	(184)	+.9	+.3	+.4	0.0	0.0
High school completed	(354)	+.9	+.7	.0	−.4	−.3
Some college	(180)	+.7	+.8	−.5	−.6	−.9
College graduate	(162)	+1.3	+1.2	−.4	−.3	−1.0
Executives	(271)	+1.4	+2.0	−.4	−.1	−.7
Natural scientists	(92)	+2.1	+2.6	−.2	−.1	−1.0
Social scientists	(90)	+1.4	+2.6	−.8	−.1	−.9
Engineers	(98)	+1.5	+2.0	−.4	−.4	−1.2

[a] Differences between ratings made on the ten-point, high-low scale. Plus scores indicate that federal service people are rated higher, negative scores show they are rated lower.

in the mass media as well as in everyday experience. For the most part, top civil servants are not often depicted in this fashion, nor does this seem to be a part of their expected role. Given the ambiguity of the phrase "getting ahead"—that is, whether it means cut-throat competition or merely trying to improve oneself—the lower evaluation of upper civil servants on this count may be no cause for alarm from a government personnel recruiter's standpoint.

There is, however, reason to be concerned about the lower ranking of top civil servants vs. top business people on "ability" and "respect." These are attributes ordinarily held in esteem; furthermore, they are the qualities that highly qualified people are likely to look for in the associates they would have in a potential employment being considered. Although the reasons why business people are judged to be more ambitious than top government people are not hard to understand, we have more difficulty when we come to the comparative evaluations of ability and accorded respect. It is possible that top-level positions in the civil service are not truly equated with those in private business—that is, the "top" may be seen as higher in some respects in business. Alternatively, the jobs may be equated, but the civil servant may be seen as falling short of the businessman. Whatever the reasons, the evidence is reasonably strong that the civil servant is at a disadvantage here. On balance, the top civil servant comes out well on "should be" qualities traditionally associated with government service, but on three other important characteristics, two of which are unequivocally desirable qualities, he places lower than his business counterpart.

A closer examination of the figures in Table 10-4 reveals that while the basic pattern is the same for virtually all groupings the range within it is considerable. The federal populations, for example, show larger plus scores and smaller negative scores than comparable nonfederal groupings do; they are sufficiently identified with federal employment and employees to emphasize somewhat more the relatively good features of top-level civil servants and to minimize the discrepancies when top-level business people have the edge.

Another interesting subpattern is the tendency of the two general work forces to see *less* difference between the two sets of top people than do the special populations. But there are marked variations by educational level within each of the two general work forces. On the three qualities where the top civil servant fares least well in the general employed public, he fares progressively worse as educational level rises. There is a similar, but less consistent, tendency among general federal employees.

In the general employed public this negative relationship is not compensated for by a counter pattern for "honesty" and "interest in serving the public," for educational level makes little difference in the comparative ratings on these two qualities. The same is true among general federal employees with respect to honesty, but there is a decided climb by educational status on the matter of service orientation. The four special highly educated and occupationally situated federal groups amplify this latter tendency; they see the greatest discrepancies of all between top-level federal and business people on the factor of serving the public. There is no question that higher occupational attainment brings a sharper differentiation in this respect.

Among the special nonfederal populations, the business groups (especially executives and engineers) are the least disposed to give an advantage to high-level civil servants on honesty and service orientation. At the same time they are the most inclined to give large disadvantages to civil servants on respect, ability, and drive. This reflects in part a natural inclination to identify with and upgrade their own kind; nevertheless the other side of the coin is that, compared with the counterpart federal groups, they rate the top civil servant decidedly lower in absolute terms on all features except respect.

The civil servant gains his best comparative ratings from the students and teachers. Students at all three levels give a decided, and virtually identical, edge to him on honesty and serving the public. And high school students rate him only a fraction lower than the top business employee on respect and ability. But again the effect of increasing education is seen in the disadvantageous comparisons made by college seniors and graduate school students on respect, ability, and drive to get ahead.

Motives for Becoming a Civil Servant

Another way of eliciting the image of the federal employee was to ask respondents this question: "What do you suppose would cause a person to become a United States civil service employee instead of something else?" The motives attributed by different groups are many and varied. The group-by-group analysis that follows indicates the different emphases.

General Employed Public

For the members of the general work force, the security and fringe benefits of government employment dominate all other motivations. The number of respondents who give this reason exceed the number mentioning the next most common explanation—financial reward—by an overwhelming margin. Moreover, many people could think of no motive for entering government service other than secuirty. The following are typical comments:

> "I think they believe they have a job with security—that the government will always be here while a company could shut down." *(Molder in an iron foundry in Cleveland, Ohio)*
> "Another thing would be the benefits; they pay good benefits—hospitalization, and so forth." *(Printer in Dallas, Texas)*
> "Well, again, I believe it would be security. Job security isn't too easy to find nowadays." *(Electric welder in a small Iowa city)*
> "It would be just like the mailman—a job as long as he lives and he can retire on it." *(Medical center maintenance worker in a southern city)*

Most people who mentioned the security motive left it at that, without indicating whether they approved or disapproved of this feature of government employment. But a few were more critical, like the sales manager of an automobile agency in Ohio who declared: "They feel it's job security. Once on the payroll they never get off—just keep graduating, through the GS ratings, to higher and higher jobs for which they are less and less qualified."

Sizable but much smaller percentages of people cited inducements of the federal pay scale and an employee's personal interest in the work. A California truck dispatcher, for instance, suggested: "Maybe the government offered a specific job that appealed to him that private industry didn't offer, such as forest ranger." And smaller numbers mentioned the physical environment and general working conditions; the fact that the person might be capable of and qualified for the work; and the opportunities for advancement in government employment. This last factor was emphasized by a number of Negroes. One, a 39-year-old Brooklyn maintenance worker who had graduated from high school and was making about $3,500 a year, said: "I believe the government is fair to its employees. I think people have more chance of advancement according to their merits—more fairness."

The major reasons attributed to federal employees for entering government work that were given by a tenth or more of the general work force (N = 1,136)—and the percentages of people mentioning them—are as follows:

Security and fringe benefits	59%
Good financial reward	21
Interest in the work	18
Person is capable of and qualified for the work	11
Good physical environment and working conditions	10
Self-advancement and desire for success	10

Variations by Education, Income, and Occupational Level. Among the more highly educated respondents, the proportion of people who feel that the working conditions or the remuneration would lure a person into the federal service declines. At the same time, two other reasons are advanced with increasing frequency: a person might become a civil servant because he was unable to succeed elsewhere or because he lacked ambition and initiative. These unflattering explanations do not loom large in the general public as a whole, but among respondents with college experience or a college diploma they are mentioned by one person in every ten. Analyses by income and occupational level also reveal this same pattern—by now a familiar one.

Perhaps the most striking finding is how few people in the general employed public say that a person might enter government work because he wants to be of service to others. Mention of this motive, to be sure, does rise with increasing educational status. In addition, as we shall see later, a desire to be of service is attributed to the person who becomes a civil servant even more often by some of the elite groups in American society. But the 7 percent of the college graduates who cite the service motive, while larger than the 3 percent mention by respondents who failed to finish high school, is scarcely of overwhelming size. It represents but one in every thirteen of the college educated members of the nation's work force. The word "service" in the phrase federal civil service is not greatly emphasized by the working public at large.

High School and College Teachers

High school teaching is not a profession that makes its practitioners rich. This may be one of the reasons why the high school teachers among our respondents are more likely than any other nonfederal group to feel that the federal salary structure might cause a person to enter government work (Table 10-5). The group does not, however, put special stress on the opportunities for serving society as a motive; in this respect they differ little from the college-educated people in the general work force.

In general, high school and college teachers share with the employed public the conviction that security is the most common factor causing people to enter federal service. And they show a small strand of negative sentiment about the service—citing lack of initiative and inability to succeed elsewhere as reasons in about the same proportions as the college-educated members of the general public. But perhaps the most significant finding is that the college teachers, and particularly the social scientists and humanists (the humanists not shown), differ in one notable way from the college-educated in the general work force. They are much more likely to feel that a desire to be of service is an important factor that attracts people into government work.

Here is how some of the college teachers developed this theme. A history professor in Ohio: "He might go with the government because he would have an opportunity to work constructively. He does very necessary work." A political science professor in Massachusetts: "They enjoy the prestige and *élan* of the 'Government Man' idea. Even the mail deliverers have pride of service." And a history professor in California: "In times of

TABLE 10-5. *Reasons Cited by High School and College Teachers for a Person To Become a Federal Civil Servant*[a]

Reasons Mentioned	High School Teachers	College Teachers	College Natural Scientists	College Social Scientists	College Engineers
Security and Fringe Benefits	69%	75%	78%	74%	62%
Specific Job Opportunities	16	22	24	25	33
Opportunity To Be of Service	9	19	12	26	7
Interest in the Work	13	15	22	16	17
Good Financial Reward	22	14	15	13	19
Self-Advancement; Desires Success	8	10	10	10	7
Lack of Ambition or Initiative	5	8	5	5	13
Unable To Work or To Succeed Elsewhere	6	7	10	14	12
NUMBER ANSWERING	(282)	(470)	(121)	(105)	(86)

[a] Based on responses to the question: "What do you suppose would cause a person to become a United States civil service employee instead of something else?"

crisis the government stands as the institution that has a call on the services of the community."

Groups in Business

Through the preceding chapters numerous analyses have documented the rather critical view of federal employment taken by the elite business groups. The figures presented in Table 10-6 are no exception. And once again security emerges as the dominant reason for a person to enter the federal service. Among the business executives, lack of ambition or an inability to succeed elsewhere are mentioned more often than such factors as the influence of specific job opportunities or a concern for public service. Very few think a person would go into government service for the money it offered. Among the business engineers, a group particularly critical of federal employment, only 2 percent mention the pay scale as an attraction.

About a fifth of the natural scientists, social scientists, and engineers in business believe a person would be in the government because he could not succeed elsewhere. But there is one distinction within the group as a whole that should be noted. The natural and social scientists are a good deal more likely than the engineers and executives to feel that the public service motive is an important factor in attracting people to government work.

Considered as a whole, these business attitudes dovetail nicely with the

TABLE 10-6. *Reasons Cited by Business Groups for a Person To Become a Federal Civil Servant*

Reasons Mentioned	Business Executives	Business Natural Scientists	Business Social Scientists	Business Engineers
Security and Fringe Benefits	83%	81%	67%	76%
Lack of Ambition, Initiative	16	6	16	12
Unable To Work or Succeed Elsewhere	14	20	18	17
Specific Job Opportunities	12	21	27	15
Opportunity To Be of Service	10	21	18	9
Interest in the Work	8	7	8	5
Good Financial Reward	7	5	10	2
NUMBER ANSWERING	(284)	(85)	(73)	(89)

popular view of what America's business leadership is supposed to be: dynamic, go-ahead, venturesome, and interested in making money. As has already been shown, the occupational values of these groups do in fact reflect special emphasis on values of this type. It is clear that many feel that the federal civil service is the reverse of these things. The resident sales manager of a firm that manufactures lighting fixtures said of government employment: "People without ambition look for it. They hold fringe benefits above everything else." A California business executive's explanation of the government worker's motives was: "I'd say, in the main, a desire for security and stability—without a tremendous amount of desire to progress." "A need for security—a lack of competitive spirit," said still another businessman. And a sales manager in Ohio attributed the choice to a "personal make-up that makes people decide that they would prefer a static job rather than a job in a competitive field."

Some high-level business employees drew an explicit contrast between civil service employment and the business world—usually to the disadvantage of the government. A few, however, implied that they did not find the situation in business ideal. A 62-year-old member of the public relations staff of a petroleum company declared: "Maybe [they enter civil service] because of the pension rights and maybe because the work is easier than in business. The work is more commonplace and more settled, whereas business has a rat-race competitive atmosphere and some people are not physically or mentally able to compete in private business." But whatever form their remarks took, one thing is clear. These business groups reflect, in exaggerated form, the tendency of most elite groups outside the federal service to regard government employment as somewhat out of keeping with the dynamic qualities widely prized by the most successful groups in American society.

Student Groups

Juniors and seniors in high school, college seniors, and graduate school students share the widespread feeling that an interest in security and fringe benefits is an important motive for becoming a federal civil servant (Table 10-7). But these data for students also shed light on a different question. At what stage in the individual citizen's development does the security image of federal employment assume dominant importance? Table 10-7 shows the marked differences between the high school stu-

TABLE 10-7. *Reasons Cited by Students for a Person to Become a Federal Civil Servant*

Reasons Mentioned	High School Students	College Seniors	Graduate Students
Security and Fringe Benefits	36%	68%	71%
Interest in the Work	36	22	18
Good Financial Reward	15	15	13
Opportunity To Be of Service	14	12	12
Self-Advancement; Desires Success	13	14	10
Specific Job Opportunities	9	21	21
Unable To Work or Succeed Elsewhere	7	12	11
Lack of Ambition, Initiative	3	8	9
NUMBER ANSWERING	(358)	(403)	(382)

dents and the two college populations. About seven in ten of the college seniors and graduate students cite security as a motive, and their responses differ but little from the proportion of college-trained individuals in the work force as a whole who mention security. But the figure for high school students who give the security explanation is much lower—36 percent. And it is lower than the comparable figures for members of the general public who failed to finish high school (48 percent), high school graduates (62 percent), and college-trained people (65 to 67 percent). Thus, although security is seen as an important reason for entering the federal service even by high school juniors and seniors, the security image of government employment appears to become dominant only *after* an individual leaves high school, with the acquisition of further schooling or through subsequent experience in his job and life.

Over all, the high school responses are rather favorable to the government—stressing interest in the work as an attraction as much as security, and emphasizing other positive factors, such as pay, opportunities for self-advancement and success, and the desire to be of service. This finding corroborates the results of other analyses presented in previous chapters—all pointing to the conclusion that high school students are, on the whole, favorably disposed toward federal employment. The responses of college seniors and graduate students to this question are not generally hostile to the government, yet they are unquestionably less favorable than those of the high schoolers. Again, as in previous analyses, it is clear that the luster of federal employment declines as one moves from broadly based groups to the elite subgroups in the population.

General Federal Employees

The reasons given by government workers for a person's becoming a civil servant may or may not indicate their own motives, but probably do indicate the motives they believe their colleagues had for entering the federal service.

Federal employees echo the public at large in stressing security and fringe benefits as the dominant factor attracting people into the federal service—in fact, in exaggerated form. Whereas three in five of the general employed public give the security explanation, three in every four of the federal employees do so. Other motives cited (though by much smaller numbers) include the federal pay scale, availability of specific job opportunities, and opportunities for self-advancement. The proportion stressing the service motive is not large, but this factor is still mentioned twice as often by federal employees as by the public at large. One federal employee in every ten, however, asserts that a person might go into the government because he was unable to work or succeed elsewhere. The main responses of 938 federal employees are distributed as follows:

Security and fringe benefits	76%
Good financial reward	16
Specific job opportunities	13
Self-advancement, desires success	10
Unable to work or to succeed elsewhere	10
Physical environment, working conditions	9
Interest in work	8
Opportunity to be of service	8

When the attitudes of women federal employees are compared with those of the men, there are only two important differences. Women are more likely than men to say that the rate of pay would attract a person into the federal service—a finding that corroborates numerous other findings presented elsewhere. Secondly, women are more favorably disposed than men toward the advancement opportunities offered by the federal service.

When educational status is examined, the usual variations in attitude are revealed. In comparison with the less-educated employees, government workers with college training place less emphasis on security, and somewhat more on opportunities for service and the availability of specific job openings. The highly educated are also more likely to feel a person might join the government because he is capable of and qualified for the work.

Two contrasts with the patterning of attitudes in the nonfederal work force should also be noted. In the general employed public, the feeling that the pay might attract a person into government work declines among the more highly educated respondents; it does not similarly decline among the better-educated federal personnel. And the belief that a person would take a government job because he cannot succeed elsewhere, which in the general public rises with increasing education, does not so rise among federal employees. Thus we have here a hint that evaluations of federal employee motives do not deteriorate among highly educated personnel in the government to the extent that they do among the better-educated in the general public.

Federal Executives, Natural and Social Scientists, and Engineers

The foregoing proposition can be tested more fully by examining the responses of the special federal populations (Table 10-8). These high-level federal employees present the most varied and, in a sense, the most positive pattern of reasons for entering the civil service of any of the top-level groups interviewed. The range of reasons they give is wide—emphasizing a host of factors besides the familiar security explanation. Security and fringe benefits are again mentioned most often, but the presence of specific job opportunities is the second most frequent explanation, and it is cited by large percentages in each of the special groups. Many respondents also stress such positive attractions of government employment as interest in the work, the compensation, a desire to be of service, opportunities for self-advancement and success, and being capable and qualified for the work.

These groups also diverge from others in that for the first time a substantial number of respondents say a person might enter government work as a result of the influence of, or contacts with, other people. They were talking, however, not so much about getting a job through "pull," as of being persuaded by someone in the federal service to join his agency. Very possibly the top-level federal employees who mentioned this factor

TABLE 10-8. *Reasons Cited by Federal Executives, Natural Scientists, Social Scientists, and Engineers for a Person To Become a Federal Civil Servant*

Reasons Mentioned	Federal Executives	Federal Natural Scientists	Federal Social Scientists	Federal Engineers
Security and Fringe Benefits	62%	67%	59%	62%
Specific Job Opportunities	38	40	47	31
Good Financial Reward	22	22	22	18
Interest in the Work	18	17	19	22
Opportunity To Be of Service	16	15	18	16
Self-Advancement; Desires Success	16	9	9	14
Influence of, Contacts with, Other People	11	7	8	4
Unable To Work or To Succeed Elsewhere	10	4	13	8
Capable of, Qualified for the Work	9	10	17	7
Physical Environment, Working Conditions	6	12	8	4
NUMBER ANSWERING	(272)	(91)	(88)	(97)

were describing their own experience. And very probably the appearance of this explanation underscores the utility for the government of positive recruiting by those who are already in the federal service.

Some members of the special groups, to be sure, say a person might enter the government because he was unable to succeed elsewhere, but taken as a whole, the data in Table 10-8 have an encouraging message for the government. The federal executives, natural and social scientists, and engineers differ appreciably from their counterparts in the academic and business worlds in their explanations of why a person would go into the federal service. In addition to the greater fullness of explanation they provide—and the marked increase in the references to the availability of specific job openings—their responses have a different *tone*. Many more of them cite various positive attractions of federal employment; for instance, there are many who say that satisfaction with the work and a feeling of dedication might attract a person to the federal service.

THROUGHOUT THE PRECEDING PAGES we have concentrated on the things the American people do say about their federal civil servants. It may be well to draw attention also to what they do *not* say. They do not say that a person might be drawn into the federal service because it has a prestige that sets its members apart from and above their fellow citizens.

They do not say that federal officials are motivated primarily by a love of power—virtually no one raises the ancient fear of public functionaries who throttle the liberties of the individual citizen. Nor are Americans deeply cynical about their public service, for very few say that people enter government work to line their own pockets. Alexis de Tocqueville, writing in 1835 when Andrew Jackson was President, stressed the non-authoritarian nature of the American bureaucracy. "A public officer in the United States is uniformly simple in his manner, accessible to all the world, attentive to all requests, and obliging in his replies."[6] Most Americans would probably agree with that judgment today.

Perceived Work Activities of Federal Civil Servants and Employees in Large Business

The image people have of federal employment is likely to be affected by their impressions of the kind of work civil servants perform. An individual who thinks of the role a federal employee may play in shaping a city's slum clearance program will probably have a different conception of federal employment than someone who thinks primarily of the man who delivers his mail. And the person to whom many kinds of federal employment readily come to mind may differ from the person who associates government work with just one kind of job.

The impression that people in the general public have of government employment forms a crucial part of the general context of knowledge and opinion within which the federal service must seek to hire the personnel it needs. Yet equally important are the views of particular groups of people who have special skills; here the key matter is whether they picture "their kind of work" in the federal service.

Our respondents were asked two "what sort of work" questions: "What do you picture a federal civil service employee as doing—that is, what sort of work?" and "What do you picture a person employed by a large private business or industry as doing—that is, what sort of work?"

In every group of interviewees, there were people who refused to generalize about government or business work, but they were in the minority. In the general employed public, only 7 percent refused to generalize about government work; 18 percent refused to do so about business

[6] Tocqueville, *Democracy in America* (Vintage Books, 1958), Vol. 1, pp. 214-215.

work. In the general federal sample, refusal to stereotype was higher, and the respondents were frequently as unwilling to generalize about civil service work (25 percent) as about business work (21 percent). In both the federal and nonfederal populations, refusal to stereotype both sorts of employment showed a strong positive association with educational and occupational levels.

What sorts of work do the people who *are* willing to generalize see in civil service and in business? Our analysis deals briefly with three broad questions:

In comparisons of civil service with business work, what kinds of comparisons tend to be made by members of all groups—federal and nonfederal alike?

What kinds of comparisons are made by some groups but not by others; and to what factors are these differences in perceptions related?

How frequently do groups with special technical skills—such as scientists and engineers—see "their kind of work" in government compared with business?

To ascertain the common elements in the images that various groups have, we shall look first at the perceptions of the general public and then indicate which of these perceptions are shared by the other groups interviewed. The principal kinds of work that members of the general employed public see in the federal service and in business are summarized in Table 10-9.

Nearly all of the groups interviewed see professional work about equally often in the government and in business, but clerical work is associated more often with the government. In *absolute* terms, however, there is some variation in outlook, both within the general employed public and among some of the other groups. Professional work in government and business, which is cited by less than one person in every ten in the general public, is mentioned by up to a fifth of some of the elite groups. And clerical work in government, mentioned often by the general public, is emphasized even more by the better-educated among the general federal work force, and by the elite groups both inside and outside the federal service. Running through all the responses is a tendency for high-status individuals to see high-level jobs more often in both types of employment.

There are three broad ways in which some of the other groups differ from the general public in the way they compare civil service work with

TABLE 10-9. *Kinds of Work Civil Servants and Employees of Large Private Business Are Perceived by the General Employed Public As Doing*[a]

Type of Work	Percentage Seeing Specified Types of Work Performed by	
	Civil Service Employees	Large Business Employees
Management	14%	38%
Sales	0	14
Crafts	4	15
Operative (assembly-line, etc.)	2	18
Labor (mainly unskilled)	2	11
Clerical	28	18
Technical and Scientific	7	3
Postal	26	0
Protective and Law Enforcement	8	0
Professional	8	7
Engineering	5	5
Office	15	14
Refused To Generalize	7	18
NUMBER ANSWERING	(1,139)	(1,138)

[a] Based on responses to the questions: "What do you picture a (federal civil service employee) (person employed by a large private business or industry) as doing—that is what sort of work?"

Percentages used in this table are based on the total number answering the questions, not just the number who would generalize.

the activities of large business. On two factors the student groups differ from virtually all other populations; on another cluster of factors, the elite nonfederal groups and federal employees differ from the general employed public; and on still another cluster, federal employees differ from all of the groups not currently working for the national government. A detailed presentation of the data that underpin these relationships can be found in the *Source Book*, Chapter 13. Here we will limit ourselves to summarizing the principal findings.

Nearly all groups except the students share the tendency of the general employed public to see engineering activities about equally in public and private employment. Students, however, see them more often in business than in the government. A parallel shift occurs with respect to technical and scientific work, which most populations see as being done more often in government than in business. To the students, these activities are equally prominent in both kinds of employment.

The general public considers office work, desk work, or paper work about equally common to business and to government. High school students share this attitude. But among the elite nonfederal groups—and among federal employees themselves—this kind of work is more often imputed to government employment. The mailman's activities form a major part of the image that the lower socioeconomic groups in the general public have of the federal service; among elite segments of the nonfederal population, and among people who actually work for the government, the influence of the Post Office on the government's image is less strong. A similar pattern prevails for the government's law enforcement activities.

Despite the fact that the government employs hundreds of thousands of blue-collar workers, relatively few members of the general public see the work of craftsmen, operatives, and laborers as part of the federal service. A substantial number, however, see these activities in business, and most of the other nonfederal populations, including the elite groups, share this perception. Federal employees (many of whom are actually doing blue-collar work) diverge sharply from this tendency. They see craftsmen about equally in government and business, and laborers almost as often. And while operatives are still seen less in government than in business by federal employees, the ratio of the discrepancy drops from 1 to 9 in the general public to 1 to 2 in the general federal sample.

Perhaps the most striking difference in perceptions between people inside and outside the government concerns managerial and executive activities. For every three federal employees who mention the management function in business, two also refer to it as part of government work. In some of the elite federal groups, the discrepancies between the proportion who see managerial activities in the government and the proportion who see them in business are even smaller. In the general public, however, 38 percent mention this kind of work as characteristic of business and only 14 percent connect it with government. And in every other nonfederal group, the business world has a long lead over the government in the extent to which it is identified with these highly prestigious activities. For example, half or more of the college seniors and graduate students mention management activities in business, but only one in five do so for government. The proportion of college teachers who cite executive work in business is 58 percent; the proportion who refer to it in government is 18 percent. Even the business executives, who might be expected to place greater emphasis on the executive function in government, are about two and a half times as likely to mention management work in business as in the federal service.

From the standpoint of the federal service, these figures are little short of astounding. In reality, federal administrators preside over and direct programs of breathtaking scope. The erection of a gigantic dam, the administration of a social security system with consequences for almost every American family, the execution of a foreign aid program that dwarfs all previous efforts of this kind are activities that require thousands of individuals with managerial skill of a high order. Yet these kinds of federal jobs are inadequately perceived by the very people whose skills the government most urgently needs and for whom such jobs would have the greatest appeal.

Other special groups are also of vital importance. For example, the

TABLE 10-10. *Percentage of the Special Groups in Education, Business, and the Federal Service Who Mention Technical, Scientific, and Engineering Work in Government and in Business*[a]

Special Groups	Average Number Answering	Percent Mentioning Technical and Scientific Work Seen in		Percent Mentioning Engineering Work Seen in	
		Federal Civil Service	Business or Industry	Federal Civil Service	Business or Industry
Federal Groups					
Executives	(271)	21%	13%	8%	4%
Natural scientists	(92)	30	15	5	4
Social scientists	(90)	30	23	7	3
Engineers	(98)	26	14	20	15
Business Groups					
Executives	(286)	5	4	2	6
Natural scientists	(84)	29	26	6	9
Social scientists	(72)	7	7	3	4
Engineers	(90)	17	10	13	15
College Teachers					
Natural scientists	(121)	41	22	3	5
Social scientists	(106)	19	7	2	4
College Engineers	(87)	31	14	25	18

[a] Based on responses to the questions: "What do you picture (a federal civil service employee) (a person employed by a large private business or industry) as doing—that is, what sort of work?"

number of natural scientists and engineers currently required by the federal government is enormous, and continues to increase each year. Two questions arise here: (1) are the people with these specialized kinds of training aware of the government's activities in their respective fields? and (2) how does this awareness factor compare with their awareness of outlets for their skills in business?[7] One rough indication that bears on the questions is provided by the frequency with which natural scientists and engineers mention their kind of work in the two employing organizations. The perceptions of natural scientists, social scientists, and engineers in business, government, and the academic world, and those of business and federal executives are compared in Table 10-10.

From the data two things are clear. Those who have special technical skills are more likely to mention their own kind of work in both government and business. Engineers in colleges, business, and the federal service are more likely to mention engineering activities, and references to technical and scientific activities are especially common—both for government and for business—among natural scientists in business, government, and the universities. But from the government's standpoint, what is even more important is that these groups see their kind of work in the federal service as often as they see it in business—and frequently more often. As has been shown, compared with business, the government's managerial activities are inadequately perceived. But awareness of the government's engineering and technical and scientific work is substantial among the groups where presumably it is most important.

Summary

1. Four fifths or more of the respondents in all groups are willing to generalize about—or stereotype—federal civil servants. The percentages of people who are willing to stereotype employees in a large private business are somewhat smaller, but still large. This willingness to stereotype both types of workers declines among the higher-status groups.

2. In the general employed public, favorable descriptions of federal civil servants heavily outnumber the unfavorable descriptions; but among

[7] In this context we are using the term "awareness" to indicate whether a particular work activity is a salient part of people's stereotype of the work in federal employment and comes to mind when they are asked an open-ended question. It should not be supposed from these results that any given proportions of a group know or do not know, in a factual sense, about these kinds of work in government and business.

the higher-level nonfederal groups, favorable descriptions of the government worker decrease.

3. Federal employees themselves are more favorable than the comparable nonfederal groups in their comments on the civil servant; but except for the federal executives, the upper-level federal groups yield fewer favorable replies than do those lower in the federal hierarchy.

4. There is no nonfederal group where the civil servant receives a higher percentage of favorable descriptions than the employee of large business. In most nonfederal groups, he receives fewer favorable descriptions than his business counterpart. On the other hand, the federal groups give him the edge over business employees, although by smaller margins.

5. The characteristics that members of the general employed public attribute to the civil servant most often are good personal character, capability for doing the work because of training and ability, being a good worker, and having an agreeable personality.

6. Among many of the elite groups outside the federal service, however, references to these favorable qualities decline, and there is an increase in the number of people who describe the civil servant as security conscious, lacking in ambition, adaptable to routine, a poor worker, and noncreative and dull.

7. Members of the general federal populations are more likely to mention favorable characteristics of the civil servant, while being less likely to make critical comments; however, people in the elite federal groups make both more positive and more negative statements about civil servants.

8. In most groups, federal employees in general are rated quite high on honesty; somewhat lower on their interest in serving the public, how well respected they are, and their ability; and lowest on their drive to get ahead.

9. In general, top-level civil servants are rated higher than top-level businessmen on their honesty and their interest in serving the public. They tend to be ranked below their business counterparts on their ability and the respect they are accorded, and especially on their drive to get ahead.

10. In all groups an interest in security is the most common reason why people think a person might become a federal civil servant. However, some groups, particularly college teachers and high school and college students, lay considerable stress on other motives, such as a desire to be of service.

11. In the general employed public, clerical work and postal work loom large in people's image of the kind of work that is done in government, both absolutely and in comparison with their image of the work in large private business. Conversely, various types of blue-collar work are attributed more often to business than to government.

12. Among groups outside the federal service, executive and managerial activities are much more visible in business than in the federal service.

13. Individuals who have specific technical skills are more likely than others to mention their own kind of work in both government and business. At the same time, natural scientists and engineers in business and the academic world are as likely—and sometimes more likely—to mention outlets for their kind of work in the federal service as to mention them in business.

11

Recommendations

IN FORMULATING OUR RECOMMENDATIONS we were influenced by most of the study results—even their details and nuances. But certain major, generalized findings played the dominant role in our identification of the needs which the recommendations should be designed to meet. These findings are as follows:

1. *No simple global evaluation of the research results is warranted.* To characterize as "good" or "bad" the public's image of federal employment and federal employees or the patterning of the appeal of federal employment is an unwarranted oversimplification. We have seen that there are many very positive elements without which the federal service would not have succeeded in employing and keeping the large numbers of able people that it has. Other positive elements have been insufficiently recognized or utilized, and should pay handsome dividends if properly capitalized on in the future. At the same time, many serious negative features urgently need correction, in some instances even at the risk of sacrificing a portion of some of the "good" aspects. Furthermore, the fact that this research revealed elements which require correction or are susceptible to fruitful exploitation suggests that further research of greater depth with groups of particular interest to the government would yield additional information of great value.

2. *Throughout the employed population, both nonfederal and federal, the level of present occupational satisfaction is high, people feel they have made marked progress occupationally, and their expectation concerning future progress in their occupation also is very high.* All three of these factors are positively related to level of education, income, occupation, and the like. In the case of students, we find that they are relatively

242

modest about where they expect to start out occupationally, but far from modest about where they expect to be five years later. Their expectations are positively related to their present level of schooling and to their academic grades. Thus, the attitudinal environment, especially at the upper levels of excellence and attainment, is one in which there is a prime need for strong positive attraction in order to compete for trained manpower—a positive appeal which fully takes into account the degree to which people expect to move ahead in their jobs.

3. *For a substantial proportion of the public, including people at the upper educational and occupational levels, the question of whether employment would be federal or nonfederal is not, by itself, a crucial factor in employment evaluation.* In addition, in all groups substantial numbers of people favor federal employment, even though in many instances the percentages are small. These findings suggest that properly designed efforts to improve federal recruitment programs now in operation would show results quickly, and should therefore be given high priority.

4. *Occupational values display a consistent hierarchical, or steplike, patterning by education, income, occupation, and other measures of attainment in the employed samples, as well as by present level of schooling and academic grades among the student groups.* The lower the level, the more simple are the occupational concerns and the greater is the emphasis on physical, material, immediate, and extrinsic values. The higher the level, the higher is the desire for personal involvement with work, the more complex are the occupational concerns, and the greater is the emphasis on abstract, long-term, ego-rewarding, and intrinsic values. Occupational values also differ significantly according to type of occupation or training, as exemplified by the results for natural scientists, social scientists, and engineers, and for college students according to major field of study. Finally, occupational values show systematic differences according to type of employing organization—as shown, for example, by the comparative results for high-level groups in colleges, businesses, and in the federal government. Differential demands call for differentiated responses.

Thus, more than in the past, the federal government should move beyond across-the-board satisfaction of the kinds of fundamental occupational values which are of general concern. To the extent possible, it should undertake to offer occupational rewards tailored to the needs and values of people at various levels and with various types of occupation and training. Beyond this, it should emphasize the special occupational rewards it can offer as an organization by virtue of its unique role in society and of the scope, importance, and nature of the missions it performs.

5. *Among people outside the federal government, the image of what the government has to offer most closely parallels the occupational values of those at the lower, rather than the higher, levels of attainment.* Also, the higher their level of attainment, the more likely are people to point to the absence in government of the kinds of occupational rewards which are of concern to them; the lower their level, the more likely are they to see in federal employment the kinds of restricted "bread-and-butter" rewards which tend to be of primary concern to them, and the less likely are they to point to any deficiencies or negative features. The same pattern prevails with respect to the evaluations people make of the motives, virtues, and faults of federal employees—persons of higher attainment are much more likely to make negative evaluations, and vice versa. These judgments have their counterpart in the degree to which federal employment appeals to people; here too the results show a strong and consistent negative relationship with income, education, and occupational level.

Thus the image of the federal service harmonizes closely with the occupational values and attitudes of those groups in society from whom its personnel needs in relation to available resources are least; it is dangerously out of phase with the occupational values and attitudes of those groups in society for whom its present and projected personnel needs are greatest, and for whom competition from the private sphere and other levels of government will be most severe.

6. *An important exception to the preceding generalization occurs in the student population. Among high school juniors and seniors, college seniors, and graduate students, level of excellence as measured by academic grades shows no negative relationship with the appeal of federal employment.* Among high school students, there is even a moderate positive relationship. In all three student groups, the better students tend to rate federal employment above large private business employment, while the poorer students tend to do the opposite. High school students with "A" grades give the government an especially great advantage, both absolutely and in comparison to large business. Thus, other things being equal, the government should have no more difficulty (and perhaps less) in attracting superior students than in attracting the less able;

in recruiting superior students it should have a significant advantage over a major competitor—large private business. However, other things are not equal, and what evidence we have suggests that things do not often enough work out this way for the government. The government should act to capitalize more fully on this attitudinal asset among students.

7. *Among the special nonfederal populations studied, those in the high schools have the most favorable outlook on what federal employment has to offer, on federal employees, and on the over-all appeal of working for the government.* This is true of the junior and senior students, especially the better ones, and of high school teachers, especially the vocational counselors. In colleges, the outlook is far more negative, among both students and faculty (especially engineers), and most, if not all, of the attitudinal advantage to the government among superior students is lost. In the business community the greatest negativism of all is found; it is especially great among the executives and engineers.

8. *Guaranteed security of job, income, and retirement dominates the image people have of what federal employment has to offer.* This is true of all groups, both in and out of government. Yet security of this kind, important though it undoubtedly is, is not currently a matter of major concern to people, especially at the upper reaches of employment and education. The evidence strongly suggests that it has no great present utility as a recruiting appeal for the highly qualified, even though it does have substantial value in retaining such people in the government, especially after ten or so years of service.

However, security of another kind does have strong appeal for the highly qualified. That is the security that comes from feeling that one is maintaining a high degree of personal qualification through utilizing continuing opportunities for further development of one's abilities and capacities. A few high-level people outside the government see in federal employment some features that reinforce security of this kind, but much more commonly such people note their absence or see features that nullify or destroy it.

9. *The patterns of occupational values and the images of federal employment among women both in and out of government are such that the federal service is viewed more favorably by women than by men, and it appeals more strongly to women than to men. And in upper-level groups, men, including those in the government, tend strongly to see federal employment as more suitable for women than for men.* These find-

ings have both a positive and a negative aspect. On the positive side is the advantage to the government in recruiting and utilizing able and well-trained women. The negative aspect stems from the fact that there is no great tendency for men and women to see different rewards in government work; rather, the rewards it is seen as offering are judged to be more closely in accord with the occupational values of women than of men. This is disquieting in view of the fact that, except in a very few occupational categories, the major source of highly trained personnel is in the male half of the population. One can scarcely deny the desirability of having a service that appeals strongly to women, nor the wisdom and morality of continued efforts to make equal opportunity fully effective for women. At the same time it should be clearly recognized that there are very real hazards involved unless steps are taken to greatly enhance in the government the kinds of occupational rewards that are of primary concern to men.

10. *The occupational image of the federal government tends to be poorly differentiated both with respect to occupational levels and parts of government.* People outside the government tend to see the occupations in the federal service in terms of a relatively undifferentiated stereotype in which there are some elements of managerial, professional, and scientific work, but in which the overwhelming element is paper work and clerical-type work. With respect to the public's perceptions of particular parts of government offering employment opportunities, most people see the government as a sort of conglomerate mass in which they identify, in a general way, one or two departments or agencies where the particular kind of work they know how to do is being performed. Although these generalizations are less true among the well-educated and the technically trained, even there they apply to substantial proportions.

11. *In many respects, the public's image of federal employment does not fit the perceptions of those who are actually in federal employment.* In general, the discrepancy is not great in the lower educational and occupational strata but is substantial at the upper levels. It is especially significant that higher-level federal employees tend to see in government service many of the kinds of occupational values which appeal most strongly to people with high-level training, while highly trained people outside the government tend *not* to see such values in federal employment. College graduates in general, executives, natural scientists, social scientists, and engineers who work for the federal government see in

federal employment elements of personal growth and development, challenge, self-determination and freedom, opportunity for service, and so on, which their counterparts outside of government, especially in the business community, do not perceive—or feel are negated—in federal employment.

One measure of what federal employment is. *really* like is what those in government employment say about it. The fact that there is such a discrepancy between what they perceive and what outsiders perceive means that the positive features of federal employment are not being adequately communicated to those outside the government.

12. *Despite the preceding generalization, federal employment is not adequately suited to the occupational values of personnel at the upper educational and occupational levels.* Several lines of evidence provide compelling support for this conclusion. For example: federal employees' ratings of their occupational satisfaction, sense of progress, and expectation for the future do not show the substantial positive relationships with educational level found in the nonfederal work force; also, the groups at the two lower educational levels yield scores equal to or above those of their counterparts outside, while the groups with some college experience or a college diploma show markedly lower ratings than those of their counterparts outside. The higher the education and occupation of the federal employee, the stronger is the appeal of nonfederal employment, and the more likely is he to feel that occupational values of major concern to him can be more fully realized in private employment. Upper-echelon personnel are much more likely than lower-level personnel to say that government employment is better suited to women than to men. The better-educated and more highly placed are more likely than others in government to see essential elements of success and opportunity as missing in the federal service.

13. *Upper-level federal employees feel underpaid relative to lower-level federal employees and compared to their counterparts outside the government, even though material considerations do not rank as high in their hierarchy of occupational values.*

14. *In all segments of the population, federal employees are judged high on honesty.* There is scarcely any suggestion, even among those groups who have the most negative things to say, that federal employees are self-seeking, dishonest, or users or peddlers of influence. On the other hand, there is a strong tendency in the general public (and a moderate

tendency even among federal employees), positively related to educational and occupational level, to characterize federal employees as unambitious, lacking in drive and initiative, security conscious, routine-minded, and the kind of people who are unable to work or succeed elsewhere.

AT THIS POINT WE WISH TO MAKE CLEAR our awareness that, although our recommendations grow out of the study findings, they are not *dictated* by them. In the research process itself, a researcher's attitudes and values inevitably play a role, but an effort is made to control their influence in the interest of clarifying what *is*. On the other hand, deciding what *ought* to be is almost entirely a matter of attitudes and value judgments, and deciding the *means* of moving from what is to what ought to be involves other attitudes and values, collateral knowledge, arbitrary choices, and, hopefully, some creative invention.

Thus, in formulating our recommendations, a number of considerations in addition to the research results were involved. In the forefront of our attention was the fact that in the economy as a whole, and especially in the federal government, manpower requirements are moving at an accelerating pace in the direction of higher levels of training and expertise. It is our conviction that the national interest requires that the federal government do a more effective job than it is now doing in attracting, retaining, developing, and properly utilizing such personnel.[1] It is to these ends that our proposals are directed.

Furthermore, other people were involved. We discussed at length the major study findings with several hundred people in and out of government, asking for their ideas and for their reactions to recommendations we had tentatively formulated. Included were personnel directors, legislators, legislative staff members, White House staff members, labor union officials, Civil Service Commission personnel, federal college recruiters, college faculty, businessmen, federal executives, and many others. During the course of these discussions we learned, not to our great surprise, that many of our specific "new" proposals have a prior history, and are "ours" only in the sense that we have put them down here, and, of course, take responsi-

[1] As indicated in Chapter 1, only a distorted view of the total needs for talented personnel of all segments of American society—both public and private—would suggest that the government should receive more than a portion of the ablest people. The situation would be equally out of balance if the government were attracting too many of the ablest individuals at the expense of other sectors of the economy. At the present time, however, any danger of this is exceedingly remote.

bility for having done so. We found that many of them have been or are being tried in some form somewhere in the government, and, furthermore, that it would be virtually impossible to enumerate in a single volume all the meritorious but highly specific actions that might be taken. We also were made aware, occasionally to an almost discouraging degree, of the manifold attitudinal, operational, and political obstacles which any set of recommendations will face. At the same time, we encountered no apathy. In all quarters we found sincere interest and, despite sharp differences of opinion concerning the value or feasibility of specific proposals, a positive response to the idea of constructive change.

With these considerations in mind we go beyond our research role, and make the following recommendations.

Specific Recommendations

Manpower Projections

There is a disturbing scarcity of organized concrete information concerning the types, amounts, and location of federal personnel needs and shortages, both present and anticipated. The fact is, there is nowhere available a comprehensive analysis of the present and projected personnel needs of the federal government. A pilot effort to make such an analysis and projection for the period 1958 to 1963 was published in 1960 by the Civil Service Commission. However, it covered only physical scientists, psychologists, technicians, engineers, and medical officers; the techniques used were not well validated; and no re-projections or evaluative follow-ups have appeared

Beginning as soon as possible, there should be provided annually a year-by-year government-wide manpower projection which takes into account both demand and supply during the next five years. This five-year projection should be corrected and reprojected each year. It should project the over-all situation by occupational classification, and provide subsidiary analyses by regions of the country, major departments and agencies, types of programs, and so on.

It should highlight not only potential needs and shortages, but also types and locations of declining need due to such matters as changing government functions and technological change. It must be planned as a continuing program with the full realization that for the first year or two many of the projections will miss the mark by considerable amounts. Several years of experience and research will be needed to achieve results that can be used with full confidence. But that should not be a deterrent; rather it should be a stimulus to beginning immediately. The information it will provide is urgently needed for better performances in planning recruitment, reducing delay between examination and appointment, planning training and retraining, adjusting emphases in public information and education, judging the feasibility of new programs and their effects on competition for personnel, improving budget estimates and justification, and in judging the government's position relative to the total national supply and the needs of other segments of the economy.

We understand that, as of autumn 1963, work on manpower projection is in progress at the Civil Service Commission. We hope that it is being done well, is backed by adequate funds, has high priority, and will be carried out as a continuing program. We have made this the first of our specific recommendations, not because it is most closely related to our study results, but because it is so fundamental to improved performance in the many areas in which our research shows improvement is needed.

Recruitment Procedures

Because of the indications in our data that improved recruitment should offer immediate and substantial payoff, we explored the problem informally with personnel administrators both in and out of government, college faculty and placement officers, college students, federal recruiters, and others. The most immediate need is for a substantial reduction in the time lag between examination and appointment. Qualified people, especially the most highly qualified, are far too often hired by others during the weeks—and often months—that elapse before the government makes a firm offer of a job. Most departments and agencies can and should improve the situation themselves through better personnel planning and forecasting and through streamlining processing procedures.

In addition, college recruitment undoubtedly would be improved if the individual college recruiters were given greater opportunity to build and maintain more enduring relationships with faculty members and placement officials. Some part-time recruiters and federal employees whose primary work is not in the personnel field have been, and are, effective in attracting people to the federal service. They should be used for this in the future. But short-term assignments to recruiting and "crash" operations during the pregraduation rush are relied upon too much. College recruiting should also be a long-term assignment for able people with special training. Repeated visits should be made to the same campuses throughout the year, year after year. Building up channels of information and influence as a means of locating able students early and interesting them in federal employment requires patience, knowledge, skill, and time.

Public Information and Education

The need for a strong, well-planned program of public information and education is underlined by the evidence that many of the positive values actually present in federal employment are not now being communicated adequately to the public, particularly at the upper levels, and that the images of federal employment and federal employees lack differentiation and are strongly tinged with perceptions of mediocrity and limited appeal. In addition, the public's grasp of factual information concerning federal employment is inadequate.

What is needed is not simply *more* public information and education, although some expansion in total amount may prove justified. Since any such program necessarily will have limited resources of money and personnel, it must be tailored to the nature of the problem. This means careful identification of the target groups as well as the content and form of what is to be communicated. Our study results make possible a number of specific recommendations concerning these matters.

1. A general program of public information and education should be directed primarily at the upper educational and occupational levels in the population. These are people for whom present and projected needs are greatest and for whom competition will be most severe, yet these very people have the most negative image of federal employment in relation to the occupational values with which they are most concerned. This recommendation has operational meaning for both the procedures and the content of the public information effort. For example, the program should use media which are the most read or listened to by the better-educated, use relevant established groups, such as professional societies, and be written or presented in a manner appropriate to the level of the intended

audience. The content, in addition to being scrupulously truthful and accurate, should emphasize those aspects of government employment and activities which appeal to the values and interests of such people. Continued use should be made of manpower projection data to further pinpoint, and appeal to, the types of upper-level personnel needed.

2. A stepped-up special program of information and education directed at colleges and universities should be undertaken with special emphasis on reaching the faculty. This program is highly desirable because of the degree to which faculty attitudes influence student attitudes throughout the college years. The means of doing this are many. They include continued and intensive contact by federal recruiters; the production of special films and monographs useful in college teaching; greater federal participation in professional and scientific societies; encouragement of federal personnel to publish in professional and scientific journals; and increased opportunity for faculty to have meaningful short-term federal employment.

3. There should be a special program, at least equal in magnitude to the college program, directed at the high school level and employing many of the same procedures. Several considerations support this conclusion. One of the most important is that the atmosphere is receptive among high school teachers and students, thus offering a great opportunity to reinforce the positive outlook and factual knowledge of young people before they are subjected to the atmosphere of negativism toward federal employment which is so much more characteristic of the college and business worlds. In general, among high school students, as compared to college students, patterns of occupational values are more congruent with the occupational values they perceive in federal employment, and this is especially true of the most able students. A program aimed at long-range results should take advantage of these facts.

IN ALL THREE PROGRAMS, occupational security—in the sense of job guarantees, retirement provisions, and the like—should be de-emphasized.[2] Security of this kind completely dominates the image of federal employment, even to an unrealistic degree, for all groups in our society, but it is not a matter of much concern to the kinds of people to whom federal employment must be made to appeal. These people take such security

[2] This is already being done by the Civil Service Commission and many departments and agencies.

for granted and judge occupational appeal in terms of more positive values. As noted before, the kind of security that concerns them comes through continued opportunity to maintain and enhance their capacities and skills.

In all three programs, but particularly in regard to the high schools and colleges, special attention should be given to increasing the differentiation of the image of federal employment, with respect both to the kinds and levels of occupations available and to the variety of activities and missions involved in governmental affairs. At present, most people show little awareness of the great variety and scope of governmental activities, a fact that can only have a depressing effect on the amount of consideration given to the federal service as an avenue of employment. Yet the reality is that the variety of jobs in the federal government is almost as great as in the entire private sphere, and that the proportion of high-level jobs is greater in the government than outside. This is one of the prime ironies of the public's image of federal employment.

Ambassadors to the Public

Upper-level career employees in government should be encouraged to act as informal ambassadors to the public. On the whole, they have a favorable constellation of values and attitudes toward their employment. They see in government work far greater elements of opportunity, challenge, self-development, self-determination, and the like than do their counterparts outside, especially in the business world. In addition—and this is our private judgment based on extensive contact—the great majority of career people at the top federal levels are impressive for their ability, intelligence, and dedication.

What we are recommending is not just a general directive to upper-level employees suggesting that they ought to spend some time on public "ambassadorial" activities. We are recommending a formal program in which carefully selected people are assigned such responsibility as a part of their job. They should, within limits, be given the authority to call on other federal personnel for aid, have the use of secretarial and other supportive help, and be reimbursed for travel, memberships, meals, and other expenses incurred. They should take an active role in community activities and organizatons, giving priority to developing good relations with business groups, colleges, and high schools.

Personnel Exchange

A large pilot program of short-term exchange of upper-level personnel between the federal career service, colleges and high schools, and, to the extent feasible, business organizations should be inaugurated. The program should be carefully designed to give worthwhile, temporary on-the-job experience in the federal career service to professional, scientific, managerial, and other high-level nonfederal personnel, while giving federal career personnel on-the-job experience outside the federal service.

The objections and difficulties such a program is likely to encounter are many. The problems involved would include security, conflict of interest, fear of loss of able personnel, the tendency to free only the most dispensable for exchange, and so forth. However, we feel that the existence of such problems does not warrant rejection of the proposal, even though the problems do underline the need for careful creative planning, for proceeding at first on a pilot basis, and for incorporating in the program from the beginning provisions for continuing and systematic evaluation.

Properly carried out, personnel exchange would encourage mutual appreciation of problems, help to educate the public concerning the career service, broaden the perspective of federal personnel, and bring fresh points of view to bear on problems. It would take advantage of the facts that federal employment offers the high-level employee a more positive experience than is presently appreciated by such a person outside the federal government, and that the upper-echelon federal employee's attitude toward federal employment is sufficiently positive to make him an effective representative.

Occupational Security Legislation and Policy

In decisions related to further legislation and policy formulation concerning job security and protective fringe benefits, it should be recognized clearly that security in the sense of protection has strong recruitment appeal only for those groups who present little or no recruitment problem. Its value in helping to solve the high-level personnel problem is in *retention*, especially of those who have been in federal employ for about ten years or more—and to most of them assurance of career opportunity and self-development is of greater concern. It is recommended that proposals for further enhancement of employment security and protective fringe benefits be looked at skeptically, and evaluated mainly in terms of how the money might be better spent on more positive measures which would contribute to the solution of the high-level personnel problem.

The government cannot, of course, afford to lag behind the private sphere in employment protection, and for this reason one area of protection is in need of immediate increased attention. Federal manpower projections should be used to forecast the types and locations of people who will be displaced due to automation and other such factors. This information should be used both in starting advance programs of training and retraining, especially of younger and more able personnel, and in creating rational programs of phasing out, and of relocation and reassignment. We feel that such measures would not merely enhance the "security" image of federal employment; they should, if done soon and done well, mark the government as a leader in meeting the impact of change through improved training and utilization of skills.

Salary Comparability

Federal salaries at all but the topmost levels should be comparable to those prevailing outside the government at comparable levels of expertise and responsibility. This principle is important not only because it provides a rational basis for salary schedule adjustments and will improve the competitive position of the government for the kinds of personnel it needs, but also because it recognizes that the worth of the federal employee is comparable to that of his counterpart elsewhere. Congress subscribed to this principle in the Pay Reform Act of 1962, but the legislation fell well short of providing actual salary increases of sufficient magnitude to bring the pay scales of upper-level federal employees into line with the pay for comparable work outside. It is extremely important for Congress to make good on its commitment to the comparability principle, and to maintain that commitment on a continuing basis through annual review and adjustment of federal salaries.

For the topmost jobs in the federal service, a realistic view suggests that the most that can be expected is a substantial increase in these salaries over their present levels. It is unlikely that the top echelons of federal employment will ever, in a prosperous economy, attain full comparability with the private sector, and such adjustments as are made will probably involve a time lag. Even below the topmost federal positions, where comparability is more feasible, it should be recognized that comparability means essentially that the federal salary for a given job would be roughly the same as the *average* pay for a similar job outside the government. In the salary competition, the more prosperous and determined private employer will continue to offer more money than the government will to those people he needs the most.

It is also important to remember that although the most highly trained and highly placed career employees display concern over their present relative financial deprivation, they are not very materialistic in outlook. Through lack of approximate salary comparability the government can lose many of them, but comparability will not guarantee that the government will retain them. The government must also be competitive in satisfying the broad range of occupational values that rank high for such people.

Because of these considerations it is imperative that we avoid the danger of focusing too narrowly on the salary question and thinking of it as a panacea. Salary comparability will not eliminate the need for the federal government to pursue a positive personnel policy on all fronts. But upper-level federal salaries should be high enough so that people who are attracted to the federal service for other reasons will feel that they can afford to take the job.

Bureaucracy

Bureaucracy as a pervasive element in the image of the federal service is inescapable. The larger the organization, the greater the need for standard procedures, formal communication, and record-keeping. In addition the governmental system of the United States splits power among the Executive, Legislative, and Judicial branches. Desirable as such a system may be, it encourages complexity, elaborate base-touching, caution, and delay. Rare indeed is the governmental activity that is carried out in an atmosphere of unanimous support or that does not restrain or run counter to the desires of many citizens. Cumulatively, this means that almost everyone finds himself on some occasion dealing against his wishes with a force which impresses him as impersonal, complex, impervious to reason, cumbersome, and powerful. This combination of forces is inherent in the operation of the federal government, and provides constant reinforcement for the bureaucratic image. It is vital, therefore, that every element of the government make a constant effort to find means of personalizing, simplifying, clarifying, speeding up, and coordinating its operations. Unfortunately, responsible officials, immersed in day-to-day activities, can all too easily lose sight of this need.

No panacea is possible, but the following suggestions illustrate the kinds of measures we feel are urgently needed:

1. The Chief Executive should equip himself—in the organization of his staff and time—to take a continuing interest in this problem. Those parts of the work of the Bureau of the Budget which are presently aimed at making governmental activities more efficient, simplified, and speeded up should be expanded.

2. Most departments and agencies should provide for greater rotation of central office personnel to the field, where the impact on the citizen may most clearly be observed, and of field personnel to the central office, where the total program may most clearly be observed. Too many central office people lack proper appreciation, not through wilfulness but through ignorance, of the consequences at the operating level of their decisions, and too many field office people become so involved with special problems and clientele that they lose sight of broader program objectives.

3. Frequently it is impossible to try out promising new administrative or other procedures because some part of the law does not permit it. Departments and agencies should actively and inventively seek authority from Congress to waive temporarily for experimental and demonstration purposes a wide variety of legal requirements.[3] Congress should look with favor on such proposals.

4. Most, if not all, committees of Congress should have a "Subcommittee on Past Legislation" composed of the chairmen of all other subcommittees. It should have a small permanent staff charged with (1) ferreting out and bringing to committee attention existing legislation which is no longer necessary, and (2) recodifying existing law to improve clarity and ease of compliance. We recognize that the first activity may not often accomplish much, because legislation which has little logical

[3] An example of such legislation is the new Section 1115 of the Social Security Act, included in the Public Welfare Amendments of 1962, which provides for such waivers and for federal support of demonstration projects in public assistance programs.

utility may have great political utility. Nevertheless, we feel that it would have a healthy effect in the long run.

Recruitment, Education, and Training of High School Seniors

We recommend an intensive program of recruitment at the high school level as part of a greatly expanded program of education and training in the civilian career service. This is not a proposal to lower the sights of the service with respect to the quality and training of its personnel. Rather it is a proposal to recruit a substantial share of the most able "coming" citizens at a time when they are most receptive, and to take an active role in their education and development.

1. *College training.* It is proposed that high school seniors, selected on a competitive basis, be sent to college with their expenses paid in whole or in part by the government with a view to their being employed, both as summer internes and after graduation, as federal civilian employees.[4] The numbers and types of openings available should be adjusted annually in relation to the long-term projected manpower needs of the civilian service. Provisions will have to be made for accommodating or adjusting postgraduation military obligations. In establishing the program, full advantage should be taken of what has been learned from the operation of the G.I. Bill and of current military-supported college training plans.

2. *In-service technical training.* It is proposed that high school seniors also be offered competitive opportunity for in-service training for a wide variety of technical positions in the career service, the need to be based upon manpower projection data. Each year there are many highly able students graduating from secondary schools who prefer not to go to college, but who would welcome immediate full-time employment as technical trainees.[5] One way of increasing quickly and permanently the government's effective supply of professional and scientific personnel is to provide such personnel with enough technical assistance so they can devote themselves more fully to the highest levels of work for which they are qualified. This should also have a very positive effect on their feeling of status and their outlook on their work and on the nature of federal employment.

---

[4] Consideration might be given to exacting a *quid pro quo*—for example, a period of federal service or reimbursement to the government in lieu thereof.

[5] Again, the problem of accommodating or adjusting military obligations would in many instances need to be solved.

Setting up a good system of in-service technical training will require the establishment of numerous schools as adjuncts to laboratories, hospitals, computer centers, and the like. Efforts should be made to establish cooperative arrangements with military technical training centers, as well as those of private industry. Private technical schools which give training of the type and excellence needed should also be utilized. It should be kept in mind that the training facilities will be needed for other than the high school recruits. Automation and technological change and the phasing out of operations will continually supply candidates for training from the regular federal work force.

As a final element in the high school senior technical training program we suggest that, for at least five years after entrance, participants should be permitted to change their minds and compete for entrance into the college training program.

WHAT IS BEING SUGGESTED here is not a small program for high school youth, but a program large enough to require expansion of technical training facilities in and out of government, and extensive use of the country's institutions of higher education; one of sufficient magnitude that its relation to such problems as youth unemployment, talent loss between high school and college, and federal aid to education should be considered. Such a program should have great long-range benefit, not only for the federal service, but for the society as a whole.

Interagency Career Planning and Training

There is a clear need in the career service among potential top-echelon personnel for greater opportunity for self-development and personal growth within the service itself. In-service education and training programs, such as those carried out under the Government Employees Training Act of 1958, are vital in meeting this need and should be expanded and improved. Equally vital, however, is the broadening of goals and the provision of new experience and a continued sense of learning through imaginative career planning. Certainly many improvements in present career planning practices are possible; here we will mention only one which seems to us to be of outstanding importance.

There is an increasing need in federal administration for generalists whose experience and understanding transcends their immediate program responsiblility—people who perceive how a given program is related to other programs and to the large missions of the government, and who are aware of changing conditions, forces, and problems in the social context. They are needed to give vitality to interdepartmental and interagency coordination and cooperation. They also are needed as a pool of administrative talent who can serve well in many programs in many capacities, and for whom lateral mobility is the norm.

For these reasons, we recommend that the President direct that interdepartmental and interagency programs of career development and training be planned and put into practice. Each element of government with a major program responsibility should be required to list the nature and location of related government programs in which their future top administrators should have had experience. Through cooperative arrangements, people with high administrative potential should be exchanged for periods of one to two years, in positions which give the greatest possible program perspective and variety of experience.

As a single illustration, let us consider the Food and Drug Administration. Its activities are closely related to many activities in the Public Health Service (biological standards, etc.), in the Departments of Agriculture (sprays and farm chemicals, meat inspection, etc.), Commerce (patents, the Bureau of Standards, etc.), and Treasury (narcotics control), to name but a few. It is our recommendation that, to the extent possible, the administrative career plan for each relevant agency provide for on-the-job experience in several of the others.

Planning and carrying out this kind of career training will be neither simple nor easy. The needed patterns of lateral movement and exchange will be complex, and, especially at first, may seem to be much like a mad game of musical chairs. Each agency must also make a sincere effort to give exchangees the most informative and worthwhile experience it can. Finally, the plan must guard against the probable tendency of some officials to assign to the temporary exchange their most dispensable personnel, rather than those with the greatest potential.

The proposal as outlined has been concerned only with exchange within the federal government. However, many federal agencies whose activities are closely related to those of state and local agencies should give serious consideration to working out career training exchanges with these other levels of government.

A Jointly Staffed Personnel Research Organization

We propose that there be established a special office for joint personnel research, probably under the Civil Service Commission. Only a very few key personnel at the top should be assigned to it on a long-term basis. They should be highly qualified social scientists who can bring to the research both scientific skepticism and the best in scientific direction. All other research personnel should be drawn on short-term assignments of one or two years, or occasionally even less, from federal departments and agencies, universities, private businesses, other levels of government, and private research organizations.

We are not suggesting that the work of this organization replace any regular government personnel research programs in the Civil Service Commission or elsewhere. It should be in addition to such programs. The purpose of a joint personnel research office goes far beyond simply getting positive personnel research done. It should serve as a training laboratory, as a center for the exchange of information and ideas and the generation of new ideas, as a means of initiating collaborative research among various agencies, as a means for those with an interest in forward-looking research to establish contacts which hopefully will endure, and as a device of exploring for the entire federal government the need for larger and better-financed programs of continuing and imaginative research and experimentation in the personnel field.

There is no present or prospective dearth of important problems which call for research and experimentation. Here are a few examples:

1. How can sufficiently valid manpower forecasting be accomplished?

2. How should the vast expansion of federal contracting outside the government, particularly for research and development, be viewed from the point of view of its impact on federal personnel problems?[6] Probably in the long run something more fundamental is called for than federal employee opposition to contracting, demands for restrictions on contractor employee salaries, trying to isolate federal employees from contractor temptations, and the like. There is a good possibility that the

[6] The Brookings Institution is currently conducting a study of federal contracting under the direction of Clarence H. Danhof, of the Governmental Studies division. While the study is not concerned primarily with the personnel aspect of government contracting, it should be helpful in that regard.

growth, through contracting, of large organizations which are neither governmental nor strictly private, is a necessary response to social and technological change, and that we are witnessing the growing pains of a new (by virtue of its magnitude) institutional means of bringing the nation's resources to bear on its problems. If so, what does it mean for the staffing pattern of the federal government? What functions should be phased out; what *must* be retained; and what new ones are required? What responsibility does the government have for the job security, training, and welfare of contractor employees who are in the in-between-land—not federal personnel, but not really nonfederal either?

3. How can certain types of authority and autonomy be decentralized while retaining necessary coordination and control?

4. It is well enough to say that seniority should be de-emphasized in favor of merit, creativity, and capacity for growth, but how are these things to be recognized or measured? Far too little is known about such matters.

5. In what ways might the present personnel classification system be changed to better meet the challenge of creating a more positive, stimulating environment for higher-level personnel?

6. What is the meaning behind the federal employees' differentially high concern with supervision?

7. What is the meaning behind the findings in this study showing a differentially high concern among federal employees with passive, as opposed to active, personal relations on the job?

8. How may creativity and innovation be fostered in the individual and in the organization? One good starting point might be to take just part of the problem and try to discover the main *barriers* to creative performance and innovation in a few key federal organizations.

9. What are the results of various types of education and training programs? Which kinds accomplish what, both immediately and in the long run? What, if any, negative effects do they have? A major share of present federal education and training is undertaken on faith—which we believe is warranted. However, efforts must be made to progress beyond faith to concrete information as a basis for planning and justifying such programs.

Corps Organization at the Top Levels of the Career Civil Service

Under the present General Schedule civil service classification system (GS 1 through 18), the occupational level of the individual is defined by the level of his job. Salary also is a function of job level, with some adjustments for merit and tenure. Thus, rank and pay reside in the job, and not in the individual. But not all federal personnel systems are of this kind. Rank-in-the-man systems, under which rank and pay are retained regardless of particular assignment, prevail, for example, in the Armed Forces, the Foreign Service, and the Public Health Service.

Careful consideration of our own data, examination of other research, and discussions with a wide variety of knowledgeable people in and out of government have led us to the conclusion that the rank-in-the-job system is inadequate at the upper levels of what are now General Schedule employees, and that some form of corps organization with elements of the rank-in-the-man system is needed. On the other hand, we feel that simply copying some other plan is not the answer. It must be tailored specifically to the needs of the upper levels of the civil service. Unfortunately, present information is inadequate to the job.

Should there be a single corps, or more than one—for example, a general administrative service and a professional and scientific service? At what level in the service should the corps begin? Should all upper-level civil service employees be included in one or another corps, or should there be a parallel rank-in-the-job system? What features of the two systems might advantageously be combined? What features present in neither are required? There is no dearth of ready answers to these and similar questions, but the answers are diverse, conflicting, and lacking solid foundation in verifiable facts. Research directly on this matter is urgently needed.[7]

At this time, however, we can set down a number of things that any plan ought to be designed to accomplish:

1. The plan should give the employee a meaningful title and a sense of occupational identification which is his, independent of the particular job he holds. To designate people as GS 17's, or GS 18's is singularly un-

[7] A current Brookings Institution research project on the higher civil service under the direction of David T. Stanley deals with this subject.

imaginative, but even these semantically unimpressive designations are merely borrowed. They belong to the jobs.

2. It should provide rank and salary independent of immediate assignment and encourage a degree of identification with the corps that will transcend, or at least effectively compete with, commitments to a particular program, agency, or job title (e.g., Director of ——). This is needed for both vertical and lateral flexibility of assignment.

3. An administrative corps plan should include plans for career training of administrative generalists who can graduate into the corps only after experience in a variety of jobs and programs.

4. Emphasis in selection, promotion, and retention should be on merit and successful experience, not seniority. As a matter of fact, reverse emphasis on seniority should be considered—that is, those who go too long without promotion would be retired or transferred out of the corps.

5. Standards of selection for and retention in the one or more corps should be very high, and subjected to periodic review in the light of changing needs of the government.

6. An administrative corps plan should take account of the fact that one of the major things a talented administrator learns is his own strengths and weaknesses. Therefore, such a person should be permitted a certain amount of latitude in accepting or rejecting job assignments. In addition, he learns how to select subordinates who will make up for his weaknesses. Therefore, he should be permitted maximum autonomy and a wide range of choice in selecting or rejecting immediate subordinates.

7. Corps trainees and especially corps members should be accorded special opportunities for education and training designed to keep them constantly in touch with new technology, new knowledge, and changes in governmental operations and policies. For professional and scientific personnel especially (should it be determined that a specific corps for them is needed), this would mean opportunities for advanced education, publication, and attendance at professional and scientific meetings.

8. The corps (or corps, plural), after being initially organized to include present upper-level personnel, should develop increasingly stringent qualification requirements. It should be regarded both by members and potential members as tough to get into and tough to stay in, but as offering amounts of opportunity, self-development, autonomy, chal-

lenge, and significant public service that make it worth while. Modest, but recurring, research checks should be made to see that these goals are being met, and if they are not in any respect, why not.

Some Suggestions to Nonfederal Organizations and Groups

The specific recommendations made thus far have been directed to elements of the federal government—because it is the federal establishment from which the main initiative must come, and where the major changes must occur. However, the responsibility is not the government's alone. Many of the measures proposed, and undoubtedly many other measures not yet thought of but which will be needed as time goes on, require not only general public support, but the active support and co operation of colleges and universities, high schools, business institutions, state and local governments, private research organizations, labor unions —especially federal employee unions—professional and scientific societies, philanthropic foundations, and those people with responsibility and influence in both the mass and specialized media of communication. We feel that these institutions and individuals not only have a responsibility to cooperate when called upon, but should actively seek out ways of providing aid. No one can anticipate fully at this time all of the many things they may be called upon to do, or ought to undertake on their own initiative. Here we will mention a few of importance for which there is present or foreseeable need.

1. Educational institutions, business corporations, state and local governments, and others should, when called upon, appoint able and responsible representatives to participate with federal officials in planning programs of personnel exchange, joint staffing of a personnel research office, subsidized higher education and technical training, and the like. Within broad limits they should be willing to undertake new or modified institutional arrangements and accept the dislocations and difficulties which accompany most new ventures.

2. Federal employee unions have political power which can be used either to impede or to support the kinds of measures suggested here. In discussions with union officials, we sensed genuine concern over the upper-level personnel problem, as well as a recognition that some such positive measures are needed for the continued welfare and vitality of

the entire federal service. We feel that a majority of the measures suggested ought to command union support. Where they do not, we feel that the unions should focus, not just on opposition to specific proposals but on the needs they are designed to meet, and propose alternative solutions.

3. We recommend that the professional and scientific societies form a joint council on federal employment. The federal government is the largest single employer of professional and scientific personnel, and such personnel have many occupational values and outlooks in common. There is a need for a mechanism whereby their societies can keep themselves informed of common federal employment problems, pool relevant information of their own which bears on such problems, adopt common policies, and represent their views before Congress and elsewhere.[8]

4. College faculty members in departments of political science, government, public administration, and public and international affairs have special responsibilities which go beyond departmental lines to the entire campus and to the community. We are not suggesting that they have failed to recognize and do something about these responsibilities; we simply feel that more should be done. For example, on most campuses it would be valuable to have an active committee on public (not just federal) employment. Such a committee could keep abreast of current public employment trends and practices; serve as a source of information and advice to college counselors, to the employment office, and to students referred to it; organize special lectures and seminars for faculty, students, and the public; and be constantly alert to correct misinformation and misunderstanding wherever it may be.

Outlook and Philosophy

Without firm foundations of outlook and philosophy appropriate to the needs of the times, any of the concrete measures proposed will lack vitality and meet with limited success. Such foundations are also needed in

[8] The Federal Professional Association, formed in 1963, is an individual membership organization created in recognition of the common interests of scientific and professional personnel. However, a joint council of societies is still needed. The Federal Professional Association would be the logical group to encourage the formation of such a council.

assessing the worth of the specific measures and in creating new and better proposals now and in the future. That is why we hope that the following recommendations on outlook and philosophy may receive greater attention, understanding, acceptance, and application than any or all of the specific suggestions we have made.

Special Presidential Responsibility for Upper-Level Employees

It should be recognized, openly and explicitly, that the President of the United States has special responsibility for upper-level career employees. Employees in the lower echelons, because of their numbers and the availability to them of union representation, will rarely fail to receive sympathetic attention from Congress. The facts of political life make it unlikely that Congress will demonstrate in legislation a similar concern for the upper echelons unless their needs receive strong support from the President. One would think that a simple concern for the effectiveness of the Executive branch would cause the President to give high priority to this matter. However, in the past, presidential support has been sporadic and too often given simply in response to impending crises or glaring inequities. When the Chief Executive fails to assume special responsibility for comprehensive planning and continuous strong support of measures designed to enhance the welfare, quality, and performance of upper-level career employees, it is an abdicaton of a major presidential responsibility, and should be regarded as such.

An Old Battle and a New One

Despite occasional skirmishes with dishonesty in the federal civilian service—which are all the more newsworthy because of their infrequent occurrence in an organization involving so many people and so much power and money—there can be little question that in the eyes of the public the battle for probity in the service has been won. Now a new challenge has been posed by the impact of social and technological change on the breadth, complexity, and importance of the national government's operations and on the nature of the duties and responsibilities required of its civilian employees.

This means that we must find ways of achieving a new and better balance in the personnel regulations that are designed to insure honesty and equity, for among them are certain restrictive rules which unduly hamper the kinds of autonomy, personal growth, creativity, and innovation for which there is now a critical and growing need. Judicious relaxation of such restrictive regulations, particularly at the upper levels of employment, are required to meet this need. This, of course, would mean greater opportunity for employees to make mistakes and to be dishonest, but it is a price we can and must afford. In a sense, the present high regard for the honesty of the civil servant is "money in the bank," part of which may be used as "risk capital" in a badly needed enterprise. It also would mean that civil servants themselves must, to an increasing degree, develop and maintain norms of excellence and integrity.

Certainly, however, we cannot abandon the independent regulatory function that has been carried out by the U.S. Civil Service Commission. The worth of the function and the continuing need for it have been amply demonstrated. But we must take a very hard and critical look at the present arrangement which places in the hands of the CSC both the regulatory function and the major responsibility for government-wide stimulation of new and positive personnel philosophies and practices. The two functions are seldom complementary—and in fact often antagonistic—both in their operational aspects and in the outlook they require of those who administer them. Furthermore, it is difficult for the people who must deal with the CSC to give full appreciation and weight to its positive functions. Its historical regulatory mission—and its continuing regulatory responsibilities—are bound to condition their view, and, in many cases, cause them to adopt a questioning or suspicious attitude. Finally, there is the very important question of whether leadership in personnel matters, which is an important executive function, ought not to be in the Office of the Chief Executive, rather than in the hands of a so-called independent agency.

However, as the other part of the picture, we must state our conviction that the Civil Service Commission has been and is providing positive leadership; that marked progress has been made in salary reform, recruitment procedures, information programs, education and training, research, and other areas. Sometimes an incongruous institutional arrangement works well when its positions of leadership are held by far-sighted and able people. We cannot recommend a change in institutional structure and responsibilities at this time.

Instead, the positive role of the CSC should be recognized and encouraged by all concerned. Needed legislation, funds, executive orders, and presidential support should be provided. In addition, it would help if agency managers and personnel directors would take a more positive approach to personnel matters and not try to perform, through anticipation and caution, so much of the CSC's regulatory job. We feel that the Commissioners would welcome being challenged more often in the interests of meeting agency and individual needs. Continuous (sensible) challenge aids the Commission in clearing up misunderstandings, making known available alternative procedures, and learning about needed changes in regulations and procedures.

Given the proper support, it is possible that the Civil Service Commission will continue for some years to perform well in stimulating positive civilian personnel reform. However, the organizational and attitudinal handicaps are such that the eventual need for institutional reform seems inevitable. We feel that the President should keep a watchful eye on the CSC's progress, and have a prepared plan available for bringing directly under the Chief Executive the leadership function in positive personnel administration, for use if and when such a step becomes necessary.

A New Personnel Philosophy

A great many of the negative elements and problems revealed by our research have their roots in over-rigid application of the historically justified federal personnel philosophy of equality of treatment and protection against inequity. This philosophy found concrete expression in emphasis on the regulatory function, as well as in a tendency to interpret *equality* of treatment as *sameness* of treatment. Very often, too, it found expression in the interpretation of inequity as lack of proper regard for seniority, as opposed to merit and creativity. Such an approach is no longer in accord with the requirements of public attitudes and the needs of government, and serves only to hamper urgently needed reform.

It should be replaced by a new and more positive philosophy which brooks no departure from equality of opportunity, but regards as a new standard and as an innovative challenge the creation of patterns of differential treatment of personnel. The traditional philosophy demands that reasons be given for treating any employee or group of employees differently from any others. The time has come to put the shoe on the other foot. We need a new approach which demands that reasons be given for *not* according any employee or group of employees the kind of special, differential treatment both uniquely suited to their needs and uniquely designed to enhance their quality, creativity, productivity, and sense of worth as individuals. This goal cannot, of course, be completely realized. The natural forces of large-scale organization place limits on it and push constantly in the direction of standardization and uniformity in the treatment of human beings. However, our society cannot afford to encourage these tendencies. We need a philosophy which will provide a strong countervailing force at all levels of personnel policy-making and at all levels of supervision.

APPENDIX

APPENDIX

The Questionnaires

Questionnaire for Employed, Nonfederal Adult Populations

WE ARE DOING A SURVEY for a major research foundation to find out something about how people feel about various ways of making a living. Most of the questions I will ask you are related to this general topic. I am sure you will find the questions interesting. Please answer them just as frankly and completely as you can.

1. First, I would like you to think about what really matters most to you in your own life. Tell me what kind of a way of earning a living would be ideal for you—that is, the very best way of doing it from your point of view. Maybe no occupation could fit your ideal. But just let yourself dream a bit and tell me the various things *about* an occupation which would make it *absolutely ideal* for you. I'm not asking for the name of a specific occupation, but for the *kinds of things about* an occupation which would make it *absolutely ideal* for you. (USE "Anything else?" PROBES)

(Has R. described *things about* an occupation, rather than just given names of occupations?)

2. Now, about the worst sort of occupation. What *kinds of things* about an occupaiton would make it the worst or least satisfying to you? (USE "Anything else" PROBES)

(Has R. described things about an occupation, rather than just giving names of occupations?)

3. (HAND RESPONDENT CARD SHOWING LADDER) Here is a picture of a ladder.[1] Suppose we say at the *top* of the ladder (POINTING) is the *very best*, the absolutely ideal sort of occupation you have just described. At the *bottom* is the *very worst* sort of occupation. Where on this ladder (MOVING FINGER RAPIDLY UP AND DOWN LADDER) would you put your present occupation, that is, what you are doing now?
    ENTER STEP NUMBER

[1] The ten-step ladder is shown in Chapter 2 of the *Source Book*.

4. Now think of what you were doing five years ago. Where on this ladder would you put what you were doing as an occupation five years ago?
　　　ENTER STEP NUMBER
　　　Not working 5 years ago

5. Thinking now of your occupational future. Where on the ladder do you expect to be five years from now?
　　　ENTER STEP NUMBER
　　　Not rated because will be retired
　　　Other (SPECIFY)

(INTERVIEWER: NOTE PARTICULARLY THE STEP NUMBER YOU RECORDED UNDER Q. 3. THEN ASK EITHER Q. 6 OR Q. 7 WHICHEVER APPLIES AND EITHER Q. 8 OR Q. 9 WHICHEVER APPLIES—THAT IS, THERE MUST BE TWO QUESTIONS ANSWERED ON THE NEXT PAGE.)

6. (FOR THOSE WHO ANSWERED Q. 3 WITH A "9" OR A LOWER NUMBER) Returning now to the present, that is, to the rating marked here in red (POINT TO Q. 3 RATING) which you gave your present occupation—what *kinds of things* about your present occupation kept you from placing it higher on the ladder? (USE "Anything else" PROBES)

7. (FOR THOSE WHO ANSWERED Q. 3 WITH A "10") Returning now to the present, that is, to the rating marked here in red (POINT TO Q. 3 RATING) which you gave your present occupation—what *kinds of things* about your present occupation caused you to place it at the top? (USE "Anything else" PROBES)

8. (FOR THOSE WHO ANSWERED Q. 3 WITH A "2" OR A HIGHER NUMBER) What *kinds of things* about it kept you from placing it lower? (USE "Anything else" PROBES")

9. (FOR THOSE WHO ANSWERED Q. 3 WITH A "1") What *kinds of things* about it caused you to place it at the bottom? (USE "Anything else" PROBES)

10. Suppose your work or occupation stayed the same but you worked for the Federal government—that is, the United States government—how much better or worse would that be? Show me on the ladder, please. The place you pointed to before is marked in red.
　　　ENTER STEP NUMBER

(Q's. 11 AND 12 ARE TO BE INTERCHANGED. IF SAME STEP OR A HIGHER STEP IN Q. 10 THAN IN Q. 3, ASK Q. 11 FIRST AND THEN Q. 12. IF A LOWER STEP IN Q. 10, ASK Q. 12 FIRST AND THEN Q. 11.)

11. What things would be likely to be better? (USE "Anything else" PROBES)
12. What things would be likely to be worse? (USE "Anything else" PROBES)
13. Suppose you were to change now and go to work for the U. S. Government doing the same thing you're doing now, how do you think your family might feel about it? Would they feel you were moving up the ladder or down?
　　　Up
　　　Down
　　　No difference
14. Again suppose for the moment that a person in your line of work *did* go to work for the United States Government. Are there any particular branches

or parts of the government that would be better to be in than others, from your point of view?

Yes

No

Don't know } (SKIP TO Q. 17)

15. (IF "YES" TO Q. 14) What particular branches or parts of the Government would be better?

16. Why do you think that?

(INTERVIEWER: BE SURE TO SHUFFLE SMALL CARDS WELL)

17. Now, I have some small cards here, each of which has a statement on it saying something about jobs or occupations. I also have this large card (SHOW LARGE SCALE CARD) which says "AGREE" on the top and "DISAGREE" on the bottom and has these spaces (MOVE HAND UP AND DOWN) in between.[2] Please take the small cards and place each one in turn on the large card according to how much you agree or disagree with the statement on it. You have ten different positions available to you. There are, of course, no right or wrong answers. Now, let's take the first small card, where would you place it? Now, just go on from there, please, as quickly as you can. We are just interested in your first impressions.[3]

1. A person has a right to expect his work to be fun
2. There are a lot of problems in this country that the federal government ought to step in and do something about
3. Employment with a large private business offers a high degree of security
4. Whenever the federal government steps into something, it just makes things worse
5. To be really successful in life, you have to care about making money
6. Work is most satisfying when there are hard problems to solve
7. After you are making enough money to get along, then making more money in an occupation isn't very important
8. To me, it's important in an occupation to have the chance to get to the top
9. It's important to do a better job than the next person
10. A person who works for the federal government generally has a good chance to get ahead
11. Success in an occupation is mainly a matter of hard work
12. Success in an occupation is mainly a matter of luck
13. All things considered, working for a large private business firm appeals to me
14. All things considered, working for the federal government appeals to me
15. Most people who work for the federal government do their best to serve the public
16. Even if you dislike your work, you should do your best
17. If a person doesn't want to work hard, it's his own business
18. Work is a good builder of character
19. It is satisfying to direct the work of others
20. Work is a way of being of service to God
21. To me, a very important part of work

---

[2] The ten-point "agree-disagree" scale is shown in Chapter 2.

[3] Each statement of the fifty-five that follow was printed on a separate small card, which the interviewee picked at random, *not* in the order given here. The numbers used here appeared on the back of the cards, for interviewers' use in recording. The cards were shuffled between interviews to insure random presentation.

is the opportunity to make friends

22. The main satisfaction a person can get out of work is helping other people

23. Work should be the most important part of a person's life

24. I would like my family to be able to have most of the things my friends and neighbors have

25. It is more important for a job to offer *opportunity* than *security*

26. To me, work is nothing more than a way of making a living

27. Most jobs in the federal government are routine and monotonous

28. Most jobs in private business are routine and monotonous

29. To me, it's important in an occupation for a person to be able to carry out his own ideas without interference

30. It would be hard to live with the feeling that others are passing you up in your occupation

31. Work helps you forget about your personal problems

32. To me, it's important in an occupation that a person be able to see the results of his own work

33. Getting recognition for my own work is important to me

34. The United States government interferes in a lot of things it should stay out of

35. Success in an occupation is mainly a matter of knowing the right people

36. To me, it's important to have the kind of work that gives me a chance to develop my own special abilities

37. A young man of ability who goes into politics has a good chance of becoming a United States Senator or Representative

38. Once a person has shown what he can do by working a number of years, he ought not to have to take a special examination to get a job

39. If I had a son just getting out of school, I would like to see him go into politics as a life's work

40. To stay honest in politics, you have to have wealth or a different occupation to fall back on

41. If I had a son who wanted to go into politics, I would want him to learn some other occupation first

42. A young man of ability who starts work in the Federal Civil Service has a good chance of ending up in one of the top level jobs

43. A young man of ability who starts work in a large private business corporation has a good chance of ending up in one of the top level jobs

44. For a young man of ability, his best chance for being *really successful* lies in going into politics

45. For a young man of ability, his best chance for being *really successful* lies in working for the federal government

46. For a young man of ability, his best chance for being *really successful* lies in working for a large private business corporation

47. For a young man of ability, his best chance for being *really successful* lies in setting up his own business

48. Sometimes it may be right for a person to lose friends in order to get ahead in his work

49. If I had a son who became a United States Senator or Representative, I would be proud of him

50. To me, almost the only thing that matters about a job is the chance to do work that is worthwhile to society

51. A person who works for a large private business generally has a good chance to get ahead

52. A person should constantly try to succeed at work, even if it interferes with other things in life

53. I like the kind of work you can forget about after the work day is over

54. To me, gaining the increased respect of family and friends is one of the most important rewards of getting ahead in an occupation

55. Employment with the federal government offers a high degree of se- **curity**

18. Now, a somewhat different type of question. If you had a son just getting out of school, would you like to see him go into politics as a life work?

    Yes

    No

    Don't know

19. Why? (PROBE)

20. Suppose he did become a United States Senator or Representative. How would you feel about that?

21. Now let's think about one particular kind of person in the Federal government. If you were to describe your general idea of a United States civil service employee, what sort of a person would that be?

22. What do you picture a Federal civil service employee as doing—that is, what sort of work?

23. What do you suppose would cause a person to become a United States civil service employee instead of something else?

24. On the whole, who would be likely to be most satisfied with civil service employment—men or women?

    Men

    Women

    No difference

    Don't know (SKIP TO Q. 26)

25. Why do you say that?

26. What is the top salary per year in the United States Civil Service—that is, not the salaries of elected and appointed officials, but the highest salary anyone in the regular United States Civil Service can get? (IF "DON'T KNOW," ASK: Well, what would you guess is the highest salary? IF GUESS, MARK "GUESS")

    $_____ per year

    Cannot even guess

27. What do you think the highest salary per year *should be* for people who hold the top level jobs in the United States Civil Service? (IF "DON'T KNOW," ASK: Well, about what do you think it should be?)

    $_____ per year

    Cannot even guess

28. Turning away from government people for a moment, how about a person employed by a large private business or industry. If you were to describe your general idea of such a person, what would that be?

29. What do you picture a person employed by a large private business or industry as doing—that is, what sort of work?

30. Now, I'm going to ask you to think a little bit more about some of the other kinds of people in our government. If you were to describe your general idea of a United States congressman, what sort of a person would that be?

31. What do you suppose would cause a person to become a congressman instead of something else?

32. Now we've talked about two different kinds of United States government people—those who are elected like congressmen, and those who are in civil service. There is a third kind—those people who are quite high in the United States Government and who are appointed to their positions. When you think about these appointed positions, which one comes to mind? Any others?

33. For talking purposes here, let's say that the appointed positions we are concerned with are mainly the administrative or executive positions together

with their assistants. If you were to describe your general idea of an appointed person, what sort of person would that be?

34. Now, here is a different set of cards. Each of these cards asks you to consider a particular group of people. They are described in red at the top of the card. Below you are asked to rate those people on some particular thing about them. Here is a card (SHOW LARGE SCALE CARD) which says "EXTREMELY HIGH" at the top and "EXTREMELY LOW" on the bottom and has these spaces (MOVE HAND UP AND DOWN) in between. Please take these small cards and place them on the large card, according to how you rate the people described, on the point made about them. This "point" is always underlined for your convenience. Now, let's take the first card. You see, it says (READ RED WORDS). Those are the people you are to consider. Then here it says (READ BLACK WORDS). Now, how would you rate them on that point? Place the card to indicate your rating. Now, just go on from there, please, as quickly as you can. We are just interested in your first impressions.[4]

1. Consider: People who are appointed to top level jobs in the United States Government

On the average, how would you rate them on their *interest in serving the public?*

2. Consider: People in the top level jobs in private business

On the average, how would you rate them on their *interest in serving the public?*

3. Consider: Federal Civil Service employees in general

On the average, how would you rate them on their *interest in serving the public?*

4. Consider: Federal Civil Service employees in general

On the average, how would you rate them on *honesty?*

5. Consider: Federal Civil Service employees in general

On the average, how would you rate them on their *drive to get ahead?*

6. Consider: People who are appointed to top level jobs in the United States Government

On the average, how would you rate them on *honesty?*

7. Consider: People in the top level jobs in the Federal Civil Service

On the average, how would you rate them on their *drive to get ahead?*

8. Consider: Members of the United States House of Representatives

On the average, how would you rate them on *ability?*

9. Consider: People in the top level jobs in private business

On the average, how would you rate them on *honesty?*

10. Consider: Members of the United States House of Representatives

On the average, how would you rate them on *honesty?*

11. Consider: Federal Civil Service employees in general

On the average, how would you rate them on *ability?*

12. Consider: Federal Civil Service employees in general

On the average, how would you rate them on *how well respected they are?*

13. Consider: Members of the United States House of Representatives

On the average, how would you rate

[4] Each of the thirty items that follow was on a separate card, numbered on the back. The first part of each item, "Consider:" (etc.), was printed in red, the second part in black. The ten-point "extremely high-extremely low" scale is not shown in Chapter 2, but is the same as the "agree-disagree" scale except for the wording at top and bottom. The cards were shuffled between interviews.

them on their *interest in serving the public?*

14. Consider: People in the top level jobs in the Federal Civil Service

On the average, how would you rate them on their *interest in serving the public.*

15. Consider: Members of the United States House of Representatives

On the average, how would you rate them on *how well respected they are?*

16. Consider: People in the top level jobs in private business

On the average, how would you rate them on *ability?*

17. Consider: People in the top level jobs in private business

On the average, how would you rate them on *how well respected they are?*

18. Consider: People in the top level jobs in private business

On the average, how would you rate them on their *drive to get ahead?*

19. Consider: Members of the United States House of Representatives

On the average, how would you rate them on their *drive to get ahead?*

20. Consider: People in the top level jobs in the Federal Civil Service

On the average, how would you rate them on *ability?*

21. Consider: People in the top level jobs in the Federal Civil Service

On the average, how would you rate

them on *honesty?*

22. Consider: People in the top level jobs in the Federal Civil Service

On the average, how would you rate them on *how well respected they are?*

23. Consider: People who are appointed to top level jobs in the United States Government

On the average, how would you rate them on their *drive to get ahead?*

24. Consider: People who are appointed to top level jobs in the United States Government

On the average, how would you rate them on *how well respected they are?*

25. Consider: United States Senators

On the average, how would you rate them on *ability?*

26. Consider: United States Senators

On the average, how would you rate them on their *interest in serving the public?*

27. Consider: People who are appointed to top level jobs in the United States Government

On the average, how would you rate them on *ability?*

28. Consider: United States Senators

On the average, how would you rate them on their *drive to get ahead?*

29. Consider: United States Senators

On the average, how would you rate them on *how well respected they are?*

30. Consider: United States Senators

On the average, how would you rate them on *honesty?*

CLASSIFICATION DATA: Now I need some information about you, so that, after we have completed all of our interviews, we'll be able to find out such things as whether men have different ideas than women, whether people who live in the country have different ideas from city people and so on.

35. First, where were you born—in the United States or in some other country?
    United States
    Other country

36. In what kind of place did you live most of the time while you were growing up (that is, up to age 15)? Would you say:

On a farm or ranch

In a town or towns under about 50,000 population

In the suburbs of a city or cities larger than 50,000 population

In the more central part of a city or cities

37. Where was your father born—in the United States or in some other country?

United States

Other country

38. What was the last grade of school your father completed?

Less than high school

High school

College—less than 4 years

College—4 years

College—more than 4 years

Trade school, nursing, etc.

39. Where was your mother born—in the United States or in some other country?

United States

Other country

40. What was the last grade of school your mother completed?

Less than high school

High school

College—less than 4 years

College—4 years

College—more than 4 years

Trade school, nursing, etc.

41. Have you yourself ever served in the United States Armed Forces—that is, in the Army, Navy, Air Force, or other branch?

Yes

No

42. Aside from military service, have you ever worked as a *civilian* for the federal government?

Yes

No (SKIP TO Q. 45)

43. (IF "YES") For how long?

Less than 6 months

6 months to 1 year

More than 1 year but less than 5 years

5 years or more

44. (IF "YES") What was the last year you worked for the federal government?

45. Now, about your present occupation. Are you now self-employed or do you work for somebody else?

Self-employed

Work for somebody else

46. Where are you employed—I don't mean the name of the place but what kind of a place is it?

47. What *exactly* do you do there?

48. What is your title?

49. (IF R. IS TEACHER, ASK:) What subject or subjects do you teach?

50. Now about your father's *principal* occupation. Was he self-employed or did he work for somebody else?

Self-employed
Work for somebody else

51. Where was he employed—I don't mean the name of the place but what kind of place was it?

52. What *exactly* did he do there?

53. What was his title?

(ASK QS. 54 THROUGH 60 IF R. IS NOT HEAD OF HOUSEHOLD, OTHERWISE, SKIP TO Q. 61.)

54. Is the head of household *now* self-employed or working for somebody else?
Self-employed
Work for somebody else
Unemployed (SKIP TO Q. 58)

55. At what kind of a place is (he) (she) employed?

56. What *exactly* does (he) (she) do there?

57. What is (his) (her) title?

58. Has head of household ever worked, as a *civilian,* for the federal government?

Yes
No (SKIP TO Q. 61)

59. (IF "YES") For how long?
Less than 6 months
6 months to 1 year
More than 1 year but less than 5 years
5 years or more

60. (IF "YES") What was the last year he worked for the federal government?

61. Getting back now to you, what was the last grade of school you completed?
Less than high school
High school
College—less than 4 years
College—4 years
College—more than 4 years
Trade school, nursing, etc.

62. What general kind of course did you take in high school?
Academic, college preparatory
Commercial
Vocational, agricultural
Other (SPECIFY)

63. (IF ANY COLLEGE EDUCATION IN Q. 61) What was your college major?

64. How old are you?

65. Generally speaking, do you usually think of yourself as a Republican, a Democrat, an Independent, or what?
Republican⎱ (ASK Q. 66)
Democrat ⎰
Independent (SKIP TO Q. 67)
Other (SPECIFY)
No choice (SKIP TO Q. 68)

66. Would you call yourself a strong (Republican) (Democrat) or a not very strong (Republican) (Democrat)?
Strong (Republican) (Democrat)

Not very strong (Republican) (Democrat)

No choice (SKIP TO Q. 68)

67. Do you think of yourself as closer to the Republican or Democratic Party?

Closer to Republican party

Closer to Democratic party

No choice

68. What is your religious preference or affiliation?

Protestant

Catholic

Jewish

Other (SPECIFY)

None

69. Present marital status:

Single

Married

Widowed

Divorced

Separated

70. Referring now to *your* occupation, the one you described for me earlier. Would you point out for me on this card the group which includes the amount of yearly income you receive before taxes, as wages or salary (including commissions and bonuses) from your present occupation. (HAND RESPONDENT INCOME CARD)

INCOME CARD

Weekly	*Yearly*
1. Under $20	Under $1,000
2. $20-$38	$1,000-$1,999
3. $39-$57	$2,000-$2,999
4. $58-$76	$3,000-$3,999
5. $77-$86	$4,000-$4,499
6. $87-$96	$4,500-$4,999
7. $97-$106	$5,000-$5,499
8. $107-$115	$5,500-$5,999
9. $116-$134	$6,000-$6,999
10. $135-$163	$7,000-$8,499
11. $164-$192	$8,500-$9,999
12. $193-$288	$10,000-$14,999
13. $289 and over	$15,000 and over

71. Which group on the card contains the amount of your *total family income?*

INTERVIEWER: ENTER FROM OBSERVATION

72. Sex:

Male

Female

73. Race:

White

Negro

Other non-white

74. Socio-economic:

Answered Q. 74:
    By observation
    Used card
        A
        B
        C
        D

INSTRUCTIONS FOR Q. 74
—circle code for Q. 74 from observation when you are interviewing respondents in *their homes.*
—present card provided for Q. 74 to respondent and have (him) (her) select a category when you are interviewing respondents in any place other than their homes.

Card presented to respondent

THINK OF THE COMMUNITY IN WHICH YOU LIVE:
Select "A" to represent your family if:
    —live in nicest section or neighborhood
    —have a relatively large, well-kept home
    —generally considered well-to-do
    —able to have a good many luxuries
    —head of house might be professional man, high business executive, owner of own business, or equivalent
Select "B" to represent your family if:
    —live in above average section or neighborhood
    —have a nice home, but not as large as some
    —generally considered to have a comfortable income
    —able to have some luxuries but not all
    —head of house might be minor or junior executive, a better paid white collar worker, owner of a neighborhood store, a plant official, or equivalent
Select "C" to represent your family if:
    —live in just about the average section or neighborhood
    —have a modest home, about average size
    —generally considered to have an adequate income, but comparatively little reserve
    —able to have few luxuries, if any
    —head of house may be clerical worker, an average white collar worker, better paid factory worker, or equivalent
Select "D" to represent your family if:
    —live in the poorest section or neighborhood
    —have a comparatively poor home, often in bad repair
    —generally considered to have an absolutely minimum income
    —able to have only the necessities of life
    —head of house might be a day laborer, less well paid factory worker, or equivalent

Questionnaire for Federal Populations

WE ARE DOING A SURVEY for a major research foundation to find out something about how people feel about various ways of making a living. Most of the questions I will ask you are related to this general topic. I am sure you will find the questions interesting. Please answer them just as frankly and completely as you can. Right now we are talking to a representative group of Federal employees, just as we talked earlier to a representative group of persons in private industry. Could you tell me, first, whether you are employed full-time or part-time by the Federal government?

1-9. [Same as questions 1-9 in the Nonfederal Adult Questionnaire.]

10. Suppose your work or occupation stayed the same but you no longer worked for the U. S. government—that is, suppose you continued in your present occupation, but went to work outside the Federal government—how much better or worse would that be? Show me on the ladder, please. The place you pointed to before is marked in red.

     ENTER STEP NUMBER

(Q's. 11 AND 12 ARE TO BE INTERCHANGED. IF SAME STEP OR A HIGHER STEP IN Q. 10 THAN IN Q. 3, ASK Q. 11 FIRST AND THEN Q. 12. IF A LOWER STEP IN Q. 10, ASK Q. 12 FIRST AND THEN Q. 11.)

11. What things would be likely to be better? (USE "Anything else" PROBES)

12. What things would be likely to be worse? (USE "Anything else" PROBES)

13. Suppose you were to change now and go to work outside the Federal government doing the same thing you're doing now, how do you think your family might feel about it? Would they feel you were moving up the ladder or down?

    Up
    Down
    No difference

14. Again suppose for the moment that a person in your line of work *did* go to work outside the Federal government. Are there any particular kinds of employment or businesses that would be better to be in than others, from your point of view?

    Yes
    No
    Don't know } (SKIP TO Q. 17)

15. (IF "YES" TO Q. 14) What particular kinds of employment or businesses would be better?

16. Why do you think that?

17. Now, returning to your present situation, do you plan to continue working for the Federal government, or do you think you might leave it?

    Continue
    Leave
    Don't know (SKIP TO Q. 20)

18. (IF "CONTINUE" OR "LEAVE" TO Q. 17) Why? What are the main things that make you feel that way? (PROBE FOR REASONS, PRO OR CON)

19. How sure are you that you will (continue in) (leave) the Federal government—very sure, fairly sure, or not sure at all?

    Very sure
    Fairly sure
    Not sure

20. Thinking now about the past. Was there ever a time when you thought

fairly seriously of leaving the United States government, and then didn't?

> Yes
> No
> Don't know } (SKIP TO Q. 24)

21. (IF "YES" TO Q. 20) About how long ago was that? (RECORD NUMBER OF YEARS AGO TO NEAREST YEAR THE LAST TIME RESPONDENT THOUGHT FAIRLY SERIOUSLY OF LEAVING THE UNITED STATES GOVERNMENT AND THEN DIDN'T)

————————— YEARS AGO

22. (IF "YES" TO Q. 20) What were the main things that caused you to think fairly seriously about leaving the Federal government? (VERBATIM)

23. (IF "YES" TO Q. 20) What were the main things that caused you to stay in the Federal government? (VERBATIM)

24-41. [Same as questions 17-34 in the Nonfederal Adult Questionnaire.]

CLASSIFICATION DATA: Now I need some information about you, so that, after we have completed all of our interviews, we'll be able to find out such things as whether men have different ideas than women, whether people who live in the country have different ideas from city people, and so on.

42-48. [Same as questions 35-41 in the Nonfederal Adult Questionnaire.]

49. Have you ever worked outside the Federal government—that is, have you ever had a private employer or been self-employed?

> Yes
> No (SKIP TO Q. 56)

50. (IF "YES") For how long?

> 1 year or less
> More than 1 year, but less than 5 years
> More than 5 years, but less than 10 years
> More than 10 years, but less than 20 years
> 20 years or more

51. (IF "YES") What was the last year you worked outside the Federal government?

52. Thinking back to the time when you last worked outside the Federal government, were you self-employed or did you work for somebody else?

> Self-employed
> Worked for somebody else

53. Where were you employed—I don't mean the name of the place but what kind of a place was it?

54. What *exactly* did you do there?

55. What was your title?

(ASK EVERYBODY)

56. Now about your present occupation with the Federal government. What is the grade of your position—that is, is it something like GS-9, WB-5, PFS-7 or something else? (ENTER GRADE RESPONDENT GIVES. IF NO GRADE GIVEN, ENTER DESCRIPTION OF GRADE LEVEL.)

57. For what major Federal government department or branch are you now working?

> Agriculture Department
> Commerce Department
> Defense: Office of the Secretary

Air Force Department
Army Department
Navy Department
Health, Education, and Welfare Department
Interior Department
Justice Department
Labor Department
Post Office Department
State Department
Treasury Department
Federal Aviation Agency
General Services Administration
Veterans Administration
All other (SPECIFY)

58. Within the (ANSWER IN Q. 57), for what bureau or major subdivision are you now working?

59. What exactly do you do here?

60. What is your title?

61. Is this the official title which your personnel office uses for your position?
Yes (SKIP TO Q. 63)
No (ASK Q. 62)
Don't know (SKIP TO Q. 63)

62. What is the exact title for your position used by your personnel office? (ASK EVERYBODY)

63. About what percentage of your work is administrative work (e.g., supervising, planning, organizing, coordinating, reporting, delegating, etc.)? Would you say it is closest to:
100%
75%
50%
25%
0%

64. How long have you worked for the Federal government?
1 year or less
More than 1 year, but less than 5 years
More than 5 years, but less than 10 years
More than 10 years, but less than 20 years
20 years or more

65-68. [Same as questions 50-53 in the Nonfederal Adult Questionnaire.]

69. Did either of your parents ever work for the Federal government for a period of 3 years or more?
Yes, father did
Yes, mother did
Yes, both did
No, neither
Don't know (SKIP TO Q. 71 OR Q. 78 WHICHEVER IS APPLICABLE)

70. (IF "YES") Was this during the time when you were growing up and living at home, or was it some other time?

Time when growing up and living at home
Some other time
(ASK Q'S. 71 THROUGH 77 IF RESPONDENT IS NOT HEAD OF HOUSEHOLD. OTHER-
WISE SKIP TO Q. 78.)
71-77. [Same as questions 54-60 of the Nonfederal Adult Questionnaire.]
78. Getting back now to you, what was the last grade of school you completed?
    Less than high school
    High school
    College—less than 4 years
    College—4 years
    College—more than 4 years
    Trade school, nursing, etc.
79. What general kind of course did you take in high school?
    Academic, college preparatory
    Commercial
    Vocational, agricultural
    Other (SPECIFY)
80. (IF ANY COLLEGE EDUCATION IN Q. 78) What was your college major?
81. (IF TWO OR MORE COLLEGE MAJOR SUBJECTS GIVEN IN Q. 80) In which *one*
of these subjects did you do the most work?
82-89. [Same as questions 64-74 in the Nonfederal Adult Questionnaire.]

Questionnaire for Student Populations

WE ARE DOING A SURVEY for a major research foundation to find out something
about how people feel about various ways of making a living. Most of the
questions I will ask you are related to this general topic. I am sure you will
find the questions interesting. Please answer them just as frankly and completely as you can.

1-2. [Same as questions 1-2 in the Nonfederal Adult Questionnaire.]
3. (HAND RESPONDENT CARD SHOWING LADDER.) Here is a picture of a ladder.
Suppose we say at the *top* of the ladder (POINTING) is the *very best*, the
absolutely ideal occupation you have just described. At the *bottom* is the *very
worst* sort of an occupation. Now, thinking of the time when you start to work
at a regular occupation, where on this ladder (MOVING FINGER RAPIDLY UP
AND DOWN LADDER) do you think you are apt to be when you start?
    ENTER STEP NUMBER
4. How about five years after you start? Where on this ladder do you expect
to be then?
    ENTER STEP NUMBER
5. Returning now to when you start out, did you have in mind starting out
working for the Federal government—that is, the United States government?
    Yes (ASK Q. 6)
    No   }
    Nothing particular in mind } (SKIP TO Q. 7)

6. (IF "YES") Tell me more about what you had in mind. Why the Federal Government? (PROBE FOR AS MUCH DETAIL AS POSSIBLE)

(NOW SKIP Q's. 7 & 8 AND ASK Q's. 9 & 10 IN THAT ORDER)

7. Suppose your first occupation was with the U. S. government. Would this be better or worse from your point of view?

Better

Worse

No difference

8. How much (better) (worse)? Show me on the ladder. The place you felt you might start out is marked in red.

ENTER STEP NUMBER

(QUESTIONS 9 & 10 ARE TO BE INTERCHANGED. IF RESPONDENT ANSWERED "WORSE" TO Q. 7, Q. 10 SHOULD BE ASKED FIRST. IF RESPONDENT ANSWERED "BETTER" OR "NO DIFFERENCE" TO Q. 7, Q. 9 SHOULD BE ASKED FIRST.)

9. What things would be likely to be better? (USE "Anything else" PROBES)

10. What things would be likely to be worse? (USE "Anything else" PROBES)

11. Let's talk for a moment about what you are actually doing and planning. In what year of school are you now?

High school	11
	12
College	1
	2
	3
	4
Graduate school	1
	2 or over

12. About what has been your grade average in school this year?

13. Do you have any plans for further education? What are they?

(CIRCLE CODE AND GIVE RESPONDENT'S OWN WORDS HERE)

No, stop before completing high school

Just complete high school

Take college work, but less than 4 years

4 years college, no more

4 years college and master's degree

4 years college and doctorate or more
  (incl. medical, law schools, etc.)

No accredited college, but special training—nursing, art school, secretarial school, trade school, etc.

14. (FOR HIGH SCHOOL STUDENTS) What general kind of course are you taking in high school?

Academic, college preparatory

Commercial

Vocational, agricultural

Other (SPECIFY)

15. (FOR COLLEGE STUDENTS) What is your college major?

16. What occupation do you hope to follow after you leave school? (CIRCLE CODE AT RIGHT AND GIVE RESPONDENT'S OWN WORDS HERE)

Professional—doctor, lawyer, etc. ⎫
Scientist—physicist, chemist, etc.
Engineering—civil, chemical, mechanical
Business or business management
Teaching of any kind
A skilled trade—carpenter, welder, etc. ⎬ (SKIP TO Q. 18)
Farmer or farming, other agricultural
Military
Social or welfare work
Clerical—secretary, bookkeeper, etc.
Sales
Art, architecture, etc. ⎭
Government or politics (ASK Q. 17)
Don't know (SKIP TO Q. 19)

17. (IF "GOVERNMENT OR POLITICS" IN Q. 16) When you say that, what do you mean?

18. What are the main things that cause you to favor that line of work instead of some other?

19-36. [Same as questions 17-34 in the Nonfederal Adult Questionnaire.]

CLASSIFICATION DATA: Now I need some information about you, so that, after we have completed all of our interviews, we'll be able to find out such things as whether men have different ideas than women, whether people who live in the country have different ideas from city people, and so on.

37-46. [Same as questions 35-44 in the Nonfederal Adult Questionnaire.]

47. Now about your father's *principal* occupation. Is he self-employed or does he work for somebody else?
    Self-employed
    Work for somebody else

48. Where is he employed—I don't mean the name of the place but what kind of place is it?

49. What *exactly* does he do there?

50. What is his title?

51. Has your father ever served in the United States Armed Forces—that is, in the Army, Navy, Air Force or other branch?
    Yes
    No

52. Has your father ever worked *as a civilian* for the Federal government?
    Yes
    No (SKIP TO Q. 55)

53. (IF "YES") For how long?
    Less than 6 months
    6 months to 1 year
    More than 1 year but less than 5 years
    5 years or more

54. (IF "YES" TO Q. 52) What was the last year he worked for the Federal government?

55-60. [Same as questions 64-69 in the Nonfederal Adult Questionnaire.]

61. Would you point out for me on this card the group which includes the amount of your family's total yearly income before taxes. (HAND RESPONDENT INCOME CARD)[5]

(INTERVIEWER: ENTER FROM OBSERVATION)

62. Sex

     Male

     Female

63. Race:

     White

     Negro

     Other non-white

64. Socio-economic: (PRESENT CARD)[6]

     A

     B

     C

     D

[5] See question 70 of Nonfederal Adult Questionnaire

[6] See question 74 of Nonfederal Adult Questionnaire.

Index[1]

Academic grades as factor in appeal of federal service, 106, *107*, 108, 118, 133

Adams, President John Quincy, 30

Administrators in federal programs of breathtaking scope, 238

AFL-CIO affiliation of federal employee unions, 43

Age: a factor in appeal of federal employment, 89; and occupational values, 66-67, 81

Agree-disagree scale, 16, 56, *63n, 64n, 65n, 76n, 94n, 95n,* 106, *109n,* 112, 147

Agriculture Department, personnel exchanges recommended for, 260

Alexander, Arthur J., *40n*

American Federation of Government Employees, 43

American society: changes in, 27, 30; recruitment from total spectrum of, 40

Ames, Fisher, 28

Appeal of federal employment: evaluative statements by nonfederal workers, *148*

Appeal of federal employment, measures of: age pattern, 89; attitudinal factors, 86, *90,* 91, 96; differences by education, income, and occupational levels, *88,* 88-89, 92, 96, 114, 118; differences between white and Negro workers, 89; "evaluation of civil servants" index, 91, 93; major subjects of college students, 108, *109;* male-female variables, 86, 87, *87n,* 92, 96, 104-5, 113; "opportunity vs. security" index, 90-91, 93; socio-economic factor, 86, *87n*

Appeal of federal employment, ratings on: by federal general employees, 110-15; by federal special populations, 115-17; by nonfederal general work force, 87-

96; by nonfederal high-level employees, 96-109

Appeal of federal employment, views on of nonfederal groups: business groups, 99-101, *99,* 117; college teachers, natural and social scientists, and engineers, 98-99, *98,* 117; high school teachers, 97-98, 117; student populations, 101-9, *101, 103, 104,* 118

Appeal of federal service vs. large private business: among federal workers, 112-13; among nonfederal general employees, 93, *94;* as related to perceptions of avenues to success, *95;* among scientists and engineers, *100;* among student populations, 102, 103, 105, *107*

Armed Services, rank and pay in, 263

Automation as factor in manpower projections, 255

Blue-collar workers, 237, 241

Brookings Institution: in coding operation of present study, 24; federal contracting study by, *261n;* research project of on higher civil service, *263n;* work of in sampling population, *18n*

Bureau of the Budget: work of in making governmental activities more efficient, 257

Bureau of the Census, *31n*

Bureau of Standards, personnel exchanges recommended for, 260

Bureaucracy in image of government as employer, 121, 123, 127, 128, 129, 132, 133, 134, 136, 139, 141, 145, 256-58

Business executives: defined, 20; unfavorable attitude of on appeal of federal service, 100, *101n,* 121, 128-30, *245*

Business groups' image of government as employer: high-level employees' nega-

[1] References to tables are in italics.